SEX MATTERS

ALSO BY MONA CHAREN

Do-Gooders
Useful Idiots

SEX
MATTERS

How Modern Feminism
Lost Touch with Science, Love,
and Common Sense

MONA CHAREN

CROWN
FORUM
NEW YORK

CROWN FORUM with colophon is a registered trademark of
Penguin Random House LLC.

Library of Congress Cataloging-in-Publication Data
Name: Charen, Mona, author.
Title: Sex matters : how modern feminism lost touch with science, love, and
common sense / Mona Charen.
Description: New York : Crown Forum, [2018] | Includes bibliographical
references and index.
Identifiers: LCCN 2018012448 (print) | LCCN 2018013091 (ebook) |
ISBN 9780451498403 (e-book) | ISBN 9780451498397 (hardcover : alk. paper)
Subjects: LCSH: Feminism. | Anti-feminism. | Sex differences (Psychology) |
Sex. | Women—Social conditions—21st century.
Classification: LCC HQ1155 (ebook) | LCC HQ1155 .C4186 2018 (print) |
DDC 306.7—dc23
LC record available at https://lccn.loc.gov/2018012448

ISBN 978-0-451-49839-7
Ebook ISBN 978-0-451-49840-3

PRINTED IN THE UNITED STATES OF AMERICA

Jacket design by Josh Smith

10 9 8 7 6 5 4 3 2 1

First Edition

For Bob:

"I am my beloved's and my beloved is mine."
—*Song of Solomon*

CONTENTS

AT WHAT PRICE?

Feminism has triumphed. No longer a movement or even a controversy, feminism has become a piety. In many respects, this is worth celebrating. Equality has borne abundant fruit and enriched the lives of women, men, and children. But feminism has carried costs too. Very high costs.

While women have dramatically increased their earning power, educational attainment, and independence, many of the crucial supports for a happy and balanced life are further out of reach than in the past, and further out of reach than they need to be. Feminism is thought to be synonymous with women's interests and women's wishes, but that is far from the case.

Every year since 1972, the General Social Survey has asked a representative sample of American adults how happy they are. In 1972, women, on average, reported being a bit happier than men. Every year since, women's reported happiness has declined, both in absolute terms and when compared with men's. Around 1990, the sexes traded places, and since then, women have reported being less happy than men, and less happy than their mothers and grandmothers were at the same stage of life. A 2011 survey found that women are two and a half times as likely to be taking antidepressant medication as men.[1]

Happiness, then, has not marched forward with feminism.

Women's lives are more varied than they once were, but also far less secure. Men and children are also unmoored in often damaging ways.

Sheryl Sandberg, in her feminist blockbuster, *Lean In,* writes, "A truly equal world would be one where women ran half our countries and companies and men ran half our homes. I believe that this would be a better world."

I don't, and it's not because I object to women running countries or companies or men running homes. It's because I don't think "equality" means "sameness." It need not frighten or bewilder us that, on average, women tend to be more inclined to choose children over work than men, and I have never understood why feminists consistently disparage women's preferences. The Pew Research Center reports that in 2012, 67 percent of mothers said their ideal was either part-time work or no work outside the home. After declining for several decades, the percentage of mothers with children under the age of eighteen who choose to be full-time homemakers has been increasing. And less than a third of mothers say their ideal working arrangement is full-time work.

Still, Sandberg speaks for millions, especially our opinion leaders. The conventional wisdom spans the political spectrum. Conservatives as well as liberals, and Republicans almost as much as Democrats, bow to the idea that equality must mean sameness. Like totalitarians everywhere, they are determined not to understand people but to regiment them.

Our society devotes tremendous resources, psychic as well as actual, to the attempt to make women and men alike. Thousands of women's studies departments catechize college students to believe in perpetual female oppression. Children are instructed that we expect them to play sports in equal measure. As they mature, young people learn that they are expected to spend the same number of hours at work, to engage in sex in the same spirit, to study the same subjects in the same numbers, to change the exact same number of diapers, and to divide all jobs in the economy right down the middle.

Women must be roofers and loggers, and men must teach kindergarten and do social work in the same proportions. (By the way, the percentage of workers who are killed on the job tends to range from 95 to 99 percent male. You rarely hear feminists decry this inequity.)[2] In our era, any story of a boy or girl doing something usually associated with the other sex is guaranteed to be hailed as a landmark in the long march toward an androgynous utopia: a girl who wants to play on her high school's football team;[3] a boy who wants to be homecoming queen.[4]

We're told that "all sex differences are socially constructed." In our time, this has expanded to the notion that the male/female binary is imaginary as well. There are not two but many genders. Sexuality is a spectrum.

Yet resistance stubbornly persists. Most Americans reject the label "feminist" for themselves. A 2016 YouGov poll found that only 26 percent of Americans call themselves feminists. Only 32 percent of women and 19 percent of men were comfortable with the term. Asked why they rejected the label, 47 percent of women and 35 percent of men said that "feminists are too extreme."[5] Twenty-seven percent of men also agreed that feminists are "anti-men." Other polls have found even fewer people accepting the feminist designation. A 2015 Vox poll found that while 85 percent believe in "equality for women," only 18 percent of Americans said they would welcome the feminist label.[6]

Our society has devoted endless effort to freeing men and women from traditional sex roles in family life. These roles are outmoded and limiting, we're told. Back in the 1970s, when second-wave feminism was gearing up, Betty Friedan asked Simone de Beauvoir whether women should have a choice between being homemakers and working full-time. "No woman should be authorized to stay at home to bring up her children," declared de Beauvoir. "Society should be totally different. Women should not have that choice, precisely because if there is such a choice, too many women will make that one."

De Beauvoir may have been onto something. I made the choice to put my family first, and as she might have put it, *Je ne regrette rien.*

By the time I became a mother, I'd been a minor public figure, a talking head on TV and radio. I'd written thousands of columns, reviewed books, written two best sellers, spoken to civic organizations, served on boards, and so forth. When children came, I assumed that I would fold them into my busy life as I had many other obligations. I learned better.

When we picked up our first son, Jonathan, from the adoption agency in 1991, we were unprepared. We knew that we desperately wanted to be parents, but we had little sense of what that would mean emotionally. At three weeks of age, Jonathan was pink and beautiful, with a soft tuft of brown hair growing only on the crown of his head like a Mohawk. His gaze was steady and trusting, and along with infatuation, I felt flutters of doubt. Do we know what we're doing? Can we give this child what he needs?

It took a few weeks for the reality of what motherhood meant to hit me, but when it did, my world rocked on its axis. The memory remains vivid.

I had a busy day planned working on a magazine piece and delivering a speech at Georgetown University. When I approached Jonathan's crib to get him up for breakfast, he seemed indifferent to me. I sang to him, played peek-a-boo, and otherwise attempted to get him engaged. He remained impassive, but when the nanny arrived—she worked five mornings a week—he lit up.

My heart froze. I'm sure my pallid face betrayed my feelings as I handed Jonathan to the nanny and headed out the door. I delivered the speech (to the College Democrats of America, as it happens) feeling as if my chest were a block of granite. I vowed to make changes immediately. The nanny's hours would be cut way back. No one could be number one with my son but me.

Perhaps the fact that Jonathan was adopted helped to clarify things. We had no biological tie to bind us. Everything, the entire mother–child relationship, rested upon care. Whoever filled that role would be the mother to this baby. It had to be me. What I came to understand only later was that this is true of all babies.

Putting family first came at a price. Much of my work life had to go. I held on to my syndicated column because I was fortunate enough to work in a field that offered this flexibility, even in the 1990s. Many women, particularly those in blue-collar jobs, don't have this luxury, though technology is offering more and more people the opportunity to telecommute.

In *Lean In,* Sheryl Sandberg warns women against cutting back at work for the sake of children. I suppose I'm Exhibit A for doing the reverse. Though I continued to work, I leaned out more than in. If I hadn't, I don't think the other four people in my family would have been nearly as well off, and I would have had profound regrets.

When I was starting my career, the culture delivered a clear message to women like me. We were supposed to "have it all": a fulfilling career, an egalitarian marriage or no marriage, children (if desired), but no more than three—four or more was considered gauche. Choosing to become a traditional homemaker, especially for a college graduate (and, soon, for everyone else), was the one option that was not respected. I cannot count how many times I've asked women what they do and seen them look down sheepishly and confess, "I'm just a mom." When I've responded that their work is incredibly important, they've often thanked me profusely, adding that I was the first person to react that way. This has remained true for decades.

In 1998, I served as a jury member for the Pulitzer Prize, which required spending three days in New York City, at Columbia University. The most enjoyable part was meeting and getting to know Joyce Purnick, then the Metropolitan editor at the *New York Times.* She was engaging and smart and insightful. We had some things in common—we had both attended Barnard College, part of Columbia. I must have burbled about my boys, who were then seven, five, and three, because it caused her to reflect on her own choices.

She offered that she could never have risen to Metro editor if she had had children, because the job was a monster that ate up a person's whole life. She hadn't intended to foreclose the option of motherhood, but her job and unanticipated family obligations had taken a big chunk of her childbearing years. Then it was too late. Though she was justifiably proud of her professional accomplishments—she was the first woman Metro editor in the *Times*'s history—she seemed wistful about the children she'd never had.

A few months later, Purnick said exactly that at Barnard College's commencement ceremonies. Noting that she rarely left work before 8:00 p.m. and often stayed until 10:00 p.m., she told graduates, "There is no way in an all-consuming profession like journalism that a woman with children can devote as much time and energy as a man can." She said, "I am absolutely convinced I would not be the Metro editor of the *Times* if I had a family. . . . With rare exceptions—in nearly all competitive professions—women who have children get off the track and lose ground. I see it all the time in my business."

Many of the women at the *New York Times* were outraged, but the statement struck me as obvious. Top jobs in the American economy require tremendous effort and time; so does raising children. Something has to give.

Purnick's speech was later described as "antimotherhood," but of course it wasn't. It was realistic.

Sexual differentiation has been a feature of life on Earth for millennia. In human history, too much has arguably been made of sexual distinctions, and men have frequently controlled and even stunted their daughters and wives, out of a misguided belief in male superiority. But the pendulum has swung way too far in the other direction. It is now a borderline thought crime even to broach the matter of inborn sexual differences in aptitudes and interests, though biologists continue to illuminate the thousands of influences that chromosomes exert on our bodies and minds.

The new orthodoxy is that most, if not all, of the sexual differences we observe in behavior, taste, and family/career choices are culturally imposed rather than innate. I disagree. I think our society has made a serious mistake. Men and women are not alike in all important respects. Sex differences are real and, in some realms, profound. Sex plays a large role not just in our reproductive lives, but also in our psyches. Rather than attempting the Sisyphean task of reforming society to meet an androgynous ideal, we are happier when we accept our natures and play to our strengths. A college woman who chooses to study psychology rather than engineering is not letting down her team. Her preferences shouldn't be derided just because they happen to be stereotypically female. As neuropsychologist Anne Moir and her coauthor David Jessel counsel in *Brain Sex,* "It is usually better to act on the basis of what is true, rather than to maintain, with the best will in the world, that what is true has no right to be so."

The feminist movement of the 1960s and '70s did some good. It was unnecessarily difficult, for example, before feminism, for women to get credit on their own. Yet the movement took a disastrous wrong turn when it rejected the family as a prison for women. Family life is a key support to the happiness of men, women, and children. Thousands of studies show that married people are happier, healthier, wealthier, and longer lived than those who are single, widowed, or divorced. As for children, there is no debate in the literature. Everyone who studies child well-being agrees that children who grow up with their married biological parents are racing ahead of their contemporaries who grow up in less stable situations.

Feminists took another wrong turn on the subject of sex. The sexual revolution could never have succeeded without the imprimatur of feminists, who endorsed it as part of women's liberation. That was a profound mistake because it flew in the face of innate sexual differences. No matter how much feminists attempt to deny it, women are and always will be more vulnerable sexually than men. Nor will they ever approach sex with the detachment men can manage (but shouldn't). Early feminists urged women to model their sexual conduct not just on men, but on the worst men.

When I was an undergraduate, the idea that a woman would simply "use" a man for sex was hailed as a triumph for the sisterhood. Having agreed that sex was recreation, feminists denied to women the vocabulary to object to what came next, which, in turn, opened the door to today's hookup culture. The sexual revolution progressed rapidly from "young people in love should not have to wait for a piece of paper to have sex" to "what's wrong with you if you're not bedding strangers after a night of heavy drinking?" No wonder we're suffering from a culture-wide case of whiplash.

The only avenue of protest that remains socially sanctioned when a woman feels used, hurt, or ashamed after a sexual encounter is to claim rape. The modern feminist thus becomes a neo-Victorian, policing each and every step of sexual encounters. The "yes means yes" orthodoxy is hopelessly unworkable (and unromantic). It also reveals the deep need for sex rules in a culture that unwisely tossed them aside forty years ago.

Additionally, the sexual revolution and the sex-drenched media of our time have given rise to a sense of entitlement on the part of some men. The drunken hookup culture seems to have been designed to the benefit of jerks, selfish creeps, and rapists. It has also confused and misled ordinary young men about what sex is and how women tend to feel, leading to misunderstandings that can turn tragic.

The sexual revolution has long since spun off the table and degraded men and women alike. "No strings attached" sexuality is debased and unnatural, especially for women—which, I submit, is why drinking to the point of blacking out has become so common among women. It is also one of the reasons that so many report being raped and assaulted in the world of drunken hookups.

Many young women would love to flirt, to date, and to form relationships in college, but find that the hookup culture is their only option. One young woman confided to Hanna Rosin in *The Atlantic* that what she really wanted was "Some guy to ask me out on a date to the frozen yogurt place. That's it. A $3 date."

Men deserve better too, and are capable of better. They crave romance. They want to fall in love. But how to behave? Traditional masculinity and the code of the gentleman have been defamed, while pornography has invaded their imaginations and degraded their understanding of relations between the sexes.

It's time to move past hookup culture and the sexual revolution to an ethic that encourages love and tenderness on the part of both men and women—a sexual counterrevolution. Most women know intuitively that such a culture would be preferable. Good men would agree.

I hope this book will help both men and women see that denying the differences between the sexes leads to unnecessary misunderstandings and miseries. Rejecting the family and—yes, I'll say it—traditional roles within the family for mothers and fathers is also causing needless hardship.

From increasing income inequality to rising levels of adolescent depression and anxiety, from falling male labor participation rates to declining levels of female happiness—the retreat from family life has had far-reaching consequences. The institution that feminists assailed as oppressive is looking more and more like the key to human thriving for both sexes, and especially for children.

Some of the latest research from Third Way, a center-left think tank, suggests that family instability is even harder on boys than on girls, which might begin to explain the drop in male educational attainment vis-à-vis women in recent decades. Boys who grow up in single-mother families are less likely to be ambitious or to attend college than their sisters who grow up in the same homes. Women now outnumber men at every level of higher education. Some cheer this as a victory for women, but I wonder: Who are those female college graduates and CEOs and doctors going to marry? Is that a politically incorrect question? It shouldn't be. Majorities of young women and men still tell pollsters they wish to wed eventually, and we know that when women marry, the overwhelming majority of them choose men who are their equals or superiors in income and education.

It is long past time we outgrow the zero-sum accounting of women's accomplishments versus men's. Women outnumber men in universities. They earned nearly 60 percent of all bachelor's degrees in 2015[7] and the margin would be even larger if colleges didn't practice silent affirmative action for men. And while this suggests that women are doing something right, it's not a cause for celebration. Both sexes would be better off and happier if men were not falling behind.

When our children were young, I felt a burning desire to be at home with them. My husband felt a deep responsibility to provide for all of us. This is common. Marriage and parenthood seem to make women more maternal and men more conscientious earners. Maybe I wanted it this way because I was a "latchkey kid" before the term was common. Both my parents had PhDs and worked full-time—my father was a physics and chemistry professor and later a community college dean; my mother was a school psychologist. My childhood was full of lonely hours home alone. When I was ten years old, my father decided they should get a dog to keep me company. She was lovely: a German shepherd named Tanya. I adored her, but our conversations were a little one-sided.

In choosing to put family first, I was not some throwback to a lost era of *Leave It to Beaver*. I was in the mainstream of married mothers. We have a photo pasted in an album somewhere of me with one of our three boys. I am standing in front of the baby, who is perched in a high chair. With one hand, I'm holding the *New York Times*; with the other hand, the baby's bottle.

Was I a victim of *false consciousness,* a term that feminists had borrowed from Marxists to refer to those who hadn't yet been taught to understand their own oppression? No. I was happy. I believe other people when they say they're happy. I want more people to be able to say it.

The question young women always ask me is how to combine career and family life. Young men seldom ask this question. The feminists explain that this is because our society expects women to make career sacrifices for their kids, but demands nothing comparable from men. That's the wrong way to look at it. Usually, one parent chooses to do the majority of the child care, and the other chooses to work harder to support the family. No iron law says it has to be the traditional way—some happy families reverse roles—but most of the time, that's what the men and women involved prefer. Nor should we be so quick to say that the mom who makes sacrifices in her career is the only one who loses something. The husbands and fathers who work extra hours to support their families lose leisure time, sleep, and ease. But the men also gain in self-confidence and a sense of life purpose.

Our culture has misled young men and women about some of the most important ingredients for human happiness and thriving. Getting the basics of life right is not difficult, though it does require discarding some pervasive myths. The most consequential is that men and women are completely alike except for obvious anatomical differences. This is false, and imagining it to be true leads to trouble, as all deceit does.

We've convinced an entire generation, at least those with lower levels of education, that marriage is optional for parents. Among high school graduates and those with only some college, marriage is rapidly becoming the exception, rather than the rule.[8] Yet highly educated people, who would never consider having children without marrying first, shrink from recommending to others that the altar should precede the nursery.

Feminists often speak in terms of power. Everything that is desirable is said to be "empowering." Women are encouraged to seize power everywhere from the classroom to the boardroom, and women have been responding. They are outperforming men in school and in many workplaces. Women now hold a majority of managerial positions in the workforce.

Yet another kind of power that women heedlessly tossed aside forty years ago was sexual power. The results of that forfeiture are rarely acknowledged. Among the well-educated elites, women must search for love and commitment among a population of young men who have ready access to sex and less incentive than in previous decades to choose monogamy.

Among the less well educated, after several decades of family decline, young men often come from single-parent homes. This makes them less likely to secure educations and good jobs, and that, in turn, makes them less attractive as husbands. Nor do they grow up with role models of responsible fatherhood.

Hand in hand with this ethic of casual sex is our culture's devaluation of men in their traditional roles. Our gender-bending age applauds a father who adopts the traditional female role of nurturer while belittling the father who remains faithful to his wife and supports his children. The truth, though, is that fathers need appreciation, first, from their wives and, second, from society, because fatherhood is a bit less ironclad than motherhood.

Except in the rarest of cases (usually involving mental illness or other extreme situations), mothers do not tend to abandon their children. The mother-child bond is the strongest to be found in nature. The father-child bond is strong too, but it depends more on the father's relationship with the child's mother. When parents divorce—particularly when fathers remarry and have new families under a different roof—fathers' relationships with their children can and often do wither.

The sexual revolution and the retreat from family stability have left women and children far worse off economically. These twin movements may have also taken a toll on many men, who find themselves aimless and unemployed, failing to meet traditional milestones of maturity or to find purpose and fulfillment in family life.

Political figures from left and right valorize single mothers. We celebrate "breadwinner moms." We're all encouraged to applaud their fortitude, praise their accomplishments, and provide assistance for their needs. Most single mothers are deserving of praise. But isn't it also clear that, in many cases, they've made poor decisions? And isn't it just as clear that men who father babies but fail to raise them deserve opprobrium?

We know that loving mothers are key to raising happy, healthy children. Yet fathers bring a special elixir to the process. Children raised by their married parents are much less likely to live in poverty, perform poorly in school, get pregnant out of wedlock, get in trouble with the law, or shoot up a movie theater than children raised in other circumstances. Fathers, numerous studies have shown, are better at discipline, more demanding that their children adhere to high standards, more encouraging of risk taking, and better able to protect their children from harm than mothers.[9] Involved fathers also seem to spur their sons and daughters to stand up for themselves. When dads are around during adolescence, their kids show less psychological distress and fewer depressive symptoms than children raised in other circumstances.[10] There is also evidence that daughters who grow up with their biological fathers reach puberty later than girls who live with their mothers and others.[11]

Feminism has taught that sex roles are confining and unnecessary. Everything can and should be different. Simone de Beauvoir argued that choices had to be withheld from women to "force [them] in a certain direction."

We've been forcing women in a certain direction for decades, and the results are disappointing, to say the least. Families are fraying, and their weakness is undermining the strength and vitality of our entire society. Is this the price we have to pay for gaining so much female power?

As someone who's never been mistaken for a shrinking violet, I can testify that my traditional family role did not diminish me or suppress my individuality one bit. On the contrary, raising children as I thought best has been the most creative and rewarding part of my life. My husband would agree. His role, equally important, has been different. Men and women bring distinctive and complementary skills and styles to parenthood.

Too many in our society encourage us to believe that our identity and our validation must come almost entirely from our profession. My own work, at its best, is stimulating and gratifying. But my husband and three sons are the treasures of my heart. Given a little luck, most of us can expect to live long lives. There is time enough for raising a family and pursuing a career. Washington Irving wrote that "A woman's whole life is a history of the affections." There is truth in that, and it applies to men as well.

The world may never (probably will never) shower the kind of adulation and respect upon good mothers and fathers that it reserves for successful entrepreneurs, athletes, or reality TV stars. But young people making choices about their futures should know that getting their personal lives right is far more important than their career decisions.

This leads to the final point. In addition to joys, parenthood also entails exhaustion, disappointment, frustration, high stress, boredom, and great expense. Those are all part of being a grown-up. It's juvenile and shortsighted to chase "having it all." We have responsibilities to our children. We owe something to our nation. Serving others is a privilege that calls forth our best selves. When I was caring for my children, even at moments of highest stress, I felt a deep sense that this was where I belonged. For me, and I believe for others, giving, not having, is the key to happiness and peace.

A Word About Pronouns

I have used masculine pronouns throughout this book as the generic for *human*—as in "If a toddler were asked which he preferred . . ." Because English doesn't contain a gender-neutral term in the singular, there are only three other options: 1) to switch back and forth between "she" and "he," which strikes me as strained; 2) to use "he or she" or "he/she" each time, which reads awkwardly; or 3) to use "she" as generic, which doesn't solve the problem of mentioning only one sex and has a whiff of political correctness about it.

The safe harbor, I think, is to default to *he* as generic. It has always been understood to refer to both sexes. People have been aware of English's missing pronouns for some time. Southerners invented *y'all* to compensate for the lack of a second person plural for *you*. If someone devises a new generic singular pronoun that isn't too ugly, I'm open to it. In the meantime, I'm sticking with tradition.

CHAPTER 1

THE FEMINIST MISTAKE

If ever wife was happy in a man, Compare
with me, ye women, if you can.
I prize thy love more than whole mines of gold,
Or all the riches that the East doth hold.

—Anne Bradstreet (1612–1672), "To My Dear and Loving Husband"

Relations between the sexes are ailing in our time. Hundreds of prominent men in fields from entertainment to sports to business to politics have been credibly accused of gross sexual harassment and other forms of boorishness. The louts span the political spectrum, from Bill O'Reilly and Roger Ailes on the right, to Al Franken and John Conyers Jr. on the left. And the toll continues to mount.

Young people hardly date much, but they feel pressured into hooking up. Some millennials are giving up on sex altogether. Eighteen-year-old Noah Patterson, a virgin, told the *Washington Post* that he preferred online porn to having a girlfriend. "For an average date, you're going to spend at least two hours, and in that two hours I won't be doing something I enjoy."[1]

Teenagers and even some preteens "sext" one another, and

sometimes find themselves facing child pornography charges.[2] The percentage of adults who have never been married is at a historic high (30 percent), and fewer than one-third of millennials say that having a successful marriage is "one of the most important things in life."[3] While many women proclaim themselves "single by choice," others express frustration with the lack of marriageable men. In 2011, Kate Bolick described the proliferation of commitment-phobic men, which she believed had created a new "dating gap." Marriage-minded women, she wrote, "are increasingly confronted with either deadbeats or players."[4] The so-called men's rights movement thrives online, encouraging men to see themselves as victims of the sex wars and to luxuriate in misogyny.

The most talked-about cultural products of the past few years only occasionally offer models of nobility or even basic integrity between men and women. They range from rampant adultery (*Mad Men*) to incest and sex slavery (*Game of Thrones*). In HBO's *Girls,* the protagonist's "boyfriend" in the first few episodes is really not a boyfriend at all but a sex partner—and not a very nice one at that. Hannah drops by Adam's apartment and is ordered to remove her clothes, to get on all fours, to stop talking, and to perform a variety of sex acts while he indulges the fantasy that she is a child with a "Cabbage Patch lunch box."

How did we become so estranged—and so strange? How did love and sex become battlegrounds where feminists decry "rape culture" while the "manosphere" hurls vicious insults at women in general?

Modern feminism, I submit, must take at least some of the blame.

Feminism deserves credit for helping women get the vote, securing equal pay, and obtaining full civil and political rights. Those are unmixed blessings. No reasonable person questions whether women should be treated as full legal equals to men—that is beyond debate. But did that full equality require the denigration of the nuclear family? Did it require the eager embrace of a sexual revolution that would dismantle the traditions of modesty, courtship, and fidelity that have protected women for centuries? Was it essential to declare a war between the sexes, and to deem men the "enemy" of women? Was it necessary to seed our culture with bitterness that continues to this day?

Let's start at the beginning. It is moving to read the pleas for women's equality from Mary Wollstonecraft, the eighteenth-century protofeminist, who argued that women could be rational creatures and deserved to be educated. In *A Vindication of the Rights of Women* (1792), Wollstonecraft wrote, "Let woman share the rights, and she will emulate the virtues of man; for she must grow more perfect when emancipated."[5]

The great British philosopher John Stuart Mill declared in 1869 that "the legal subordination of one sex to the other—is wrong itself, and is now one of the chief obstacles to human improvement; and it ought to be replaced by a principle of perfect equality that doesn't allow any power or privilege on one side or disability on the other."[6]

In his treatise "The Subjection of Women" (1869), Mill scoffed at the notion that women were less intelligent than men (a widely held view at the time) and rebutted those who protested that women had achieved little in the arts and sciences. Mill was scornful: "Our best novelists have mostly been women," he wrote, mentioning in particular Madame de Staël and George Sand. Of the latter, he wrote that it would be impossible to find "[a] finer specimen of purely artistic excellence than the prose of Madame Sand, whose style acts on the nervous system like a symphony of Haydn or Mozart."[7]

It was fully understandable that women had not achieved excellence in other fields, Mill noted, since they were denied the education men received, and he added that women had original ideas all the time but, lacking the wherewithal to publish or publicly demonstrate their insights, often passed along these ideas to husbands or other male relatives.[8] Mill freely acknowledged that "a very large proportion indeed" of his ideas originated with the women in his life.

He also explained women's comparatively less prodigious production of original works of art by noting that "very few women have time for them. . . . Even when the superintending of a household isn't laborious in other ways, it's a very heavy burden on the thoughts; it requires incessant vigilance, an eye that catches every detail, and it constantly presents inescapable problems to be solved."[9] Bravo, Mr. Mill. Too few men appreciate this core female competency.

In the intervening centuries, women's roles have changed dramatically. In our own time, we've been encouraged to believe that women's history is one long tale of exploitation and denigration, oppressions that lifted only when feminism arrived to free us. But this narrative always seemed forced to me. Of course, some men have treated some women badly throughout human history. But declaring that all women have been oppressed by all men seems overly simplistic. Relations between the sexes, starting in families, are too complex to reduce to oppressors and victims.

The First Wave You've Never Heard Of

Feminism's "first wave" is usually dated to the late nineteenth century's suffrage movement, though some people agitated for equal rights before then. The suffragists are now included in the feminist pantheon. On the evening before the 2016 presidential election, feminists gathered at Susan B. Anthony's grave, assuming that Hillary Clinton would become the first woman elected president. Anthony has been honored on the U.S. currency, and Elizabeth Cady Stanton's home is a National Park Service site. In April 2016, the Treasury Department announced that Stanton, Lucretia Mott, Sojourner Truth, and Alice Paul will be featured on the ten-dollar bill to mark the one-hundredth anniversary of the Nineteenth Amendment, which enfranchised women coast to coast.

These women may be the ones most often cited in textbooks, but as the American Enterprise Institute's Christina Hoff Sommers has pointed out, Frances Willard and Hannah More were far more influential and popular with women during the nineteenth century. More (1745–1833), an English novelist, poet, political reformer, and pamphleteer, championed what Sommers calls "maternal feminism." She didn't deny differences between the sexes but urged women to use their special abilities to improve the world. Religiously inspired, she founded Sunday schools that taught poor children their ABCs, but also instilled thrift, sobriety, and piety. Her novels and pamphlets excoriated the rich for their amorality, for their hedonism, and for ignoring the needs of the poor.[10]

Frances Willard, who founded the Woman's Christian Temperance Union, spoke for many more women than the suffragists. We look back on Prohibition as an idealistic blunder, but women's intensity about the question indicated that they were more concerned about what excessive drinking was doing to families than they were about the right to vote. As Sommers notes, the National American Woman Suffrage Association had only about seven thousand members, though the WCTU could boast one hundred fifty thousand. The women's suffrage movement needed help from the WCTU before it could begin scoring political victories. Like More, Willard embraced women's "separate sphere" while also believing that women had a duty to improve the world. In addition to temperance, the WCTU lobbied for prison reform, child welfare, and care for the disabled.[11]

The women reformers of that time, unlike those who would lead second-wave feminism some decades later, avoided grievance-mongering. They saw women's issues as being linked to men's and children's. Though the temperance movement highlighted the damage excessive alcohol use did to wives and children, it also focused on husbands and sons who drank.

Second-wave feminists, by contrast, would explicitly link women's struggles with the cause of civil rights for African Americans. In 1963's *The Feminine Mystique,* Betty Friedan declared that "What we need is a political movement, a social movement like that of blacks."[12]

In a 1969 piece for *New York* magazine titled "After Black Power, Women's Liberation," Gloria Steinem wrote, "Finally, women [recognized] their essential second-classness, forming women's caucuses inside the Movement in much the same way Black Power groups had done. And once together[,] they made a lot of discoveries: that they shared more problems with women of different classes, for instance, than they did with men of their own."[13]

This is overwrought, particularly when compared to the approach taken by the women leaders of the first wave. The women's suffrage movement did share roots with the movement for abolition. Lucretia Mott, Elizabeth Cady Stanton, Susan B. Anthony, Angelina Emily Grimké, and Sarah Moore Grimké were prominent abolitionists who also campaigned for women's rights. But suggesting that the condition of women could be compared to that of black slaves or black citizens is a huge leap.

It has become fashionable for various interest groups to hijack the vocabulary and moral standing of the civil rights movement. Women, Latinos, the handicapped, homosexuals, transgender individuals—all have sought to compare their situations with that of blacks. But no group in American history has suffered the kind of dehumanization, persecution, exclusion, terror, and discrimination that blacks were subjected to for more than three hundred years.

Even leaving aside slavery, with its incalculable suffering, African Americans were the victims of thousands of lynchings, systematic torture, discrimination, and abuse. In the years between 1883 and 1927, more than three thousand blacks were lynched.[14] As historians Stephan and Abigail Thernstrom note, these crimes were designed to terrorize all African Americans. "They were not usually the furtive work of masked men wearing sheets, as is sometimes thought. Rather they were highly public events; the perpetrators were not only known to the community but sometimes even posed for 'before' and 'after' photographs in the local paper first with their victim and then with their victim's corpse!"[15]

Now consider how Steinem described the "oppression" of women in her 1969 article: "[M]ore backstage work, more mimeographing, more secondary role playing around the revolutionary cells and apartment communes. And to be honest, more reluctance to leave the secondary role and lose male approval."[16]

Steinem believed women deserved a revolution because "subtler, psychological punishments for stepping out of women's traditional 'service' roles were considerable. (Being called 'unfeminine,' 'a bad mother,' 'a castrating bitch,' to name a traditional few.)"[17]

Or, as one New York woman complained during a consciousness-raising session in 1969, "I have to keep reminding myself that there's nothing wrong with body hair, and no reason for one sex to scrape a razor over their legs."[18]

Comparing women's "plight" to what blacks experienced trivialized the true suffering of African Americans, yet feminist-influenced textbooks increasingly stressed this, maintaining that women have been ignored by a "patriarchal," man-centered history. One widely used women's studies textbook argued for "radical reconceptualizations" that would "overcome the bias that has been built into what has come to be known as 'knowledge.'" Another insisted that "traditional systems of knowledge have ignored women altogether or frequently portrayed them in stereotypical or demeaning ways."[19]

I was educated before this victim narrative took hold, and accordingly, I learned that American history (and world history, for that matter) is brimming with stories of women who were brilliant, brave, righteous, inventive, and worthy of emulation—as well as treacherous, greedy, cruel, lazy, and insipid. I could never escape the suspicion that women were human beings, with all the virtues and vices of the human condition.

But cringing victims bent under the weight of patriarchy? I don't think so.

American women have been at the forefront of many of our country's most momentous reform movements. Anne Hutchinson, a charismatic preacher (and mother of fifteen), provoked a schism among Puritans in seventeenth-century Boston. Harriet Beecher Stowe gave abolitionism its greatest weapon in *Uncle Tom's Cabin,* while Harriet Tubman helped to run the Underground Railroad. As I've noted, the temperance movement and Prohibition were primarily the work of the Woman's Christian Temperance Union, led by Frances Willard. Dorothea Dix successfully campaigned to reform the treatment of the mentally ill. Mother Jones was an influential labor activist. Mary Baker Eddy founded the Christian Science church, and Ida Tarbell was a crusading Progressive Era journalist. Jane Addams was a pioneer of urban reform. Rosa Parks helped ignite the struggle for civil rights, and Dorothy Day was a leader of the Catholic Worker Movement. Additionally, millions upon millions of unsung women married, bore children (without anesthesia until quite recently), kept households running, ran businesses, took in boarders, and were the anchors of stable and fulfilling family lives.

And every one of the male oppressors who are said to be women's enemies had a mother, usually a wife, and often sisters and daughters and cousins and aunts and nieces and friends. Those women sometimes made the lives of their men miserable, but more often they made life worth living.

Let's face it, some women have always inspired awe and fear in men. P. G. Wodehouse described one such woman in his comic novel *Right Ho, Jeeves*: "It isn't often that Aunt Dahlia lets her angry passions rise, but when she does, strong men climb trees and pull them up after them."

The Second Wave's Historical Revisionism

The so-called second wave of feminism dawned in the 1960s, and its leaders instituted the narrative of female victimhood. Creating their own version of history, they maintained that before second-wave feminism, women were passive overgrown children, able to express themselves only through domestic drudgery. They suggested that women had been brainwashed into wanting limited lives as caregivers and homemakers while men enjoyed the challenges and rewards of careers in the wider world. This myth arose during the post–World War II era, which was characterized, for understandable reasons, by a longing for domesticity.

First, let's look back a bit further. Before the Industrial Revolution, women and men worked primarily in agriculture and trades, where the tasks were less rigidly divided by sex. Men and women shared the work on farms: caring for animals, fetching water, making candles, preserving food for winter, chopping firewood, and plucking chickens. Men performed the heavier work, such as clearing and plowing fields, while women spun wool, preserved food, and cared for babies. Everyone, including children, worked from dawn to dusk six days a week, year-round, and cows had to be milked and animals fed and watered even on the Sabbath. Beyond farm work, tradesmen and women made and sold cloth, wigs, soap, horseshoes, whiskey, and other products. Only a tiny wealthy elite was spared hard daily toil.

Life was rapidly transformed by the Industrial Revolution. After 1800, in cities and, later, rural areas, factory and mine work became more common for men than agricultural work. Though many women worked in factories, particularly in the clothing trades, or in domestic service, most nineteenth-century women aspired to be supported by a working husband while they cared for home and children. Work itself was not the goal of most people, male or female. Everyone envied the rich, or leisure class, who didn't need to scrape for a living. The idea of work as a source of satisfaction or pleasure didn't become common until the postindustrial economy, with the rise of "knowledge work." This isn't to say that no one ever took satisfaction from a job well done before the industrial era, but work was not seen as a defining feature of one's identity, nor necessarily as a source of self-esteem.

The decades preceding the modern feminist movement were

particularly turbulent. Technology began to deliver products and services that transformed the lives of people worldwide, particularly those of women. But the early to mid-twentieth century also brought catastrophes of unprecedented proportions. The 1920s saw the debut of automobiles and movies and radio, but the 1930s brought mass unemployment.

In 1913, just fifty years before second-wave feminists decried the cruel tyranny of housework, Southern California Edison first brought electricity to Los Angeles. In 1940, 25 percent of U.S. homes were still heated only with wood stoves,[20] and fully one-third had no flushing toilet,[21] yet by the late 1940s, home refrigerators and freezers came into wide use.

In 1929, the Great Depression plunged the nation into an economic disaster that didn't truly lift until the end of World War II in 1945. During this time, millions of Americans lacked for the basics. My mother, born in 1923, vividly recalled many years later having only one dress to wear for each of her high school years. Her brother, whom she adored, was sent to live with relatives. They didn't go hungry, but millions did. We are not speaking of getting by on beans and rice or having to cut back on meals out, but of true hunger.

The ordinary comforts that even the poorest Americans now take for granted were luxuries during the war years. In 1943, only half of American farms had electricity, and by 1960, about one out of ten Americans still worked on farms, with the heavy physical labor that required. (Today, only 2 percent of Americans are employed in agriculture.) In the 1960s, I recall seeing in my grandmother's basement the old washboard and basin she used for hand-scrubbing clothes. She was born in 1895.

During the Great Depression, marriage rates plunged, as young people, unsure about their futures, delayed or canceled plans to wed. The birth rate declined as well, for the same reasons.[22]

World War II left no aspect of American life unaltered. Though Americans were not as devastated by the war as Europeans or Asians, they did have to cope with rationing, shortages, prolonged family separations, and other civilian hardships. Though the economy picked up during the war, Americans were imbued with an ethic of sacrifice. They purchased war bonds with their extra cash. The war obliged millions of American women to take factory jobs while men were overseas, drove the development of enormous defense industries, and cost the lives 420,000 Americans.

I say that women were "obliged" to take factory jobs, but many feminist-inflected histories describe women's entry into factory work during the war as a boon, and the postwar withdrawal from such jobs as a setback for women's progress. That romanticizes the situation. The federal government, together with compliant popular culture outlets, launched a tremendous propaganda push to get women to take factory jobs because such jobs were often hard and dirty. At the behest of the federal government, Norman Rockwell created "Rosie the Riveter," the iconic *Saturday Evening Post* gal wearing overalls and holding a riveting gun, as a propaganda icon. A popular 1943 song lauding "Rosie's" role in keeping war materiel flowing included the line "She's making history, working for victory."

In addition, the government sponsored 125 million print advertisements, as well as film and radio spots, encouraging women to take all kinds of jobs, not just those in war industries. According to the Basic Program Plan for Womanpower in the Office of War Information, "These jobs will have to be glorified as a patriotic war service if American women are to be persuaded to take them and stick to them. Their importance to a nation engaged in total war must be convincingly presented."[23]

Some women found their war work gratifying. Inez Sauer recalled that "At Boeing[,] I found a freedom and an independence that I had never known." Bethena Moore already had a job as a laundress when she went to work in the Kaiser Shipyards. Her tasks included climbing down a narrow ladder into the unlit bowels of ships, sometimes four stories in depth. She was tethered to the welding machine. "It was dark, scary," she recalled. "It felt sad, because there was a war on. You knew why you were doing it—

the men overseas might not get back. There were lives involved. So the welding had to be perfect."[24]

Dot Kelley, another welder, worked nights so she could be with her children during the day. Her neck and face became covered with tiny burn marks, a commonplace injury for welders. By 1945, at the Redstone Arsenal in Huntsville, Alabama, about 60 percent of the workforce was female. The work was hard and dangerous and involved handling chemicals and munitions. A number of women were killed on the job.[25]

Is it really surprising that after sixteen years of the worst poverty and deprivation in the history of the nation a period of grateful domesticity and consumerism followed?

The First Feminist Blockbuster

Our image of twentieth-century life, at least for women, was forever altered by one woman and one book.

Betty Friedan, born in 1921, experienced the Great Depression and World War II, though she was insulated from the worst effects of both. Friedan, born into a prosperous family, was a bright, ambitious graduate of Smith College. In *The Feminine Mystique,* she portrays herself as a frustrated housewife, but we've since learned that she created that mystique to serve her own purposes.

In her youth, Friedan was a committed leftist, a labor union activist who had written for the left-wing Federated Press, and later for the United Electrical, Radio, and Machine Workers of America, which *The New Yorker* described as the "largest Communist-led union in the United States."[26] Her feminism may have been sincere, but her discontent with being a suburban housewife probably owed more to her unhappy marriage and her leftist views than to a dispassionate critique of the plight of women.

It is important to remember that when *The Feminine Mystique* was published in 1963, the Great Depression and World War II were still fairly fresh in people's memories—as recent for them as the Monica Lewinsky scandal and the First Gulf War are for us today.

Sociologist Amitai Etzioni has described *The Feminine Mystique* as "one of those rare books we are endowed with only once in decades, a volume that launched a major social movement." It led to the founding of the National Organization for Women, the revival of the Equal Rights Amendment (though the measure was ultimately defeated), and thousands of imitators. Above all, it influenced the entire nation's sense of women's roles and desires. Self-styled "futurist" Alvin Toffler declared that the book "pulled the trigger on history." As one reader put it, "It literally changed (and perhaps saved) my life."[27]

The Feminine Mystique achieved pop-culture status, but it was a deeply flawed work that presented a tendentious version of history, relied upon discredited theories, and—this is often missed—demanded changes that were already underway.

This much-quoted opening passage describes the plight of the 1960s mother and wife:

> The problem lay buried, unspoken, for many years in the minds of American women. It was a strange stirring, a sense of dissatisfaction, a yearning that women suffered in the middle of the twentieth century in the United States. Each suburban wife struggled with it alone. As she made the beds, shopped for groceries, matched slipcover material, ate peanut butter sandwiches with her children, chauffeured Cub Scouts and Brownies, lay beside her husband at night—she was afraid to ask even of herself the silent question—"Is this all?"[28]

The Feminine Mystique was ambitious—in fact, overly ambitious. It surveyed women's magazines, popular psychology, a seemingly endless parade of anonymous psychiatrists and psychologists, anthropologist Margaret Mead, Sigmund Freud, Alfred

Kinsey, as well as her own college cohorts to arrive at sweeping generalizations about women's place in the postwar world. A *New York Times* review gushingly described *The Feminine Mystique* as a "highly readable, provocative book." Well, that's not true. It's long-winded, repetitive, and dubious as social science. Even the liberal *New York Times* columnist Gail Collins acknowledged in her introduction to the fiftieth-anniversary edition that it's "a little whiny."

Before Friedan wrote the book, she had a large house in the suburbs, a husband, three children, domestic help, and a thriving career as a freelance journalist,[29] yet she was unhappy. She and her husband, Carl, fought constantly and sometimes violently. It was not a love match. Betty wished Carl were better educated. He had dropped out of college. He wished Betty were prettier. Betty found a letter Carl had written to his parents announcing their engagement. His fiancée, he wrote, wasn't much to look at but was "so bright that they would never have to worry about money."[30]

Friends recalled a 1956 dinner party: "The women decided to dress for dinner. It was very pleasant, and Betty brought out the main course, a beautiful fish on a platter. Carl said, 'Jesus, Betty. Fish? You know I don't like fish.' He took the platter and threw it at her."[31]

Still, according to biographer Judith Hennessee, Friedan was not a classic battered wife. She gave as good as she got. Carl showed up for an important job interview with a face so scratched that his interviewer said he looked as if he'd been mauled by a tiger.[32] He was also seen knocking Betty to the ground upon leaving a dinner party when both were drunk.[33] They divorced in 1969.

Second-wave feminists introduced the slogan "The personal is political" and meant it as a rallying cry. Friedan certainly poured the bitterness over her unhappy marriage into political activism. It's possible to read *The Feminine Mystique* as a bid to ennoble her private misery by transforming it into a cause. The book pulses with grievance. There is hardly an ailment, complaint, or social pathology Friedan doesn't blame on the culture's imposition of a false and unsatisfying feminine ideal of domesticity (i.e., the "feminine mystique").

Friedan thundered that a great con had been perpetrated on the female sex, and that women had sometimes participated in their own victimization. Beneath the Stepford wife surface (though that term wouldn't enter the lexicon until later) lay lives of quiet desperation. "A family doctor in Pennsylvania"—anonymous, like so many Friedan quotes—told Friedan about "great, bleeding blisters" that broke out on women's hands and arms. He called it "housewife's blight" but advised, "It isn't caused by detergent, and it isn't cured by cortisone."[34] One woman cried for no reason. Another paced the house while the children napped, just waiting for them to awaken and give her life meaning again. Friedan diagnosed a "high rate of emotional distress and breakdown among women in their 20s and 30s,"[35] though she did not provide evidence to support this.

In her telling, the feminine mystique was responsible for men's infidelity (p. 325), the rise of "increasingly overt homosexuality" (p. 327), "malaise, nervousness, and fatigue" (p. 299), and "obesity and alcoholism" (p. 299). It also prompted promiscuity among teenaged girls (p. 331), women's irritation with their husbands (p. 413), and increased hostility toward women among men (p. 310). It caused a rise in depression, suicide, and "maternal psychoses" (p. 351), and led to young mothers suffering from an "impairment of the ovarian cycle—vaginal discharge, delayed periods, irregularities in menstrual flow and duration of flow, sleeplessness, fatigue syndrome, [and] physical disability" (p. 318). It might have a role in menstrual cramps, backaches, nausea during pregnancy, and menopausal symptoms (p. 320).

Though mostly well concealed, Friedan's leftist sympathies occasionally peeked through. She quoted Dr. Benjamin Spock, another well-known leftist, as wondering if Russian children weren't "more stable, adjusted, mature" than American children because Russian mothers "work in medicine, science, education, industry, government, art" and have "a serious purpose in their own lives."

He believed these Russian mothers were "more sure of themselves as mothers" and weren't "dependent on the latest word from experts, the newest child-care fad."[36]

Of course, the women of the old Soviet Union probably spent hours every day waiting on long lines for basic goods, and reporting to jobs that paid far, far less than the same jobs in free societies. The old Soviet joke was "They pretend to pay us, and we pretend to work."

Like many other leftists, Spock was a committed Freudian. His mega-selling *Baby and Child Care,* the bible of child rearing for several generations of American parents, was imbued with Freudian categories. He warned that ordinary tickling, nursing, playing, and toilet training were capable of scarring a child for life with neurosis.[37]

Friedan mocked American mothers for consulting experts or indulging the latest fad about child rearing. She may have been onto something there, though she saw no contradiction in asking women to put their faith in *her.* In any case, others were better at debunking this faddishness. Critic Lionel Trilling described the American rage for expertise this way in 1950: "This is the public that, on scientific advice, ate spinach in one generation and avoided it in the next, that in one generation trained its babies to rigid Watsonian schedules and believed that affection corrupted the infant character, only to learn in the next decade that rigid discipline was harmful and that cuddling was as scientific as induction."[38]

Friedan detected among the children of blighted American women "strange new problems." She wrote that children "whose mothers were always there, driving them around, helping them with their homework" showed a worrying "inability to endure pain or discipline or pursue any self-sustained goal of any sort, a devastating boredom with life. Educators are increasingly uneasy about the dependence, the lack of self-reliance, of the boys and girls who are entering college today."[39]

None of this is sound social science. Friedan opines upon this or that study, this or that clipping from a women's magazine, a conversation with a neighbor, and dozens upon dozens of anonymous quotes from doctors to spin a theory about the suffocating conditions housewives were enduring. For every assertion she backs up with a study or a statistic, she offers fifty more that are supported by nothing more than anecdotes from anonymous psychotherapists, often psychoanalysts (Freudians), or her own theories.

She questions a White House conference on children's fitness by asking, "Were they being over-nurtured?" even though the conference had nothing to do with nurturing. It began when President Eisenhower noticed a rising level of obesity after World War II. President Kennedy inaugurated an exercise program for the nation's schoolchildren that I remember to this day because of the "Chicken Fat" song sung by Robert Preston, which was supposed to help us with our calisthenics in gym class. (This program didn't succeed; obesity is a more serious problem today.)

But Friedan put an anti-housewife spin on children's fitness, by shoehorning everything into that Procrustean bed.

It is the mystique of feminine fulfillment, and the immaturity it breeds, that prevents women from the doing the work of which they are capable. It is not strange that women who have lived for 10 or 20 years within the mystique, or who adjusted to it so young that they have never experienced being on their own, should be afraid to face the test of real work in the world and cling to their identity as housewives—even if, thereby, they doom themselves to feeling "empty, useless, as if I do not exist."[40]

Friedan devoted an entire chapter to women's magazines, arguing that the independent, striving woman featured in previous decades (a woman pilot, for example, in *Ladies' Home Journal* of 1949) had been supplanted by the dull, childlike, cosmetics-wearing, bed-making, pie-baking baby machine of the 1950s and '60s. "In 1958, and again in 1959," Friedan wrote, "I went through issue after issue of the three major women's magazines . . . without finding a single heroine who had a career, a commitment to any work, art, profession, or mission in the world, other than 'Occupation: housewife.' One in a hundred heroines had a job; even the young unmarried heroines no longer worked except at snaring a husband."[41]

On the book's fiftieth anniversary, in 2013, *The Feminine Mystique* was reissued and again hailed as "remarkably inspiring" and "changing the way women viewed themselves."

There's no question it inspired something, though it's doubtful it was an accurate account of history or the experiences of most women, even most white, upper-middle-class women. It certainly warped our perceptions of women's wants and needs and devalued the most precious part of life.

Historian Joanne Meyerowitz, acknowledging that she had been influenced by Friedan's depiction of postwar American culture as repressive and limiting for women, was surprised to find that the reality was much more complex. She examined 489 nonfiction articles that appeared between 1946 and 1958 in popular magazines of the era, including *Reader's Digest, Harper's, Atlantic Monthly, Ladies' Home Journal, Woman's Home Companion,* and two aimed at black readers, *Ebony* and *Negro Digest.* "All of the magazines sampled advocated both the domestic and the nondomestic," she wrote. "In this literature, domestic ideals co-existed in ongoing tension with an ethos of individual achievement that celebrated nondomestic activity, individual striving, public service, and public success."[42]

Reader's Digest, a staid voice of middlebrow sensibilities, ran an admiring profile of Dorothy McCullough Lee, describing her as an "ethereally pale housewife who tipped the scales at 110 pounds." But "she was also the mayor of Portland, Oregon, who had defeated, single-handedly it seems, the heavyweights of organized crime."

Meyerowitz concluded that only *15 percent* of the profiles focused chiefly on women's roles as wives and mothers. Many fell into the Horatio Alger, up-by-the-bootstraps inspirational category, celebrating uncomplaining hard work. Meyerowitz quotes a typical article as saying, "You can't be busy and sorry for yourself at the same time." About a third of the articles featured women who were single, divorced, or whose marital status was unknown. There were doctors, teachers, athletes, entertainers, civil rights activists, authors, politicians, and humanitarians.[43]

In 1953, *Woman's Home Companion* recognized six women for outstanding achievement. They had excelled in medical science, education, literature, the theater, human rights, and social betterment. First Lady Mamie Eisenhower was quoted as saying, "We can all take pride in the forward steps women have taken during our own generation to a role of leadership in community and even national affairs."[44]

Continuing to refute Friedan's stereotype, Meyerowitz found that "the postwar popular magazines were . . . unequivocally positive on increased participation of women in politics" and favored women working for wages. Then, as now, there was much discussion of the merits of part-time versus full-time work for mothers, but the articles stressed the psychic as well as financial benefits of work.

Friedan claimed she was the first to unlock the secret dissatisfaction of millions of American women, but Meyerowitz found many articles published before *The Feminine Mystique* that examined the stresses and special challenges of suburban homemaking. Among those difficulties were "confinement, isolation, loneliness, boredom, frustration, dissatisfaction, and nervous and physical fatigue." Some proposed remedies included "recreation, part-time jobs, volunteer work, 'outside interests,' more prestige for mothers, more help from fathers, cooperative babysitting, and nurseries."[45]

Meyerowitz's examination also showed that Friedan had cherry-picked her magazine examples to suit her fable that Madison Avenue had imposed a stifling domesticity on American women. Meyerowitz's more systematic study unveiled a far more mixed picture. She discovered in the magazines an assumption that most women wanted to be married and that they would be their children's chief caregiver. Glamour was celebrated, but in a particularly democratic fashion. Women's magazines stressed that every woman could be attractive with a little effort. Allure was considered an "accomplishment," not a gift, and women were encouraged to achieve it with subtlety, not with "vulgar" sexuality.

Meyerowitz concluded that Friedan's portrayal of domestic propaganda was "unabashedly hyperbolic," and noted that "postwar magazines . . . rarely presented direct challenges to the conventions of marriage or motherhood, but they only rarely told women to return to or stay at home. They included stories that glorified domesticity, but they also expressed ambivalence about domesticity, endorsed women's nondomestic activity, and celebrated women's public success."[46]

When Friedan has come under fire, it has been chiefly from her left. The feminist author and activist bell hooks, for example, was scorching in her contempt for Friedan's upper-middle-class white parochialism:

> Friedan's famous phrase, "the problem that has no name," often quoted to describe the condition of women in this society, actually referred to the plight of a select group of college-educated, middle- and upper-class, married white women—housewives bored with leisure, with the home, with children, with buying products, who wanted more out of life. Friedan concludes her first chapter by stating: "We can no longer ignore that voice within women that says: 'I want something more than my husband and my children and my house.'" That "more" she defined as careers. She did not discuss who would be called in to take care of the children and maintain the home if more women like herself were freed from their house labor and given equal access with white men to the professions. She did not speak of the needs of women

without men, without children, without homes. She ignored the existence of all non-white women and poor white women. She did not tell readers whether it was more fulfilling to be a maid, a babysitter, a factory worker, a clerk, or a prostitute than to be a leisure-class housewife.[47]

These are all fair points, and hooks was right that Friedan's glamorization of jobs and careers was aimed at an elite audience. Most men and women did not then (and do not today) have the "careers" Friedan rhapsodized about. Most people, especially those without college educations, work at jobs to put food on the table. Poor and working-class women have been no strangers to the workplace. That's why there is an International Ladies' Garment Workers' Union and why women have been dominant in the National Education Association and other teachers' unions.

In 1964, only around 8 percent of women had college degrees that could prepare them for the careers Friedan spilled so much ink over. Even in 2016, college graduates remain a minority (32 percent) of all women.[48] Some jobs are rewarding and intellectually or emotionally stimulating, but many are not. For many women, raising their own children is more gratifying than paid employment.

Is it really better for a woman with a high school diploma to work as a salesperson or checkout clerk rather than stay home to raise her children? Is it preferable that she and her husband pay another high school graduate to care for their babies, a person who may or may not share their values and certainly does not love their kids as they do? Many women who work for low wages do not have husbands, and accordingly have no good choices. They must either work or receive welfare. Is this preferable to the married housewife's lot? And how does it improve the lot of women as a class when some women subcontract out the care of their children to other women?

This is a big part of Betty Friedan's patrimony (driving American women who have a choice away from caring for their own children), and though she came to regret it later, and even essentially reversed herself in a later book called *The Second Stage,* it was too late.

Lesbians were outraged at what they regarded as *The Feminine Mystique*'s anti-homosexual bias and Friedan's posture generally. She had dubbed the rise of lesbianism in the women's movement the "lavender menace," fearing it would repel most mainstream women.[49] Friedan later retracted this.

Other weaknesses in the first feminist manifesto have grown more evident over time. Critic Alan Wolfe noted that many of the book's factual claims have since been shown to be deeply flawed if not outright fraudulent.[50] Friedan devoted thousands of words to Freudian psychoanalysis, the work of anthropologist Margaret Mead, and the sex research of Alfred Kinsey. The work of none of these influential twentieth-century figures has held up well.

Freud continues to enjoy some status in psychology as a shrewd observer of human behavior, but he is viewed more as a literary than a scientific figure. His schema of id, ego, and superego; his theory about oral, anal, and genital stages of development; his interpretation of dreams; and the Oedipus complex—all have been dismissed by modern psychology as works of imagination, not science. In 1996, the journal *Psychological Science* declared flatly that "[T]here is literally nothing to be said, scientifically or therapeutically, to the advantage of the entire Freudian system or any of its component dogmas."[51]

Wolfe also described how Margaret Mead fell for one of the great hoaxes in the history of science:

One need not accept the sociobiological determinism of Mead's critic Derek Freeman to recognize that he has undermined the empirical claims of *Coming of Age in Samoa*. In *The Faithful Hoaxing of Margaret Mead: A Historical Analysis of Her Samoan Research* (1990), Freeman shows in detail how Mead's most important informant, a young product of a culture that placed great emphasis on female virginity before marriage, was so embarrassed by Mead's probing that he responded in typical Samoan fashion by jokingly telling Mead the opposite of the truth.[52]

Wolfe went on to write that "For Friedan, the hoaxing of Margaret Mead was particularly unfortunate. It was precisely those of Mead's books that Friedan liked best that have not withstood later scrutiny."[53]

Friedan often quoted Alfred Kinsey on the frequency of extramarital sex, sexual desire within marriage, and women's sexual satisfaction. Considering what we've since learned about his research methods, none of those data can be considered reliable.

By the time Friedan was using his research, Kinsey was a pop-culture star, the father of sexology, and the author of the influential *Kinsey Report on Human Sexuality.* His much-vaunted 1948 report, *Sexual Behavior in the Human Male,* convinced America that, among other things, 10 percent of American men were homosexual and that 37 percent had had at least one homosexual experience. (A 2012 Gallup survey found that only 3.8 percent of the U.S. population identified as gay, lesbian, bisexual, or transgender.)[54]

Kinsey was an entomologist by training, which meant he studied insects, and his biographer revealed that he was a man of peculiar sexual tastes. He had several affairs with men, encouraged so-called open marriages among his staff, and filmed sexual encounters between them in his attic for "research." His personal sexual practices included inserting tubes into his urethra and using ropes for sexual gratification. All of this suggests he *may* have had an interest in persuading the world that sexual deviance was normal and common.[55]

His methodology was also highly suspect. Rather than interviewing a representative sample of the population, he chose people whom he and his colleagues met in bars, along with prisoners and others eager to talk about their sex lives. He then asked those subjects to recruit their friends. His methods would certainly be considered "junk science" today, due to the self-selection bias of his sample. One man he interviewed claimed to have had sexual

experiences with women, men, children, and animals, yet his accounts were disguised to seem as if they came from multiple study
participants.[56] That is fraud. Kinsey's methods were criticized at
the time, including by Abraham Maslow, a psychologist Betty
Friedan admired, so she would certainly have been aware of the
controversy.

In contrast to the feminists who came right after her, Friedan
was not especially anti-male or anti-family. Her fault, as I see it,
was that she thoroughly stigmatized motherhood as a full-time
commitment. Housewives, Friedan wrote, "devour their children
[and] sow the seeds of progressive dehumanization, because they
have never grown to full humanity themselves."[57]

Millions of American women (and billions worldwide) still devote themselves full-time to the job of raising children and maintaining a home. Thanks to Betty Friedan, many of them feel they
must apologize for, justify, and/or explain this decision.

The Feminine Mystique's most offensive chapter, the one that
really marked Betty Friedan's fathomless moral vacuity, was titled
"The Comfortable Concentration Camp." Friedan callously compared the "dehumanization" of housewives to that of Jews in Nazi
concentration camps. "Strangely enough," she wrote, "the conditions which destroyed the human identity of so many prisoners
were not the torture and the brutality, but conditions similar to
those which destroy the identity of the American housewife."[58]

Actually, no. Being despised as subhuman "vermin"; robbed of
all one's worldly goods; shipped off to camps in cattle cars without food, water, or sanitation; separated from loved ones; starved;
stripped naked; and marched into gas chambers holding babies is a
little different from staying at home with children, making peanut
butter and jelly sandwiches, and keeping a warm, safe home in
smooth running order.

Friedan seems to have gotten carried away by her grand theory
of women's oppression, to the point where she lost sight entirely
of the pleasures of mothering. Nowhere in Friedan's nearly five
hundred pages of bitter complaints about the crushing demands of

domesticity is there any hint at what makes home and children so appealing. F. Carolyn Graglia protested that "it is profoundly sad that one who bore children could think the experience of raising them was so valueless. For the sake of market production, Friedan would have women abandon what many of us believe is the single greatest opportunity for human growth."[59]

Perhaps if Friedan had read some economic history instead of burying herself so deeply in Freud and Kinsey, she would have been aware of the seismic changes that were already underway. The great movement of women into universities and the workforce predated *The Feminine Mystique* and had nothing to do with consciousness-raising or women believing that raising children was beneath their dignity. In the years following the Depression and World War II, increasing wealth and technological changes naturally opened up a pent-up desire for secure homes and large families. The birth rate famously rose during the postwar years, creating the "baby boom." But the baby boom did not imprison women in their homes. Starting in the 1950s, married women began a steady march into the workforce.

Writing in *Fortune* magazine in 1956, sociologist Daniel Bell said, "Today, a girl who announces that she is being married is asked by her supervisor, 'Are you taking a trip, or will you be back on Monday?' Whichever the answer, it is becoming increasingly rare that she does not return at all."[60]

Between 1940 and 1956, Bell noted, the number of married women in the workforce doubled from 15 to 30 percent, and it continued its steady rise for the next six decades. This corresponded with the march of single women into the workforce that had begun in the 1920s. By 1955, more than half of married women without children were in the workforce, and increasing numbers of mothers were getting jobs as well.

Data from the Bureau of Labor Statistics demonstrate that the number of women in the workforce grew steadily from 1950 to 2000. There was no spike in the late 1960s or '70s, after feminist ideas came into fashion, though the number of women entering professions such as law, medicine, and engineering did jump in the '70s.[61]

In 1936, the Gallup organization asked a cross-section of the American public, "Should a married woman earn money if she has a husband capable of supporting her?" Only 18 percent of respondents said yes. By 1960, 50 percent approved, and the number was soon more than 80 percent.[62] These changing perceptions about women in the workforce predated Betty Friedan.

What *did* propel women to work? Lots of things. The expanding economy created many job opportunities that did not require heavy labor. Prepared foods, wash-and-wear clothing, and labor-saving devices made housework easier and less time-consuming. Rising levels of education gave women remunerative skills. Most of all, after years of depression and war, Americans wanted the many things money could buy. In the late 1940s and '50s, that supply of new goods and services was expanding rapidly.

The United States had long led the world in providing higher education to women. In 1880, for example, one-third of university students were female.[63] In 1950, women earned 23.9 percent of bachelor's degrees. By 1960, the percentage had jumped to 35.3.[64] The 1950 figure was lower than the percentage of women who received degrees in 1920 (34.2), but the total number of students, male and female, who attended college at all in that era was tiny, just above 3 percent.[65] In the late 1940s and into the 1950s, millions of men swelled college ranks as they took advantage of the GI Bill.

Among white Americans in the 1950s, the old cultural standard of a husband working to support a wife who stayed home had already changed. Women were following a new pattern: working while single, cutting back or working only part-time while their children were young, and then resuming full-time employment after their children were grown. Daniel Bell called this the U-shaped pattern. The more education a woman had achieved, the more likely she was to be employed outside the home. The exception was married African American women, who left the labor force if their husbands earned enough to enable it. The long history of poverty and the necessity for African American women to work makes this choice understandable.

Did feminism free women from artificial restrictions on which jobs they could choose? Friedan suggested that the only fields open to women were nursing, teaching, and clerical jobs. Though many women did populate those fields, Bell showed that in the 1950s "females [were] to be found in such unlikely jobs as railroad trainmen, baggage handlers, furnace tenders, glaziers, auctioneers, plumbers, and jumper men (i.e., connecting cable terminals) in the telephone field . . . there was not one category in the published census of occupations that did not have at least a few females."[66]

Bell noted that women were sometimes paid less than men for the same job, but he suggested this was likely to change. In 1963, Congress passed the Equal Pay Act, an update of the Fair Labor Standards Act of 1938, to forbid the practice (though lawbreakers are still to be found). Bell also predicted, in 1973, that women would play an ever larger role in the "postindustrial" economy because it would reward services rather than goods production. "What counts is not raw muscle power, or energy, but information."[67] He was prescient.

What about Friedan's descriptions of the tyranny of the patriarchal family? Were women timid servants of domineering husbands? Some no doubt were, but there is reason to suspect that this model was already on the way out by the time Friedan's book was published.

Within families, decisions were shared between husbands and wives. A 1959 study of 400 Washington, DC, families found that most day-to-day decisions (such as what children wore and what the family ate) were made by mothers. Larger decisions were shared by both parents about 80 percent of the time, and were imposed by the father in only 20 percent of cases.[68]

A larger survey, of 650 families in the Detroit area, found that equal decision-making was the norm. Donald Wolfe, one of the study's authors, wrote, "Neither the farm families, nor Catholic families, nor the older generation, nor poorly educated families adhere to a patriarchal way of life."[69]

A popular joke in the 1960s captured the spirit. A man explains that he and his wife agreed on their wedding day that the husband would make all the big decisions and the wife all the small ones. After thirty years of marriage, he marveled, they had never made a big decision.

Most women prefer the arc of work-life balance that emerged in the 1950s—the U-shaped curve of work, marriage, childbirth, cutting back on work, and finally returning to work after children are older or grown. Even today, despite a continuing drumbeat of encouragement from the culture and government to prioritize careers, most women still choose to put family first.[70]

If feminists had stuck to lobbying for equal pay, opening more job categories to women, securing the right to serve on juries, and other equity issues, they would have made significant contributions to social advancement. Instead, they chose to become revolutionaries, howling at the nature of femininity, love, marriage, and motherhood. The deepest irony is that their "radical" new ideas owed more to two nineteenth-century European men, Karl Marx and Sigmund Freud, than to any woman.

The Sexual Revolutionaries

The sexual revolution is commonly dated to 1960, the year the Food and Drug Administration approved Enovid, the first oral contraceptive. But it's doubtful "the Pill" actually sparked the revolution. As historian Alan Petigny argues in *The Permissive Society: America, 1941–1965,* Enovid was difficult to obtain for many years after it received FDA approval. It was relatively expensive then and required a doctor's prescription. Physicians in the early 1960s were loath to prescribe it for unmarried women, and even as late as 1971, when the price had come down, only about 10 percent of women between age fifteen and nineteen said the Pill was their form of contraception.

Many factors played a role in the first sexual loosening of the twentieth century. The technology to vulcanize rubber made condoms and diaphragms widely available in the years after World War I. Booze played a role too. The most obvious unintended consequence of Prohibition was the expansion of crime and the empowerment of criminal gangs. But another change ushered in by the law was the normalization of public drinking by women. Before Prohibition, most drinking occurred in saloons and bars that were male-dominated. Carrie Nation, the flamboyant six-foot-tall temperance crusader, attacked saloons with an axe. But the Volstead Act stimulated the invention of the speakeasy, which catered to both sexes. "Under the new regime, not only the drinks were mixed, but the company was as well."[71]

The 1920s in America also saw the emergence of the automobile, especially the closed automobile, which put couples out of sight of parents and other chaperones. The divorce rate doubled between 1910 and 1928 (though it was still low by today's standards), and the number of Americans who approved of pre- or extramarital relationships grew, though more slowly than it did later in the century.

The relaxation of American standards was evident to the British in the 1940s. During the Second World War, Britons played host to thousands of American GIs, about whom they sniffed, "They're overpaid, oversexed, and over here."[72] Apparently, American women were feeling randy as well: unwed pregnancies doubled between 1946 and 1958.[73] Though the 1950s are now remembered as a period of stuffy respectability, the American appetite for sexual information and entertainment was already rumbling ravenously. The steamy 1956 novel *Peyton Place* flew off the shelves. Americans pored over the Kinsey Reports, first on male and then on female sexuality, and teenagers swooned as Elvis Presley gyrated his hips.

Feminists did not invent the sexual revolution, but they

certainly joined it and, by doing so, ratified it. Without women's seal of approval, the sexual revolution would have been nothing more than another attempt in a long history of men urging women to let down their guard. Thousands of years of civilizational evolution had been necessary to get men to subordinate their natural desire for lots of sex with many partners to women's preference for monogamy and faithfulness. One of recent history's greatest scams was persuading women that offering men commitment-free sex was a victory for womankind.

Pre- and Extramarital Sex Goes Mainstream

The first woman to embrace the sexual revolution was not a self-described feminist, but Helen Gurley Brown, a slick saleswoman who would go on to a lucrative career turning *Cosmopolitan* into a soft-core porn magazine. Her 1962 blockbuster, *Sex and the Single Girl,* was a triumph of titling, especially considering how little of the book concerned sex (though an early draft apparently included advice on birth control and abortion).[74] It was a self-help book in the tradition of Dale Carnegie's *How to Win Friends and Influence People.* Brown, too, pitched her book to aspiring young people hoping to make their way in the world. With brisk confidence, she offered advice on everything from renting and decorating apartments to dressing well to job hunting to plastic surgery. Brown seemed to regard men and love as just another way to get ahead in the world.

In some respects, *Sex and the Single Girl* is old-fashioned. The assumption throughout is that young women will scrimp, save, reuse, scheme, flirt, and plan for success in the world of work. Brown advised them not to be ashamed of a low-level starting job. Get your foot in the door, and who knows where your energy, drive, and propinquity might lead? Many of her tips stand up well, as does her commonsense practicality. The following words would raise shrieks from most of today's college-educated women (and it's doubtful they would appear in the pages of today's *Cosmopolitan*), but fifty years later, they remain pretty accurate: "The Ultimatum: Hardly any bachelor wants to get married. Even the most adorable, non-phobic one has to be gently but firmly prodded into matrimony. If the truth be known, many of your married girlfriends who you thought were the pursued darlings used everything from vapors to bloodletting to get their man. It's nothing to be ashamed of."[75]

Although some of *Sex and the Single Girl*'s advice sounds like an updated version of Horatio Alger, it's important to remember that Brown was addressing a new class of women. Until the mid-twentieth century, most unmarried women lived with their parents or other relatives, or if work took them to another region, they found a respectable boardinghouse. With the economy's expansion in the 1950s and '60s, women could afford to rent (or more often share) their own apartments.

Brown saw in this new independence an opportunity for sexual adventure, or at least she saw the financial possibilities for herself in peddling the idea. "Theoretically," she wrote, "a 'nice' single woman has no sex life. What nonsense! She has a better sex life than most of her married friends." This is a dubious claim. Many surveys have found that married women enjoy sex more than their single sisters, but Brown had books to sell. She was among the first to suggest that women think of their "sex lives" as separate from their family lives. Much would follow from that.

She unblushingly itemized the benefits of having affairs with married men: "Plusses: good sex, admiration, even adoration from him. We're not talking about outright being kept, but delicious prezzies and trips are often in his portfolio." Years later, she claimed to be the first feminist. She acknowledged that Gloria Steinem "worked her brains out," but "I was one of the first to tell women, 'Make up your own mind about your life and don't just be somebody's appendage. Create your own identity.'" She continued, "I was among the first to say that sex before marriage can be the best sex of your life."

Apparently overcome by her own insight, she added, "Sex is pleasurable. I can't think of anything better than having an orgasm. It's just yummy. Sex is one of the three best things you have—and I don't know what the other two things are."[76]

Americans are ambitious and always looking for ways to improve their lot. *Sex and the Single Girl* offered a road map for career and personal success. That women might be the losers in a sexual free-for-all (particularly the married women whose husbands were now ripe targets for single "girls") doesn't seem to have troubled Brown. She encouraged young American women to toss aside sexual restraint the way they did last year's fashions. As for children, they didn't interest her. But Brown wasn't on fire with rage against men, marriage, and the female plight the way the feminists who soon dominated the movement were. On the contrary, the song "I Enjoy Being a Girl" could have been written for her.

The Dead Hands of Marx and Freud

The feminists who came next were in a different mood. If Brown's book told women how to get the most out of men, the new feminists were determined to change what women wanted altogether. The second-wave feminists were radical, unhappy, and, ironically, enslaved to the ideas of two nineteenth-century "dead, white, European males": Karl Marx and Sigmund Freud. The worldview of second-wave feminists was completely wrong about women, history, and human nature—and it left a lot of wreckage in its wake.

The second-wavers might quibble with Marx and deviate from Freud on some points of doctrine, but they were firmly within the Marxist and Freudian traditions. They saw themselves as transgressive, but they also reflected the intellectual currents of their time. They believed in the Marxist assertion about classes vying for supremacy. They also accepted the Freudian view (which traces back to Jean-Jacques Rousseau) that human beings in their natural state are essentially "free," and that civilization imposes on them costly and unnecessary limitations on their natural desires. For them, the first step in liberation is recognizing that one belongs to an oppressed class; the second is throwing off "repressions" and "taboos."

Feminists were Marxists with an asterisk. They fully embraced Marx and Engels's concept of class war, but they threw "sex" into the mix of classes. The radical feminist Redstockings issued a manifesto that proclaimed that because women lived with their "oppressors," they had been "kept from seeing our personal suffering as a political condition. This creates the illusion that a woman's relationship with her man is a matter of interplay between two unique personalities, and can be worked out individually. In reality, every such relationship is a class relationship, and the conflicts between individual men and women are political conflicts that can only be solved collectively."[77]

In 1970, three furious feminist tracts dominated the best-seller lists: Germaine Greer's *The Female Eunuch,* Shulamith Firestone's *The Dialectic of Sex,* and Kate Millett's *Sexual Politics.* When I arrived at college in the mid-1970s, Greer in particular was all the rage. Gloria Steinem, who described herself as a Marxist, was also in vogue, but she was better known for one-liners than for a worked-out philosophy.[78]

Greer wrote that "Women have somehow been separated from their libido, from their faculty of desire, from their sexuality. They've become suspicious about it. Like beasts, for example, that are castrated in farming in order to serve their master's ulterior motives—to be fattened or made docile—women have been cut off from their capacity for action. It's a process that sacrifices vigor for delicacy and succulence, and one that's got to be changed."[79]

Greer, an Australian with a Cambridge University pedigree, became a pop-culture sensation. She did not achieve this with the lurid prose and intellectual pretensions found on page after page of *The Female Eunuch*. No, she did it the way nearly all pop sensations do: she sold sex. In the foreword to the twenty-first-anniversary edition, Greer mocks reviewers who interpreted her magnum opus as "telling women to go out and do it," but the critics were more right than wrong. "In the final analysis," she writes, "women aren't really free until their libidos are recognized as separate entities."

Greer described herself at times as an anarchist and at others as an anarchist/communist—so there's Marx's ghost hovering over her work. Freud is well represented too. Though she takes some much-quoted shots at the father of psychoanalysis and other Freudians in her chapter "The Psychological Sell," she accepts Freud's basic schema of the mind throughout the rest of her book.

"Women have very little idea of how much men hate them,"[80] Greer advises. Her counsel—which she herself did not follow—was that women should never marry. The entire social system was a conspiracy to keep women down. When one looks back at *The Female Eunuch* forty-five years later, it isn't clear that Greer loved women very much. She describes women as "masked menials" whose blighted lives are enlivened only when they vie for the attention of husbands—sometimes their own, sometimes not.

Greer's book was greeted as a brave manifesto for female empowerment, but the tone throughout is bitter and cynical. She devotes a mocking chapter to romance literature, yet acknowledges the powerful influence such books exerted on her own teenage self. "I cannot claim to be fully emancipated from the dream that some enormous man, say six foot six, heavily shouldered and so forth to match, will crush me to his tweeds, look down into my eyes and leave the taste of heaven or the scorch of his passion on my waiting lips."[81] (Greer is six feet tall.)

She considered a loving marriage to be a myth. "What many women mistake for happiness is in fact resignation," she told an Australian reporter the year *Eunuch* was published.[82] She could not accept that reality sometimes falls short of one's adolescent fantasies. British housewives often work, she complained, because their husbands do not earn enough to support them. "Still more know that their husbands are paunchy, short, unathletic, and snore or smell or leave their clothes lying around."[83]

Germaine Greer was thrice married but had no children, and her treatment of maternity was heavily ideological and detached. She accepted the Freudian view that children were caught in the terrible tragedy of Oedipal conflict. Imagining the typical mother, she wrote, "Her child is too much cared for . . . and[,] when her husband returns from work, soon banished from the adult world to his bed, so that Daddy can relax. The Oedipal situation which is always duplicated in marriage is now intensified to a degree which Freud would have found appalling."[84]

In other moods, Greer offered daydreams about how children ought to be raised that are about as compelling as a sumo wrestler's advice on ballet. When she was not disparaging childbearing as "breeding," she was spinning tales of utopia. She envisioned raising her child in a farmhouse in Calabria together with other women. The children's fathers would visit from time to time, and the children would explore nature, work on the farm, garden a bit, and perhaps never even know who their actual "womb mother" was.

Naturally, none of the women would be married to the fathers of their children. "If women are to effect a significant amelioration in their condition," Greer wrote, "it seems obvious that they must refuse to marry."[85] As sexually dominant creatures, they would have sex whenever and wherever they liked. But mothering by mothers would be unnecessary, even undesirable. "A group of children can be more successfully civilized by one or two women who have voluntarily undertaken the work than they can be when divided and tyrannized over by a single woman who finds herself bored and imposed upon."[86]

Women who followed Greer's advice would have to be "brave" enough to abandon their most sacred promises and responsibilities. "Most women, because of the assumptions that they have formed about the importance of their role as bearers and socializers of children, would shrink at the notion of leaving husband and children, *but this is precisely the case in which brutally clear rethinking must be undertaken*"[87] (emphasis added). The word *brutally* is apt.

The revolt against marriage and family was part of a larger revolutionary project for Greer. Society was profoundly corrupt and needed to be remade from the bottom to the top. "Women's liberation, if it abolishes the patriarchal family, will abolish a necessary substructure of the authoritarian state . . . [L]et the demolition begin."[88] And so it has.

In the chapter titled "Family," Greer reveals that her own family was miserable. "Our society has created the myth of the broken home which is the source of so many ills, and yet the unbroken home which ought to have broken is an even greater source of tension as I can attest from bitter experience."[89]

Greer's mother suffered from Asperger syndrome, and her father was apparently remote and unloving. "I can recall being beaten for giving away all my toys when I was about four," Greer writes.[90] Her biographer described Greer's mother as a "terrorizing force."[91] Greer recalled in a 2011 radio interview that her mother would "slap me in the face," while adding that "in those days, all mothers did that."[92] No, they didn't.

Many of the leading second-wave feminists seem to have had difficult relationships with their parents. Betty Friedan felt she could never compete in femininity with her beautiful mother. Gloria Steinem's parents divorced when she was ten years old, leaving her the sole caregiver for a mother who suffered from severe mental illness. Robin Morgan, a founder of New York Radical Women and other feminist organizations, had a stage mother who pushed the five-year-old Robin into acting. After struggling against her mother's dominance for a decade, Robin quit acting at the age of fourteen. Andrea Dworkin, who famously argued that all sexual intercourse was a form of rape and who described "romance" as "rape embellished with meaningful looks," was raped or molested at age nine. Kate Millett's father was an alcoholic who beat his daughter and abandoned the family when Kate was fourteen.

People deserve sympathy and often admiration for the difficulties they overcome. It is clearly not the fault of the girl that her parents were unfaithful, alcoholic, or otherwise. I mention the personal struggles of the second-wave feminists only because they explicitly insisted that "the personal is political." Of the major second-wave feminists, none had a lifelong successful marriage. Few were mothers. The conventional life script of marriage, work, home, children, and grandchildren (something most women hope for) was not their goal. They seemed determined to persuade American women that these things were traps and snares.

Second-wave feminists believed that women had been hood-winked for centuries into wanting marriage and children. To deprogram (or, depending upon your point of view, indoctrinate) them, feminists proposed "consciousness-raising" sessions. *Life* magazine profiled one that met weekly in New York City. A poster on the wall invoked the Chinese Communist Revolution, the civil rights movement, and the "final revolution," summing up with "Bitch, sisters, bitch!"

Often, the focus was not just "the patriarchy" but also nature and its unjust burdens. The most quoted section of *The Female Eunuch* was: "If you think you are emancipated, you might consider the idea of tasting your menstrual blood—if it makes you sick, you've a long way to go, baby." Greer's dubious point was that women had been taught disgust about bodily functions. Perhaps she mistook manners and good taste for shame. "Women still buy sanitary towels with enormous discretion, and carry their bags to the loo when they need only carry a napkin."[93] She didn't ask why neither sex headed to the restroom clutching rolls of toilet paper. She went further, and howled at nature herself. "Menstruation," she wrote, was a "horror" and a "bad joke." Why, she demanded, "should women not resent an inconvenience which causes tension before, after, and during; unpleasantness, odour, staining . . . there is no rational ground for maintaining that menstruation as we know it . . . must be irreversible."[94]

Note that in this passage, Greer is not protesting patriarchy or inequality or women's oppression by society. She is rejecting biology. She is not urging relief from menstrual discomfort but demanding that medical science treat menstruation as a form of illness. "The new assumption behind the discussion of the body is that everything that we may observe *could be otherwise*" (emphasis in original).[95] And with this, a leading feminist pathologized femaleness.

Celebrity seems to have been the one great love of Greer's life. Her specialty was shock value, as seen in the dramatic calls for women to taste their menstrual blood. Since that was a hard act to follow, she later reached for greater vulgarity, posing for nude photos, publishing articles with titles such as "I Am a Whore" and "Welcome to the Shit-Storm," and sitting for an interview with *Playboy* magazine. So did the feminist and sexual revolutions join hands.

Her prescriptions for women's happiness (sexual experimentation, aggressiveness, and radical independence) were unconnected to the needs and desires of most women. "There is no such thing as security," she writes. "There never has been."[96] As a matter of metaphysics, this may be true. But Greer is not referring to mortality or even to the vicissitudes of fate. She is arguing that marriage and family provide the illusion of security. "A lover who comes to your bed of his own accord is more likely to sleep with his arms around you all night than a lover who has nowhere else to sleep."[97]

Rubbish. A married couple, secure in each other's love, trusting in each other's loyalty, and forsaking all others, are far more reliable lovers than anyone who wanders into one's bed on any given night.

Later, she careened into different policy prescriptions like an intellectual pinball. She endorsed chastity and denounced birth control. She decried breast cancer screening and, to the dismay of many feminists, abortion. She even condemned efforts to combat female genital mutilation in Middle Eastern countries as attacks on others' "cultural identity."

In the updated introduction to the book, published in 1981, Greer reveals second thoughts about her embrace of sexual promiscuity. "Twenty years ago," she wrote, "it was important to stress the right of sexual expression and far less important to underline a woman's right to reject male advances." But times had changed. Now she was interested in the "the right to reject penetration by the male member, the right to safe sex, the right to chastity, the right to defer physical intimacy until there is irrefutable evidence of commitment, because of the appearance on the earth of AIDS."[98]

Actually, women had excellent reasons to demand commitment before AIDS entered the picture. It's a measure of Greer's shallowness, her misunderstanding of the realities of male/female sexual differences, that she was unable to see it. She was the diva of sexual experimentation and transgression in 1970. That was the spirit of the age, without a doubt. Greer embodied it, celebrated it, and dined out on it for decades. Twenty years on, she was having second thoughts, but rather than face the truth (that sexual promiscuity was terrible for women, men, and children), she grabbed the AIDS scare as a fig leaf and hid behind it.

Second-wave feminists are often cited for their critique of Freudian concepts such as "penis envy" (and that was certainly a Freudian flight of fancy that cried out for ridicule), but even when feminists assailed Freud, their embrace of the sexual revolution had the effect of ratifying him.

The popular understanding of Freud, which has dominated American thought for a century or more, is that sexual repression is the cause of various neuroses, and that sexual liberation should represent a giant leap toward health. Freud wrote that "No neurosis is possible with a normal *vita sexualis.*"[99] Feminists saw sexual inhibitions, later derided as "hang-ups," as evidence of male oppression, while at the same time male sexual revolutionaries saw them as inconvenient barriers to commitment-free sex.

Freudian influence on the intellectual life of the twentieth century (from theater to literature to criminal justice to education) cannot be overstated. The critic Alfred Kazin summed up Freud's influence: "In the same way that one associates the discovery of certain fundamentals with Copernicus, Newton, Darwin, Einstein, so one identifies many of one's deepest motivations with

Freud. His name is no longer the name of a man; like 'Darwin,' it is now synonymous with a part of nature. This is the very greatest kind of influence that a man can have."[100]

Or, as the poet W. H. Auden wrote, "To us he is no more a person / Now but a whole climate of opinion." Feminists lived in that same climate. Shulamith Firestone, another best-selling feminist fire breather who burst onto the scene in 1970, argued that Freudianism and feminism had common roots because "Freud grasped the crucial problem of modern life: sexuality."[101] She acknowledged that some of Freud's views were "absurd," yet agreed that sexual repression was the root of all social ills. Firestone protested that Freud had not gone far enough. There could be no escape, she thought, from the pathologies that sexual repression and Oedipal conflicts create without the destruction of the incubus—the nuclear family.

Firestone hoped to upend pretty much everything about relations between men and women. "Genital" distinctions between the sexes would no longer matter culturally. If that sounds familiar, it's because modern feminism adopted this goal, if not Firestone's wild language. Yet just a few sentences from Firestone's *The Dialectic of Sex* reveal the fantasy world she was spinning:

A reversion to an unobstructed *pansexuality*—Freud's "polymorphous perversity"—would probably supersede hetero/homo/bi-sexuality. The reproduction of the species by one sex for the benefit of both would be replaced by (at least the option of) artificial reproduction: children would be born to both sexes equally, or independently of either, however one chooses to look at it; the dependence of the child on the mother (and vice versa) would give way to a greatly shortened dependence on a small group of others in general, and any remaining inferiority to adults in physical strength would be compensated for culturally. The division of labor would be ended by the elimination of labor altogether (cybernetics). The tyranny of the biological family would be broken.[102]

The Dialectic of Sex accepts Freud and Marx the way Islam accepts Moses and Jesus, as precursors to the final, true revelation. Firestone promised that her philosophy would go beyond Freud and beyond Marx. And it does—into incoherence. She claims that everything about civilization, from the economic system to the family, had to be reimagined in light of the oppression women face due to biology. Until women were freed from giving birth, women's liberation would stall.[103]

Firestone's life was blighted by mental illness. She died, age sixty-seven, alone, in a fifth-floor walkup in Manhattan. When they found her body, she'd been dead for several days. There was no food in the apartment. She had been suffering from schizophrenia for decades. I mean no disrespect to the mentally ill, but the marks of a disordered mind are plainly evident in *The Dialectic of Sex*. There are dozens of bizarre arguments along with odd graphs and charts with heavily bolded arrows and symbols. One chart shows a category labeled "Culture: based on psychological division of responses for: realization of the conceivable in the possible." This is followed by scribblings in a neighboring box called "control of the tool-fire-wheel" and then "religion" in another box, and so on. Another graphic features text reading horizontally and vertically with arrows and male and female symbols along with dashes and ellipses. These are not sane exercises.

Even so, Firestone was a critical voice of the radical feminists. Most of them were not insane, of course, though they often believed in insane ideas. Journalist Susan Faludi described Firestone's 2012 memorial service as verging "on radical-feminist revival." She said, "women distributed flyers on consciousness-raising, and displayed copies of texts published by the Redstockings, a New York group that Firestone co-founded." In the same piece, Faludi wrote about a proposal for a "Shulamith Firestone Women's Liberation Memorial Conference on What Is to Be Done."[104] "What Is to Be Done" is a reference to a pamphlet published in 1902 by an aspiring Russian revolutionary named Vladimir Lenin.[105]

That *The Dialectic of Sex* was ever taken seriously shows how unhinged the second-wave feminists, and particularly the radical feminists, could be. Here was a book proclaiming "all children" to be oppressed, all families to be unhappy, and demanding a science-fiction "solution" to the problem of childbirth that contemplated real test-tube babies. To be clear, Firestone was imagining not just in vitro fertilization, the union of gametes in a petri dish, but gestation, somehow, of babies for nine months in laboratories.

Yet Kate Millett would say of Firestone, admiringly, "I was taking on the obvious male chauvinists. Shulie was taking on the whole ball of wax."[106] That "ball of wax" was reality itself.

Schisms

By the 1980s, feminism had been riven by quarrels. Warring camps declared themselves "sex-positive" or "sex-negative." Ellen Willis, one of the "sex-positive" feminists, published a monograph in the Duke University journal *Social Text* arguing that feminists had an urgent duty to continue the path of feminist sexual revolution. "Organized feminism," she wrote, "has been united in endorsing sexual freedom for women . . . to engage in sexual activity for our own pleasure, to have sex and bear children outside marriage, to control our fertility, to refuse sex with any particular man or all men, to be lesbians." The phrase "control our fertility" clearly includes abortion, though Willis chose to leave this implicit.[107]

Willis rejected the idea then gaining purchase among some feminists that "heterosexual relations [are] more or less synonymous with rape, on the grounds that male sexuality is by definition predatory and sadistic,"[108] yet her endorsement of sexual libertinism rests firmly on Freud's utterly debunked phantasm of the Oedipal conflict and "castration anxiety." Acknowledging that American society in 1982 was quite liberated sexually, Willis was at pains to explain why both men and women were unhappy with the results. Her answer is a labored, one might even say excruciating, restatement of the Freudian theory of the primal family melodrama, in which infantile boys (between ages three and five) desire to copulate with their mothers and fear that their fathers will castrate them in retaliation. Boys and girls alike are supposedly traumatized when they learn that girls do not have penises. For boys, this realization awakens "castration anxiety," and for girls, "penis envy" and feelings of inferiority.

Willis goes on at length in this vein, sounding like an eager psychoanalysis acolyte in 1920s Vienna. She speculated that young girls live out the fateful Oedipal drama this way: "Her moment of awful truth comes when she understands that her father will neither restore her penis nor choose her over her mother."[109]

But what if Freud was wrong? Where does that leave the sexual revolution and the feminism that unwisely endorsed it?

Freud is credited with inventing the "talking cure," the foundation of modern psychotherapy. There is little doubt that a variety of therapists are able to help patients through sensitive listening and dispassionate advice. But Freud was no scientist. His work has been debunked in any number of professional journals, books, and conferences.

Philosopher Edward Erwin, in a detailed analysis of Freudian psychology, noted flaws with nearly every specific insight Freud advanced. He found no support for Freud's concept that paranoia arises from repressed homosexuality, nor for the notion that dreams are wish fulfillments, nor for the idea that excessive tidiness in adults results from poor toilet training, nor any other theory. "The amount of confirmation of distinctively Freudian hypotheses is close to zero," he wrote in 1996, stating further, "Has the effectiveness of Freud's therapy been established? No. How much of his theory has been confirmed? Virtually none of it. These verdicts are likely to be final."[110]

As critic Frederick Crews, in a heated exchange with Freud's defenders in a series published in the *New York Review of Books,* summed up: "Freud's theories of personality and neurosis—derived as they were from misleading precedents, vacuous pseudo-physical metaphors, and a long concatenation of mistaken inferences that couldn't be subjected to empirical review—amount to castles in the air."[111]

As for Karl Marx, his legacy is one of the greatest tragedies in human history. Marx's economic theories have been debunked. He predicted, for example, that the income gap between the proletariat and the bourgeoisie would continue to increase, that workers' wages would steadily decline, that profits would fall, that capitalism would collapse due to its own "contradictions," and that revolutions would break out in the advanced countries of Europe. In fact, in the century and a half since Marx's death, standards of living for workers have dramatically improved, market economies have not collapsed but have instead thrived (even, ironically, in formerly communist states like China), and communist revolutions happened in backward nations like Russia and China.

More important, the nations that came under communist control in the twentieth century suffered mass starvation, oppression, and state terror on a scale that has few historical precedents. According to the *Black Book of Communism,* communist regimes were directly responsible for the murders of between 85 million and 100 million people.[112]

On that note, let's return to the banner year of 1970, when second-wave feminists dominated the landscape and Kate Millett achieved instant celebrity with the publication of *Sexual Politics,* an ambitious polemic that interpreted all of human history through the lens of male power and female enslavement. *Time* magazine, not unkindly, dubbed Millett the "Mao Tse-tung of Women's Liberation." It's likely that Millett had more humanity than the monstrous Mao (who was responsible for the deaths of 65 million Chinese), but her ambitions to remake society were quite as radical. Hers was a comprehensive outline for the new world that feminists hoped to create. For Millett, "A fully realized sexual revolution would require . . . an end to traditional sexual inhibitions and taboos, particularly those that most threaten patriarchal monogamous marriage: homosexuality, 'illegitimacy,' adolescent, pre- and extra-marital sexuality . . . The goal of revolution would be a permissive single standard of sexual freedom, and one uncorrupted by the crass and exploitative economic bases of traditional sexual alliances."[113]

"Crass and exploitative economic bases" were feminist code words for marriage. Millett sometimes abjured the code words altogether, endorsing Friedrich Engels's belief that "the family, as that term is presently understood, must go."[114]

"[T]he great mass of women throughout history," Millett writes, "have been confined to the cultural level of animal life in providing the male with sexual outlet and exercising the animal functions of reproduction and care of the young."[115]

Millett was an enthusiastic sexual liberationist, waxing rhapsodic about women's superior capacity for sexual pleasure. "All the best scientific evidence today unmistakably tends toward the conclusion that the female possesses, biologically and inherently, a far greater capacity for sexuality than the male."[116]

Sex roles, she argues, were wholly an artifact of culture, not founded in nature. Though first articulated by Millett, this theme would be echoed and elaborated by later feminists and would become part of the academic and "enlightened" view of society. This is where we find the roots of our current confusion about whether masculinity and femininity are natural or whether they are "socially constructed." Here is the origin of the movement on college campuses to have students declare their preferred pronouns.

In *Sexual Politics,* Millett calls for the eradication of sex roles and the complete financial independence of women. Professional child care, which Millett imagined would be far superior to parental care, would also free children from their status as "chattel."

Millett's book is part literary criticism, part rant. She takes swipes at some well-known writers, notably Norman Mailer, D. H. Lawrence, and Henry Miller. No doubt they deserved their rebukes, but her analysis is utterly paralyzed by her relentless obsession with female victimization. She has her innings with Freud too, but sadly, instead of critiquing his science, she complains that the "effect of Freud's work . . . was to rationalize the invidious relationship between the sexes."[117]

In 2016, Columbia University Press published a new edition of *Sexual Politics,* which attests to the book's continuing relevance/ popularity in academic circles. Catharine MacKinnon, often dubbed the "godmother of sexual harassment law," contributed the enthusiastic introduction.

Feminists joined the sexual revolution because they were good Marxists and more or less good Freudians, and because they were part of the New Left counterculture that rejected nearly every aspect of American (and Western) culture. Anger was the feminist métier. The celebrated feminist poet Adrienne Rich raged that "a thinking woman sleeps with monsters" and coined the term *compulsory heterosexuality.* When she died in 2012, the *New York Times* obituary nearly swooned with admiration of her "unswerving progressive vision and a dazzling, empathic ferocity." Her poetry, the obituary continued, "brought the oppression of women and lesbians to the forefront of poetic discourse and kept it there for nearly a half century."[118]

Compared with Rich, Gloria Steinem was the girl next door, but she was certainly an eager enlistee in the sexual revolution. When, in 1962, the president of Vassar College expressed the view that premarital sex was "offensive and vulgar behavior," Steinem took to the pages of *Esquire* magazine to mock her. The 1962 Steinem was not yet a feminist firebrand, and her tone was mild. "For better or worse," she wrote, "the emphasis is now on the individual, and group judgments of individual actions are out-of-date."[119] She praised birth control and the new sexual freedom for young women—though, interestingly, the word *abortion* is completely absent from her piece.

Later, Steinem remembered the pre–sexual revolution days with revulsion. "There was always the fear that you might be punished for being sexual," she told David Allyn, author of *Make Love,*

Not War: "The young miss, for example, must never take any real initiative in courtship . . . must never go home with a man whom she has just met at a dance, lest he consider her 'just a pick-up' . . . must not act too intelligent when she's with a boy because 'boys don't like you to be smart' . . . must never phone a fellow unless she is going steady with him."[120]

Sexual pleasure became a rallying cry. A revolutionary cell calling itself New York Radical Women published a pamphlet called "The Myth of Vaginal Orgasm." The National Organization for Women lobbied for abortion on demand. The National Abortion Rights Action League was founded. Everyone quoted a best seller called *The Hite Report,* which proposed that women were miserably unhappy in their sexual relations with men. Shere Hite's methodology was so poor that even reviewers from friendly publications such as the *Los Angeles Times* and *Time* magazine felt obliged to note that her data were not at all representative of American women. Hite claimed that 98 percent of women were dissatisfied with their relationships with men, but a *Washington Post*/ABC News poll in 1987 found that 93 percent of women said their relationships were good or excellent. Hite's various reports were, like those of Alfred Kinsey, textbook cases of junk science.[121]

Other sexual revolutionaries, such as Hugh Hefner, welcomed feminists' support for eliminating traditional obstacles to male sexual license. Hefner, the founder of Playboy Enterprises, offered financial support to the NOW Legal Defense and Education Fund, supported the Equal Rights Amendment, and filed amicus curiae briefs in abortion cases before the Supreme Court. "I was a feminist before there was such a thing as feminism," he boasted.[122] The crusaders for "free love" got the "free" part. Whether people got the "love" is another matter.

Examining the origins of the feminist embrace of the sexual revolution, Barbara Ehrenreich, Elizabeth Hess, and Gloria Jacobs reflected the common view: that sexual freedom and female power were linked. "Early feminist writers on sex . . . insisted, at least implicitly, that sex should have no ultimate meaning other than pleasure, and no great mystery except how to achieve it. They realized that for women to insist on pleasure was to assert power."[123]

Is any of that true?

Surely if power is one's chief goal, joining the sexual revolution was the worst move for heterosexual women. As Ellen Willis acknowledged, "Sexual liberalism has allowed many men to assert these patterns [to delink sex from love and responsibility] in ways that were once socially taboo, and to impose them on reluctant women."[124] As George Orwell reminded us, "Sometimes the first duty of intelligent men is the restatement of the obvious." So let's say it: Women's desire for sex is less urgent and powerful than men's. Accordingly, nature has given women an advantage or bargaining chip with men. Why should women give that up? Why did they?

Besides, in loving relationships, power is not the highest good. A willingness on the part of men and women to think of the other, to share, to support, to cherish—those are the marks of ideal human relationships. Contests of power are demeaning and coarsening for both sexes.

And while pleasure is nice, elevating it to the highest personal or political goal is childish. Pleasure is only one aspect of a relationship, and of life. It is, by definition, pleasant, but it is not the highest good. It may not even be the highest good of sex; that distinction may belong to the bonding that sexual intercourse promotes between spouses. And there is an irony in the feminist demand for sexual license in the pursuit of sexual pleasure. Women, more than men, find their greatest sexual pleasure in the context of committed relationships.

Surveys reviewed at the International Academy of Sex Research showed that women were only half as likely as men to experience orgasm in a casual hookup.[125] "The notion of sexual liberation, where men and women both had equal access to casual sex, assumed a comparable likelihood of that sex being pleasurable," explained Kim Wallen, a professor of neuroendocrinology at Emory

University who presented his findings. "But that part of the playing field isn't level."[126] Fully 75 percent of women in committed relationships, the Academy found, had orgasms.

Many studies show that when women feel safe in a relationship, they experience more sexual pleasure, but you hardly need studies to imagine why this should be so. Communication, trust, and experience are necessary for women's maximum sexual pleasure. A man who is committed to a woman on many levels, who has an ongoing relationship with her, a need for her, and an awareness of who she is as a human being, is more likely to put in the effort to please her sexually than a casual bedmate would be.

Ehrenreich and her fellow authors denied, perhaps a bit too defensively, that the sexual revolution was a "victory for men and a joke on women."[127] They, like other feminists, are convinced that the old sexual mores were a yoke on women. If love, sex, and childbirth were the chains that held women down, the first step toward freedom was to dump the sexual "double standard." If men could have premarital sex without too much loss of reputation, the same should be true of women. If men could sow their "wild oats," then women must do the same.

When I enrolled in college in 1975, promiscuity was a political cause. A popular slogan of the era was "Chaste makes waste," and the spirit of the age was that sex was "no big deal" or "no different from a handshake." Feminists railed at the patriarchy for making unhappy wives feel that something was wrong with them. Yet women who shrank from the new sexual dispensation felt equally, if not more, judged. Women who were reluctant to treat sex as mere sport were derided for being "uptight." Yet few could shed their natural reticence entirely. Drugs and alcohol could anesthetize women, and with time, female drunkenness would skyrocket.

The counterculture view was that middle-class morality was inauthentic and stifling. As Hillary Rodham declared in her 1969 graduation speech from Wellesley, her generation was finished with all that, and was seeking "more immediate, ecstatic, and penetrating modes of living." The dean of students at Columbia

University explained to the *New York Times* that it was becoming increasingly acceptable for undergraduate couples to live together: "It reflects what's happening in America today: The breakdown of the Victorian and Protestant Ethics; the creation of a whole new set of values, and a new emphasis on honesty and integrity in interpersonal relationships." This was the purest claptrap. There may have been a breakdown in ethics, but honesty and integrity didn't enter into it.

Perhaps the most representative expression of the spirit of the sexual revolution was the 1966 best seller *The Harrad Experiment*, by Robert Rimmer, a utopian novel set in a New England college. The college is the site of a sociology experiment in which students are assigned roommates based upon sexual compatibility (determined by a computer). In this lubricious, polyamorous atmosphere, young people learn to shed "embarrassment, envy, shame, and other forms of sexual repression." As David Allyn wrote, "students discover" in the story, "that heterosexual relationships can be based on full equality between men and women. They realize that most of the differences . . . (especially the differences in sexual attitudes) are shaped by society, not by biology. In the state of nature . . . men are gentle and considerate while women crave sexual variety."[128] Monogamy, the book taught, arises from the idea of women as property. In the new world, women and men will be free to "explore their sexuality."

In the novel, men and women, once freed from sexual repression, embrace group marriages and ascend the evolutionary ladder to, "a world where men and women can and must relate their sexual drives and needs for one another into a unified whole so that the act of sex is a perfectly wonderful consummation of a much larger ecstasy and pride and joy and respect for the amazing fact that each of us, man and woman, are human beings."[129]

Despite writing of that caliber, *The Harrad Experiment* was a blockbuster. It sold 2.5 million copies in the first eighteen months and was, unsurprisingly, extremely popular on college campuses.

Feminists were among Rimmer's most enthusiastic boosters. Betty Friedan personally invited him to join the National Organization for Women, and the American Association of University Women sought his views on the cultural construction of gender roles.[130]

Regrets

Soon after joining forces with the sexual revolutionaries, some feminists began to have second thoughts. According to Ellen Willis, one feminist faction concluded that "the sexual revolution simply legitimized the age-old tendency of men in a male-supremacist society to coerce, cajole, or fool women into giving them sex without getting anything—love, respect, responsibility for the children, or even erotic pleasure—in return."[131]

Ti-Grace Atkinson, head of the New York chapter of NOW, told *Life* magazine in 1969 that "The more I understand what's going on with men, the less I miss male companionship and sex. Men brag about domination, conquest, trickery, exploitation. It gets so I can't even respond. Male chauvinism comes out in waves—every gesture, every word."[132]

Like many radical feminists of the day, Atkinson soon gave up on sex with men altogether. "Feminism is the theory," she said, "lesbianism is the practice."[133] A significant percentage of radical feminists saw lesbianism as a political statement. One group called the Furies issued a manifesto explaining that "Lesbianism is not a matter of sexual preference, but rather one of political choice which every woman must make if she is to become woman-identified and thereby end male supremacy."[134] The men of the left, who tended to be the only men radical women interacted with, were clearly behaving in ways that the feminists found wanting.

The late Andrea Dworkin is not a household name, but she continues to influence modern feminists. Actress and writer Lena Dunham called upon the "spirit of Andrea Dworkin" when she mused about her fantasy girl band, which she said would also include Rep. Debbie Wasserman Schultz, Dr. Jill Biden, Sen. Kamala Harris, and Cindy McCain.[135]

Dworkin's radical feminism grew out of disillusionment with a particular subset of men—those in the New Left, as *New York* magazine confirmed in a sympathetic appreciation published after her death.[136] Dworkin was a model of the angry feminist. Eschewing makeup and fashion, she made lesbianism an anti-male cause rather than an affirmation of female homosexuality. "Men are shits and take pleasure in it," she writes in her memoir, *Heartbreak.* In another book, *Intercourse,* she writes that "Intercourse is the pure, sterile, formal expression of men's contempt for women."[137]

Dworkin was an extreme case. But Todd Gitlin, a former radical himself, speculated about the kind of behavior among left-wing men that might have offended even less sensitive women: "Men sought them out, recruited them, took them seriously, honored their intelligence—then subtly demoted them to girlfriends, wives, note-takers, coffeemakers."[138]

Cathy Wilkerson, who had been a member of the radical Students for a Democratic Society (SDS) in the 1960s, recalled the atmosphere between radical men and women in a 1985 interview with the Columbia Center for Oral History: "The men in our organizations demanded that we assert and reassert constantly our loyalty to them, and not to the independent women's movement. Women within SDS had to denounce separatism, you know, every five minutes in every discussion of women's issues or they would not be allowed to continue."[139]

When women radicals gathered on their own, the same authoritarian impulse was indulged in reverse: "Yet when women tried to get together with separatists," Wilkerson noted, "they were again challenged to say that working with men was bad, you know, all the time."[140]

Stokely Carmichael, later Kwame Ture, a leader of the Student Nonviolent Coordinating Committee before becoming a member of the Black Panthers, was explicit about the respect women could expect from radical men: "The only position of women in the SNCC," he said, "is prone."

Some feminists turned their energies toward battling pornography, which sprouted in the post–sexual revolution world like a noxious weed. I recall, as a high school student in the 1970s, attending a taping of *The Dick Cavett Show* in New York City. The topic was whether to liberalize laws regulating porn. The proponents—I think they were representatives of the American Civil Liberties Union—argued that once pornography was unregulated and freely available, it would quickly lose its allure as people grew bored with it. That worked out well.

Of course, what was considered pornography in the 1970s (*Playboy* and *Penthouse* magazines, mainly) is part of mainstream entertainment now. Today it's more challenging to avoid soft porn in media than to encounter it. And the hard-core variety is available on every smartphone, cable provider, and computer in the world.

Feminists saw porn—accurately, in my judgment—as a degradation of women. Yet they always interpret life through the narrow lens of women's oppression by men, which prevents them from seeing that its harm is to human dignity and not just to women as a class. Porn encourages immorality because it treats people as means, not ends—which is exactly what casual sex does. Porn is, in a sense, the logical end point of the sexual revolution because it completes the separation of sex from love and relationships. Sexual release is commodified, packaged, and sold. The right to pleasure may be assured, 24/7, but it carries with it the debasement of human beings.

Helen Gurley Brown got the ball rolling by promising young women that their "sex lives," as distinct from their romantic or family lives, would be delicious when they dove into casual sex. For men, with far greater sex drives and visually oriented arousal, their "sex lives" could easily become porn lives and prowling sexual harassment.

Feminists have proved incapable of admitting their own role in assisting the trends they so condemned. The pornography industry could not have flourished without the green light provided by the sexual revolution. Though porn has a long history that stretches back centuries, it did not go mainstream until the 1960s, when the culture was in the midst of a sexual revolution.

Sexual harassment has a long history too, but the libertine sexual ethic of the past few decades fueled its foul expansion. Feminists played a large role in opening this particular Pandora's box. Once opened, it's difficult to close. Still, it's worth recalling that in the original myth, after evils such as misery and sickness flew out of Pandora's box, there remained one last thing: hope.

CHAPTER 2

VIVE LA DIFFERENCE

"Why can't a woman be more like a man?"
—"A Hymn to Him," *My Fair Lady*

People have strong intuitions that men and women are different, and they are right. Even though it rarely makes headlines, a steady drumbeat of scientific research shows that differences between men and women are real, quantifiable, and even fun.

Brain research, the study of hormones, and animal studies all confirm that males and females are innately, inherently different. These dissimilarities are not drastic, mind you—we are not different species, though it may feel that way when men forget to lower the toilet seat—but they can be significant.

One reason so many American women aren't drawn to feminism is that feminists so often come off as scolds, not just of society but also of other women. Many women detect that the feminist agenda is about making women more like men, instead of speaking for women as they really are. And men don't like hearing feminists portray them as the eternal enemy of women.

Women's studies departments at universities marinate students in topics such as "Gender, Sexuality, Racializations, and Postcolonialities in Political and Religious Conflict" (Berkeley), "Gender,

Race, and Class in the U.S." (University of Iowa), and "The Development of Gender Roles in Children" (Purdue). Yet precious little attention is paid to the vast literature about sexual differentiation in neuroscience, evolutionary biology, and other fields.

For a number of years, it was an act of courage for academic researchers to study sex differences at all. The political pressure against such inquiries was intense. Gloria Steinem called research on male/female brain differences "anti-American crazy thinking."[1] Dissident feminist scholars Daphne Patai and Noretta Koertge, in their 2003 book *Professing Feminism,* explained that they became refugees from women's studies in part because of "biodenial"— that is, feminists' refusal to grapple with biological reality.

Researchers who study sex differences frequently say they were warned off the topic by advisers or professors. Dr. Larry Cahill, who teaches neurobiology at the University of California, Irvine, confided that even as late as 2000, "senior colleagues strongly advised me against studying sex differences because it would 'kill' my career."[2] Leonard Sax, an MD and PhD, recalled in his 2005 book *Why Gender Matters* that, in the 1980s, his psychology professor at the University of Pennsylvania asked rhetorically, "Why do boys and girls act differently?" The answer, at Penn and throughout academia, was "Because we *expect* them to."[3]

Psychiatrist Louann Brizendine was struck, as a young physician, by the two-to-one ratio of depression in females compared with males. "Because I had gone to college at the peak of the feminist movement, my personal explanations ran toward the political and the psychological. I took the typical 1970s stance that the patriarchy of Western culture must have been the culprit."[4] But then she noticed that the higher rates of depression in girls did not show until after puberty. If depression were caused by patriarchy, wouldn't its effects show up in childhood, when girls were supposedly being devalued and oppressed? This spurred Brizendine to investigate the role of hormones in brain function. She found that the brains of boys and girls differ in their responses to puberty. "Many gene variations and brain circuits that are affected by estrogen and serotonin are thought to increase women's risk of depression," she wrote.[5]

Geneticist Anne Moir and coauthor David Jessel, reviewing the science of mental differences, noted in their book *Brain Sex* that "Some researchers have been frankly dismayed at what they have discovered. Some of their findings have been, if not suppressed, at least quietly shelved because of their potential social impact."[6]

In 2005, Larry Summers, then president of Harvard University, while speaking to a meeting of the National Bureau of Economic Research, mentioned that sex discrimination remained a problem in American life, but speculated that one reason men outnumbered women among academics in the hard sciences might be that more men than women were at the high end of math and science aptitude. Well, a firestorm ensued. A member of the faculty told the *Harvard Crimson* that "In this day and age to believe that men and women differ in their basic competence for math and science is as insidious as believing that some people are better suited to be slaves than masters."[7]

Nancy Hopkins, a professor of biology at MIT, who was present at Summers's speech, told the *Boston Globe* that Summers's remarks made her so physically ill that she had to flee the room. Two-thirds of the Harvard faculty later voted to express their "regret" for what Summers had said, and Summers felt obliged to apologize and grovel repeatedly.[8] He was out of his job within the year.

But did Summers speak the truth? Feminists seemed indifferent to that. The truth frightens feminists because they worry that any differences between males and females discovered by biology, anthropology, or neurology will be cited as proof of women's inferiority to men.

Their fear is not groundless, but it's outdated. In the past, some have misused sex differences to keep women in a subordinate status. Doubtless some obtuse individuals cling to these ideas today—I'm sure they have an online forum. Aristotle believed in female inferiority, as did most of the great thinkers of the world. Cultures as diverse and far-flung as the Persians, the Chinese, the Mayas, and the Norwegians seem to have believed that the larger, stronger sex was also the superior. But is it worth getting hysterical about this today? In times past, many also believed in slavery, witches, child labor, executing horse thieves, and the unhealthful effects of night air.

Even we, enlightened modern folk that we are, may not have the Truth as firmly within our grasp as we think. Trusting science, I was an anti–dietary fat fanatic for at least thirty years. The best minds of the time told me to shun butter, cheese, roast beef, and cream like the plague. And now—whoops—it turns out that conventional wisdom was wrong, and I missed out on years of prime rib without (probably) improving my health at all.[9]

Early in the twentieth century, when medical researchers confirmed that men's brains are larger than women's (even adjusting for body size), the French scientist Gustave Le Bon said women's lower intelligence was "so obvious that no one can contest it for a moment."[10] Today we reject Le Bon's views not because they were uncongenial, and not because legal equality depends upon the sexes being identical in all respects, but because we're committed to the truth, and Le Bon was wrong. Women's brains, though smaller, are simply different from men's. They have more gray matter, for example. Overall, there is no difference in average IQ between men and women. If the evidence showed something else, we would have to cope with it, not deny or silence it. The commitment to equal rights for women arises out of respect for the human dignity of each person, not from the notion that the sexes are identical.

On average, men are physically stronger than women. That doesn't mean that every man is stronger than every woman. It probably *does* mean that even the strongest woman is not as strong as the strongest male. She's probably not stronger than many males. But even though physical strength is nice—one would hope a firefighter called upon to carry you out of a burning building has it—strength is not a moral virtue. A physically strong person has no more essential human worth than an incapacitated person.

Given this, it's inexplicable why some feminists choose to con-test whether men are, on average, stronger than women, especially when they're trying to prove how smart they are. In 2013 there was much celebration of the fortieth anniversary of the iconic 1973 tennis match, the so-called Battle of the Sexes, between Billie Jean King and Bobby Riggs. Robin Roberts of ABC News recalled King's "stunning triumph." ESPN explained to younger viewers that King "won for all women." The coverage generally echoed the 1973 *New York Times* editorial, which had proclaimed that "In a single tennis match, Billie Jean King was able to do more for the cause of women than most feminists can achieve in a lifetime."

Really? King was a twenty-nine-year-old, five-time Wim-bledon female champion. She defeated a *fifty-five-year-old* former Wimbledon male champion, Bobby Riggs. It is true that Riggs had defeated champion Margaret Court about three weeks before, and was surely a good player, but the likeliest explanation of this "battle of the sexes" match is that it was a gimmick. Riggs adopted the moniker "male chauvinist pig," and King presented herself as the symbol of women's lib.

King won. Did it change tennis? Not one bit. Women still com-pete only against women. King would not have been so foolish as to challenge the 1973 male Wimbledon champion, Jan Kodes. Nor would Serena Williams challenge Roger Federer today. It would be no contest.

That's brawn. What about brains? Well, we have different dis-tributions of abilities. On average, men and women have the same intelligence, but women are more bunched toward the center of the bell curve, and men are more distributed at the ends. In other words, men outnumber women among people with the lowest IQs and also outnumber women among people who are geniuses. This is true of traits other than intelligence as well. As the irrepressible Camille Paglia quipped, "There is no female Mozart because there is no female Jack the Ripper."

Paglia overstates for effect. There are female geniuses, of course, though there has never been a female genius quite like Mozart. I can live with this, because there has never been another male genius like Mozart either. Actually, I could live with it either way, because the truth doesn't frighten me.

Females outperform males in many areas: psychological insight, grades in school, high school graduation rates, college graduation rates, lawfulness, social connectedness, longevity. So why are we so obsessed with the few realms, such as high-end mathematical wizardry, in which men excel?

Females, on average, outperform males on language skills right out of the womb, which undermines the socialization argument. Female babies typically start speaking earlier and advance to whole sentences sooner. Males catch up, but only much later. Girls speak faster than boys and make fewer mistakes. Girls, on average, score better than boys on reading and writing throughout their school years.[11]

These overviews still don't tell you anything about any particular woman or man you meet. Shakespeare was a man, and he was a genius with words. Marie Curie was a woman, and she was a scientific genius. Ability is distributed along a spectrum. We've all known many people of both sexes who are smarter and dumber than we are. So what? I have met quite a few more men who are computer geeks than women, and I'll bet you have as well.

Differences in body size and strength between men and women are the most obvious and least interesting ways we differ, which brings us back to the brain. Consider what Diane Halpern, a former president of the American Psychological Association, wrote in the preface to the first edition of her book *Sex Differences in Cognitive Abilities*:

> At the time [I started writing this book], it seemed clear to me that any between-sex differences in thinking abilities were due to socialization practices, artifacts and mistakes in the research, and bias and prejudice. After reviewing a pile of journal articles that stood several feet high and numerous books and book chapters that dwarfed the stack of journal articles, I changed my

mind. . . . There are real, and in some cases sizable, sex differences with respect to some cognitive abilities. Socialization practices are undoubtedly important, but there is also good evidence that biological sex differences play a role in establishing and maintaining cognitive sex differences, a conclusion that I wasn't prepared to make when I began reviewing the relevant literature.[12]

Males tend to dominate in mathematical brilliance. As Steven Pinker notes in *The Blank Slate,* "In a sample of talented students who score above 700 (out of 800) on the mathematical section of the Scholastic Assessment Test, boys outnumber girls by 13 to 1."[13]

In 1932, Scotland tested the IQs of every eleven-year-old in the country and found that, at the highest end, among those with IQs above 140, boys outnumbered girls 277 to 203, and among those with the lowest IQs, boys outnumbered girls by a similar amount.[14] Outnumbered. That's it. There are always some girls at the very top, just fewer than the number of boys.

The same is true at the bottom of the scale. In general, boys have more difficulties than girls. They're more likely to experience mental retardation, dyslexia, stuttering, and behavior problems than girls. Color blindness is found among about 8 percent of males but only 0.5 percent of females. Autism is five times more common in boys than girls. ADHD is three times more common. Hemophilia affects one in five thousand males but almost no females.[15] Some of this can be explained by chromosomes. Men have an X and a Y chromosome. Women have two copies of the X. Girls have fewer disorders carried on the X chromosome because they have a spare.

There is wide agreement among researchers—and this includes many female scholars—that male and female brains differ anatomically and operate in a slightly different fashion. As with strength or height or musical ability or many other traits, there is a spectrum. Still, on average, women are superior to men at interpreting facial expressions, noticing different tones of voice, mathematical calculation, visual memory, empathy, and spelling.

(The calculation and spelling skills eluded me!) Men outperform women on spatial relations skills (mentally rotating an object in space); abstract mathematical thinking; map reading, which is related to spatial skills; and hand-eye coordination.[16] Anne Moir and David Jessel report that women have "tactile sensitivity so superior to men's that in some tests there is no overlap between the scores of the two sexes."[17]

Men are better at reading maps; women at reading people.

Psychologist Susan Pinker could have been thinking of my mother-in-law when she explained this male/female distinction: "Men are better at forming mental maps of a route (go north for three miles, then turn east for half a mile). Females are more likely to navigate using landmarks (drive until the red-roofed church, turn right, and continue until the river)."[18] My sense of direction is so awful I've gotten lost in my own city (before the GPS rescued me). My mother-in-law gives directions using landmarks paired with relationships. She'll say, "Go down Township Line Pike until you pass where the Goldblooms used to live. Their son Kenneth was in the same class as Rick. Make a right."

Are these differences imposed by culture? Surely culture plays some role. That's why men and women in Guinea-Bissau behave differently from men and women in Tibet. But when differences are found in the first minutes of life, or when patterns are found across cultures, it points to biology. A shocking number of human behaviors and values are universal, including lying, turn taking, redress of wrongs, the mother/son incest taboo, ethnocentrism, the proscription on murder, the classification of kin, and hundreds of other things.[19]

In *Taking Sex Differences Seriously,* Steven E. Rhoads notes that some differences are evident from the first days of infancy:

Compared with one-day-old male infants, one-day-old females respond more strongly to the sound of a human in distress. One-week-old baby girls can distinguish an infant's cry from another noise; boys usually cannot. . . . Four-month-old girls can distinguish photographs of those they know from people they do not; boys the same age generally cannot. On the other hand, five-month-old boys are more interested than girls in three-dimensional geometric forms and in blinking lights.[20]

Women have more acute senses of smell, touch, and hearing, and see better in the dark.[21] Women are more sensitive to acute pain but are better able to handle long-term discomfort than men. Women's brains are denser than men's in the centers that regulate hearing and language. The hippocampus, the center for governing emotion and memory, is larger in women.[22]

Men's brains are also more compartmentalized than women's. In the 1960s, Dr. Herbert Lansdell, a Maryland psychologist, studied epileptics who had had parts of their brains removed to help them cope with extreme seizures. He noticed that when one particular brain part was removed from men's brains, they lost nearly all their capacity for spatial reasoning. Women did not, which indicated to Lansdell that spatial relations skills are located in one particular part of the male brain but in several places in the female brain. Also, women use both sides of their brains for tasks, whereas men's brains are more specialized, with tasks performed predominantly by either the left or the right hemisphere.

Innovations such as PET scans and fMRI tests have provided new insights into the brain's functioning as it solves problems and responds to stimuli. These tools, along with the studies of brain injuries, have helped clarify differences in how men and women process information. Men have two and half times the brain space devoted to sex drive, and larger areas devoted to aggression and action.[23] The corpus callosum, which links the left brain to the right, is thicker in women than in men, meaning it can pass messages from one part of the brain to the other more readily. This may grant an advantage in some skills, such as verbal fluency, and a disadvantage in others, such as doing two tasks simultaneously.[24]

For the first six weeks or so after conception, human embryos develop similarly—the human brain's default mode is female—but then male zygotes are flooded with testosterone, causing cells in the male brain's communication centers to die off and those in the sex and aggression areas to increase. The female fetus sprouts more connections in the regions of the brain that process language and emotion.[25] Hormones later in life reinforce the anatomical differences.

Humans receive another dose of sex hormones in infancy (at about five months), and of course, a great fire hose of hormones drenches the mind and body during puberty, ushering the boy or girl out of childhood. Boys' voices crack and then deepen; their beards grow, their bones enlarge, and their thoughts turn to sex. Girls begin to menstruate, develop breasts, and acquire body hair. Both sexes spend inordinate amounts of time in the bathroom.

Though feminists continue to resist the importance of sex differences, there is no longer any respectable argument that they don't exist. A number of medical studies have shown that female-to-male organ transplants are more likely to fail than male-to-male, even when controlling for body size.[26] Scientific journals, such as *Biology of Sex Differences,* were founded to highlight research on sex differences in areas as diverse as responses to lung cancer, heart disease, and pain sensitivity. Arthur P. Arnold, distinguished professor of integrative biology and physiology and director of the Laboratory of Neuroendocrinology of the Brain Research Institute at UCLA, explained that *"Biology of Sex Differences* serves as a forum for discussion of the forces that make females and males different, and the downstream pathways that are affected by sex-specific forces. This information will be critical for discovery of factors, often more prevalent in one sex than the other, that alleviate disease."[27]

Margaret McCarthy, PhD, president of the Organization for the Study of Sex Differences, notes that "Sex is a biological variable that profoundly influences the physiology of every organ in the body."[28] The brain is an organ.

Larry Cahill, writing in the journal *Cerebrum,* grants that human brains are in some sense "mosaics," but he emphatically rejects the argument that males and females share an essentially "intersex" brain. "Evolution," he writes, "has produced in men and women bodies that are filled with similarities and differences, including in the heart, liver, lungs, immune system, and even knees. To insist that somehow—magically—evolution did not produce biologically based sex differences of all sizes and sorts in the human brain . . . is tantamount to denying that evolution applies to the human brain."[29]

Dr. Simon Baron-Cohen of Cambridge University postulated that autistic spectrum disorders are examples of extreme male orientation in the brain. Individuals with autism and related disorders such as Asperger syndrome are often good at tasks requiring systematizing abilities such as math, music, mechanics, or computer skills, but they lack, sometimes completely, the ability to understand other people's emotions or what goes on their minds. Baron-Cohen has labeled this "mind-blindness." In other words, the autistic brain is an extreme version of the typical male brain: stronger on math and weaker on emotions.

Baron-Cohen predicted that prenatal testosterone levels would foretell the later onset of autism. He seems to have been onto something. The journal *Molecular Psychiatry* published the results of a 2014 study from Denmark in which testosterone levels of unborn children were measured during pregnancy. The children were followed after birth, and as Baron-Cohen predicted, elevated levels of testosterone in utero were associated with higher rates of autism.

There are examples of genetic defects that result in masculinized brain organization in females as well. A rare condition called congenital adrenal hyperplasia (CAH) causes female babies to receive a large dose of testosterone in utero. At the age of one year, CAH baby girls make less eye contact than other girls.[30] They demonstrate a noticeable preference for toys such as trucks and less interest in dolls. They engage in play fighting and are less interested in clothes or their appearance than other girls. They also demonstrate better spatial relations skills.[31] The same pattern occurred in girls born to women who were given progesterone (which is chemically similar to testosterone) during pregnancy to prevent miscarriages.[32]

Girls with Turner syndrome have a damaged or completely missing second X chromosome, do not develop ovaries, and do not receive testosterone (secreted in small amounts by the ovaries) at all during their lives. Turner syndrome girls who receive their X chromosome from their mothers display exaggerated feminine behaviors and preferences (a strong interest in dolls, mothering, and caretaking).[33]

Testosterone levels vary in women. Perhaps not surprisingly, women with high levels of the hormone smile less than other women, are more likely to be unfaithful spouses, and have stronger handshakes.[34]

Simone de Beauvoir, the intellectual godmother of French feminism who was influential among second-wave feminists, said, "One is not born but becomes a woman." In the 1960s and '70s, people thought this was literally true. There was a famous 1965 case of an eight-month-old boy (one of a pair of identical twins) whose penis was accidentally severed in a botched circumcision. The distraught parents sought out Dr. John Money, coeditor with Dr. Richard Green of *Transsexualism and Sex Reassignment* (1969). Money taught that sex differences were partly the result of conditioning—that is, reward and punishment meted out by parents—and he coined the term *gender identity*. He argued that children could be molded into a sexual identity by the way they were treated, and he recommended that the little boy be surgically transformed into a girl. The parents agreed. The boy was castrated and had an artificial vagina created for him. The parents raised him as a girl. The *New York Times* cited this as an example of how pliable human nature was. "Brenda," the paper breezily assured readers, was "sailing contentedly through childhood as a genuine girl."[35]

When "Brenda" was seven years old, Money published a paper citing his success with her sex reassignment at a speech before the American Association for the Advancement of Science. Because

Brenda had a twin brother, the case was hailed as the perfect ex-periment on the essential mutability of sexual identity. *Time* maga-zine hailed Money's "success" and said it provided "strong support for a major contention of women's liberationists: that conventional patterns of masculine and feminine behavior can be altered."[36]

Psychologist Steven Pinker describes what was later discovered: "The facts were suppressed until 1997, when it was revealed that from a young age, Brenda felt she was a boy trapped in a girl's body and gender role. She ripped off frilly dresses, rejected dolls in favor of guns, preferred to play with boys, and even insisted on urinat-ing standing up. At fourteen she was so miserable that she decided either to live her life as a male or to end it, and her father finally told her the truth. She underwent a new set of operations, assumed a male identity, and today is happily married to a woman."[37] Sadly, that was not the end of the story. The man who had been called Brenda never completely surmounted the psychic scars of his tragic situation and committed suicide in 2004.

We cannot experiment on people (Brenda's heartbreaking story began with a freak accident), but animal studies shed light on the role that genes and hormones play in behavior. Experiments on rhesus monkeys and other animals have shown that if a female fetus receives a dose of testosterone while the brain is at a key phase of development, the adult that results will not display the usual female interest in infants. She will also be more inclined to mount other monkeys, engage in rough-and-tumble play, and dis-play other behaviors usually observed in males. Experiments with rats found that the presence or absence of testosterone at crucial developmental phases will determine if an adult rat's brain adopts female or male structures and if the adult animal displays male or female behavior patterns.

Examples of intriguing similarities in other animals are legion. Researchers at the Yerkes National Primate Research Center in Atlanta found that young male monkeys preferred toy dump trucks and wheeled vehicles to plush dolls. Females played with both kinds of toys.[38] Other studies of monkeys have found even more pronounced gender selection (or, if you like, stereotypes) in the choice of toys. Is this socially constructed? Are they behaving differently because we "expect them to"?

Some caution about comparisons to animals is always in order. No animals write sonnets or build rockets, yet some commonalities are notable. Leonard Sax itemizes some of these: "Wherever you look among the primates, you'll find that young females show much more interest than young males do in taking care of babies. That's certainly true of baboons, rhesus monkeys, marmosets, and vervet monkeys. It's also true for humans: girls, on average, are much more likely to embrace little babies and be interested in babies than boys are."[39]

As a matter of evolution, this differentiation in behavior makes sense. Evolutionary psychology infers things about human nature from our past. For millennia, human beings lived as hunter-gatherers. The traits that were successful in prehistory have left their mark on our biology. For a male to pass on his genes successfully, he needs only to impregnate a female. Sexual intercourse requires just a few minutes of his time. For a female to pass on her genes, she must be pregnant for many months, give birth, and then nurse the baby. The female is more likely to succeed at raising offspring who survive long enough to reproduce themselves if she is nurturing, attentive to her baby's needs, and a good judge of mates. For males to succeed, they must appeal to (or possibly rape) the largest number of females, and if males stick around to protect and feed the mothers, the kids are more likely to survive.

We may think it's unjust that women are the smaller and weaker sex; that only women menstruate, often painfully; that only women give birth (speaking of pain!) and suckle. But these are the realities. They shaped our ancestors, and they shape us. If evolutionary psychology is right, then the nature of men (to be more aggressive and risk taking) is the result of women choosing those traits in the men they had sex with (i.e., through sexual selection). In any case, it's surely not worthwhile to chew over grievances with our prehistorical foremothers and forefathers. It *is* useful to consider whether to be at peace with our natures or at war with them.

Sugar and Spice

Every preschool teacher can testify to the average differences between boys and girls. So can parents. One way to describe people who insist there are no innate differences between the sexes is "childless."

When my oldest child, who had some developmental issues, was four, I accompanied him to preschool a couple of days a week to ease his transition to school. When the children were released to the playground, the boys, mine very much included, acted as if they'd been shot out of a cannon. They careened around the play equipment, shouting at the top of their lungs, zigzagging, chasing, and throwing whatever came to hand. Some of the girls played on the swings and other equipment, but in a much less frenzied fashion. Their preferred location seemed to be under the slide, where a committee would gather to talk.

Little girls tend to take turns far more often than little boys, and are less likely to treat a toy as a weapon.[40] Boys can turn anything, even a Barbie doll, into a play gun. Again, these are generalizations, not absolutes. Our second child, also a boy, was much less active and rough than his older brother. He was more talkative, though his preoccupations were also quite typical of his sex. He adored dinosaurs, and learned all their names and geological eras. During the phase when dinosaurs dominated his life, I remember coming across a quote from a paleontologist about why boys in particular were so drawn to dinosaurs. "It's simple," he explained. "They're big, they're mean, and they're dead."

As the mother of three boys, I had to repress my own natural disgust at snakes and other reptiles because the little guys found them delightful. When a snake curled up on the windowsill outside my office, I suppressed the urge to scream, and instead called the kids to come see the "cool snake." At the zoo, you could find me, plaster smile in place, admiring the Komodo dragon or the alligator snapping turtle. My reward was dragging everyone to the exhibits featuring sea otters and great cats. The boys enjoyed the cute animals as well, though not with the passion they brought to poisonous, dangerous, creepy things.

Reams of research confirm what common observation tells us: boys on average are more physically aggressive than girls. They push, elbow, and grab more than girls. Girls tend to express their aggression verbally. The cutting gossip or slur is their métier, and it can be more painful than a punch in the gut. If physical aggression in boys were socially learned behavior, you would expect it to increase as the child grows. Yet boys are at their most violent at age two and gradually learn to control themselves through social conditioning.[41]

If male aggression and violence were not biologically based but completely cultural, you'd expect to find some society somewhere in which men were the more nurturing, more socially connected sex and women the more dominating and warlike. The ancient Greeks sang ballads of the Amazon women, fearsome female warriors who cut off one of their breasts to improve their aim with a bow and who killed all their male children. The great Greek male warriors, including Hercules and Achilles, were said to have battled the Amazons. Very interesting—but no more historical than the Augean stables, the Nemean lion, or any of the other tales of Hercules. They're called myths for a reason.

Evolutionary psychologist David Buss studied mate preferences in thirty-seven cultures over five years and found that women's and men's ideal mates were stable and differed little by culture. Whether women were from Iran or Vietnam, they valued material resources, social status, and ambition in men more than physical appearance. Men preferred women who were young and attractive. Once Buss and his colleagues knew a person's ideals in a mate, they were able to predict that person's sex with 92 percent accuracy.[42]

Matt Ridley, in *The Red Queen,* his tour d'horizon of evo-lutionary theories about human nature, quotes John Tooby and Leda Cosmides as saying that "The assertion that 'culture' explains human variation will be taken seriously when there are reports of women war parties raiding villages to capture men as husbands, or of parents cloistering their sons but not their daughters to protect their sons' virtue, or when cultural distributions for preferences concerning physical attractiveness, earning power, relative age, and so on show as many cultures with bias in one direction as in the other."[43]

We've all known men who are gentle, compassionate, and sensitive. We hope to instill these traits when we raise sons, along with self-sufficiency, a strong moral code, a sense of responsibility, and so forth. Yet we recognize (or should) that the male comes into the world as the less tractable, more violence-prone sex. Among prison inmates, men outnumber women by fifteen to one.

Men commit murder at thirty to forty times the rate women do. This is true around the globe and has been, as far as we can tell, throughout human history. Two-thirds of these murders, according to an analysis of homicide records from many different societies over seven hundred years, did not involve other crimes but were matters of pride/honor.[44] Young males who feel their dignity or "manhood" has been challenged defend it with violence unless they are strongly socialized not to. Men commit fif-teen times as many robberies and three times as many assaults as women.[45] Simon Baron-Cohen notes that in preindustrial societ-ies, the murder rate among young men was one in three, an as-tounding figure.[46]

"Aha," you may say. "You concede that socialization changes behavior." Of course it does. But the question is not whether cul-ture affects behavior, but whether *everything* is socially constructed. When you plant a tree, it will not thrive or grow unless it gets water and sunshine. But no amount of careful tending will cause a pear tree to become a birch.

Also, considering that there are costs to encouraging and

discouraging behavior, it takes more effort to suppress a strong natural inclination than a weak one. It's harder to discourage men from treating women as sex objects than it is to inhibit women from violence. It's difficult to get women to part from their newborns, but comparatively easy to ask men to go back to work. How much effort is it worth to paddle upstream? Speaking for myself, I'd devote a great deal of effort to discouraging sexually predatory behavior by men and little to encouraging women to leave their infants.

Both women and men produce testosterone, which promotes self-confidence, risk taking, competitiveness, aggression, and sex drive. From puberty on, and continuing throughout the rest of their lives, men have between ten and one hundred times more testosterone in their bloodstreams than women. Andrew Sullivan, who was prescribed testosterone for a medical condition, wrote about its effects for the *New York Times Magazine*:

> Late last year, mere hours after a T shot, my dog ran off the leash to forage for a chicken bone left in my local park. The more I chased her, the more she ran. By the time I retrieved her, the bone had been consumed, and I gave her a sharp tap on her rear end. "Don't smack your dog!" yelled a burly guy a few yards away. What I found myself yelling back at him is not printable in this magazine, but I have never used that language in public before, let alone bellowed it at the top of my voice. He shouted back, and within seconds I was actually close to hitting him. He backed down and slunk off. I strutted home, chest puffed up, contrite beagle dragged sheepishly behind me. It wasn't until half an hour later that I realized I had been a complete jerk and had nearly gotten into the first public brawl of my life. I vowed to inject my testosterone at night in the future.[47]

There is no debate over the connection between testosterone, sex drive, and aggression. Boys experience a twenty-five-fold jump in testosterone between the ages of nine and fifteen,[48] and it affects the mind as well as the body. Starting at puberty, boys begin to experience sexual thoughts an average of four to five times as frequently as girls. Boys become more competitive and more assertive. The male hormone delivers a sense of well-being, invulnerability (which can be a problem in some teenagers), and a drive for dominance.

Andrew Sullivan quoted a woman undergoing hormone treatments for a female-to-male transition: "My sex-drive went through the roof," [she] recalled. "I felt like I had to have sex once a day or I would die. . . . I was into porn as a girl, but now I'm really into porn."

Teenagers of both sexes are flooded with steroids at puberty. Estrogen also increases sexual desire, though not nearly to the degree that the male hormone does, and it counteracts some of the other effects of testosterone (e.g., aggression).[49]

Louann Brizendine, in *The Female Brain,* writes, "Just as women have an eight-lane superhighway for processing emotion while men have a small country road, men have O'Hare Airport as a hub for processing thoughts about sex whereas women have the airfield nearby that lands small and private planes. That probably explains why 85 percent of 20- to 30-year-old men think about sex many times each day, and women think about it once a day."[50]

Brain imaging studies have found that, in men, the base of the brain (the thalamus and the hypothalamus) lights up in response to sexual stimuli. In women, there is comparatively more activation of the cerebral cortex. Leonard Sax, a psychologist and family physician, described teenaged boys' responses to being asked why they had sex: "Boys usually answer that question with a snort. 'Why *wouldn't* I have sex? As long as the girl wants it, too—I mean, as long as she doesn't kick me or slap me or yell 'Fire!'—why shouldn't I?' Boys want to have sex because they feel sexually aroused. Simple, base-of-the-brain motivation."[51]

For girls, sexual arousal hardly enters the picture. "Girls may hope that having sex will earn them points in the popularity contest," Sax observed, "or they may just want to please the boy they happen to be hooking up with, or they may feel pressured either by the boy or by other girls who are having sex."[52] Boys almost never initiate sex as a means of sparking a romantic relationship. They know that showing interest in a girl as a person, taking her out on dates, and talking with her is the way to begin a romance. Yet girls, under pressure from a hypersexualized culture, often initiate or at least agree to sex with the hope it will lead to romance.[53]

Males, in general, desire casual sex more than females do. Letitia Anne Peplau, a psychologist at UCLA, summarized the research on differences in sexuality for the American Psychological Society in 2003 and found that men think of sex as an act, a release, a physical pleasure, whereas women are more likely to think of it as an expression of intimacy and love. Men were found to rate their sexual desire as stronger than that of women, to be more stimulated by images, to want to engage in sex more frequently, and to masturbate earlier in life and more often.[54] Women, more than men, "emphasize committed relationships as a context for sexuality."[55]

When I was a teenager, a great fuss was made about the debut of a version of *Playboy* for women, called *Playgirl*. It featured nude pictures of attractive men, and was greeted as—you guessed it—a huge step forward for equality of the sexes. Women could now ogle men just as men had ogled women.

Another way men and women differ is in what they find arousing. Men find depictions of bodies alluring, whereas women are less interested in purely visual stimulation. Men are the overwhelming consumers of pornography, and to the surprise only of deluded naïfs, *Playgirl*'s readership wound up being mostly gay men. When women look for stimulation, they choose romance novels that deliver erotica in the context of relationships. Women comprise 91 percent of the romance fiction market.

The behavior of homosexuals of both sexes can tell us a lot about the differing sexualities of men and women. Gay men, whose sexuality is not mediated by women, have sex more frequently and with more partners than heterosexual men. Lesbians, who do not need to adjust to men's needs, have less sex. Among heterosexual married men, 7 percent say they have had sex with more than twenty women. Among homosexual couples, 43 percent say they've had sex with twenty or more partners. Among lesbians, only 1 percent have had twenty or more liaisons.[56]

The aforementioned Andrew Sullivan, widely credited as the father of the gay marriage movement in the United States, told a joke that reflects this difference well: "Question: What does a lesbian bring on a second date? Answer: A U-Haul. Question: What does a gay man bring on a second date? Answer: What second date?"[57]

Here's a question: If men's sex drive were indistinguishable from women's (if men valued relationships and emotional connection as much as women and if women valued sexual release as much as men), would prostitution still cater almost exclusively to male buyers? I don't mean to suggest that I am defending or justifying prostitution. I part company with some feminists, such as libertarian Wendy McElroy (whose work I respect), who believe prostitution should be legal. Prostitution seems to me to be a prime example of men's oppression of women, particularly because it seems always to involve some degree of coercion, exploitation, and violence by pimps.

Leaving aside the immorality of prostitution, let's look at just how revealing the trade is. I suppose you could argue that female prostitution is "socially constructed," that is, subtly encouraged by social norms, but since prostitution is illegal and suppressed nearly everywhere, world cultures are promoting it in an odd fashion. The sellers are overwhelmingly female (though some male prostitutes cater to men), and the buyers are pretty much 100 percent male. Has anyone even heard of a lesbian prostitute? When I googled the term, I got page after page of porn videos, but no news stories. (Admittedly, I gave up after about five pages.)

A famous 1989 study tested the stereotype about women being less interested in casual sex than men. Attractive young men and women approached forty-eight male and forty-eight female strangers on the campus of Florida State University and opened a conversation by saying, "I have been noticing you around campus. I find you to be very attractive." Next, the "student" (actually a confederate of the researchers) asked a series of questions: (1) Would you go out with me tonight? (2) Would you come over to my apartment tonight? (3) Would you go to bed with me tonight?

Men and women were similarly open to going on a date. Among men, 50 percent said yes; among women, 56 percent agreed. Sixty-nine percent of the men agreed to go to an interested stranger's apartment, but only 6 percent of the women said yes to this. And 75 percent of men approached for casual sex by an interested stranger agreed. Among women, zero did. (Note how many more men agreed to meet for sex than to meet for a date.)

The emotional responses of the subjects were illuminating too. When attractive women asked men if they'd like to have sex, men commonly responded eagerly with replies such as "Why do we have to wait until tonight?" The women, by contrast, tended to be appalled. "You've got to be kidding" or "What's wrong with you?"[58]

An old saying—at least when I was growing up—goes that "Women give sex to get love. Men give love to get sex." It's an overstatement that minimizes men's capacity to fall in love and maintain emotional intimacy. And it dramatically understates women's enjoyment of sex. But there is more than a grain of truth to it.

Feminists have been so suspicious of the science of sex differences that some of the most important effects of hormones and other differences have been buried. I was astounded by how many college students told me they did not believe there were any particularly important differences between men and women when it came to casual sex. This does a deep disservice to both genders. If young men are encouraged to believe that young women view sex with the same detachment they themselves feel, they are more likely to behave in ways that women will find insensitive and offensive, and may, in the worst cases, find themselves accused of sexual assault. Correspondingly, young women who don't recognize that young men approach sex differently might put themselves in harm's way both physically and emotionally.

If both sexes can be realistic about their average differences, it should relieve them of a sense that something is wrong with their wives, husbands, boyfriends, girlfriends, or children. If more women knew that men are simply less wired for deep conversations about relationships than they are, they might be less frustrated with the men in their lives.

As my late friend Kate O'Beirne put it, "These young women think that their husbands should fulfill all of their emotional needs. That's not going to happen. That's why you have sisters and girlfriends!"

Gender

Some feminists, when faced with evidence that one of their fundamental assumptions about human nature—that sex differences are only skin deep—is wrong, adjusted their views and sought deeper understanding. I've quoted a number of them. I suspect that Louann Brizendine, Anne Moir, and Diane Halpern would call themselves feminists, but they respect the truth and acknowledge that men and women are different.

Others—and they are the majority—have responded with a sleight of hand. Perhaps that's too gentle. More accurately, they remain in denial of reality. They now grant that "male and female," "men and women," "masculinity and femininity" are true things, but their way of wiggling out of the clear lessons of brain science and other disciplines has been to invent a novel concept: gender identity.

At one time, *gender* was a grammatical term with no biological definition and little relevance for English speakers. Its introduction into the study of human sexuality has generated confusion—

which, I suspect, was not accidental. If one's gender identity is distinct from one's sex, which in turn is separate from one's sexual orientation, then the concept of "normal" becomes lost in a fog of infinite permutations. Not only that, but because "gender identity" is totally subjective (based upon how one feels, not on one's clear biology), it becomes possible to smuggle back into our understanding of sexuality the discredited idea that "male" and "female" are entirely socially constructed.

Please note that this entails a complete contradiction of earlier orthodoxies. The idea that a not insignificant number of human beings have the bodies of one sex but the minds of the other sex requires admitting that the brains of males and females are indeed different. It also leads gender theorists into territory they previously disdained. Only yesterday, they denied that the sexes behaved in identifiable ways due to their biology. Now they grab stereotypes with both fists. Caitlyn Jenner proves his "femininity" by posing in a bathing suit for the cover of a magazine, as if flaunting one's body is what it means to be female. Parents of little boys who like to play with dolls or of girls who like to climb trees rush to doctors to determine whether their children might be transgender.

The American Psychological Association outlines the new thinking: "Sex is assigned at birth, refers to one's biological status as either male or female, and is associated primarily with physical attributes such as chromosomes, hormone prevalence, and external and internal anatomy. Gender refers to the socially constructed roles, behaviors, activities, and attributes that a given society considers appropriate for boys and men or girls and women. These influence the ways that people act, interact, and feel about themselves. While aspects of biological sex are similar across different cultures, aspects of gender may differ."[59]

The APA, sensitive to social fashion, is reflecting the gender theory popularized by feminists such as Ann Oakley, Suzanne Kessler, and Wendy McKenna. The latter two collaborated on *Gender: An Ethnomethodological Approach* (1978), which argues that "gender is a social construction, that a world of two 'sexes' is a result of the socially-shared, taken-for-granted methods that members use to construct reality."[60] Gayle Rubin says she looks forward to an androgynous society in which "obligatory sexualities and sex roles" are swept away and "one's sexual anatomy is irrelevant to who one is, what one does, and with whom one makes love."[61]

The "gender binary" is out. "Queer theory" is in. But isn't this merely old wine in new bottles? This is, again, the denial of sex differences with a gloss of lesbian/gay jargon—or what the late Supreme Court justice Antonin Scalia might have called "jiggery-pokery." When your ideas are not founded on reality, you are driven to clothe them in impenetrable word fogs. On that score, few can match Judith Butler, Berkeley professor and author of *Gender Trouble: Feminism and the Subversion of Identity* (1990). The mother of "queer theory," Butler is capable of sentences like this one: "The move from a structuralist account in which capital is understood to structure social relations in relatively homologous ways to a view of hegemony in which power relations are subject to repetition, convergence, and rearticulation . . ."[62] It goes on (and on) from there.

To its credit, the journal *Philosophy and Literature* gave Butler its 1998 "award" for bad writing. Yet the idea of "gender identity," though based on nothing more than activists looking to revive androgyny after its rout at the hands of neuroscience, evolutionary psychology, and biology, has achieved broad social acceptance.

With lightning speed, gender identity was accepted as part of the progressive view of human sexuality. A joint statement by the Obama Justice Department and Education Department (its guidance since withdrawn under the Trump administration) asserted that:

- *Gender identity* refers to an individual's internal sense of gender. A person's gender identity may be different from or the same as the person's sex assigned at birth.

- *Sex assigned at birth* refers to the sex designation recorded on an infant's birth certificate should such a record be provided at birth.
- *Transgender* describes those individuals whose gender identity is different from the sex they were assigned at birth. A transgender male is someone who identifies as male but was assigned the sex of female at birth; a transgender female is someone who identifies as female but was assigned the sex of male at birth.[63]

Is it true?

As we've already seen, there is convincing evidence that male and female brains are innately different. The differences in brain organization are no longer in doubt (though there is debate over how much behavior the observed differences affect). Turner syndrome, CAH, and possibly autism point to the likelihood that hormonal malfunctions or differentials affect the masculinity/femininity of the brain.

This leaves us open to the possibility that some biological females may have more masculine brains, and some biological males more feminine brains, but it does not support the proposition that male and female *identities* are subjective, fluid things. The recklessness with which our society is embracing gender identity is troubling when the evidence is so scanty, the stakes are so high, and the chances that children could be harmed so troubling. Gender identity is not even being proffered as a hypothesis—as is, for instance, the theory that vaccines cause autism, which was subject to being disproved (and has been). Instead, gender identity is asserted as fact, and doubts are treated as prejudice or bad faith.

We are in the midst of a mania, and it is not about medicine but politics. Progressives have made the question of how to understand and treat transgender individuals, especially children, into yet another "civil rights" question. Crowning transgender people as the newest category of victims serves two ends for progressives: it creates new avenues for them to display empathy and compassion, and it offers an opportunity to sneak in their ideological preference for androgyny and sexual mutability even though scientific evidence doesn't support it.

Let's not forget there is a huge spectrum of behavior within the sexes. We've all known masculine women and effeminate men. Sometimes they're homosexual, sometimes not. Perhaps their genes are mostly responsible for where they fall on the masculine-feminine axis. Probably, as with most traits, there's an interplay of genes and environment. Yet there have always been sensitive, verbal, expressive boys who don't like sports and prefer to read quietly in their rooms. And there have always been girls who disdain makeup, get dirt under their fingernails, and love cars and trucks. Perhaps the sensitive boys become therapists or composers. The girls may go on to become engineers or Yellowstone Park guides. But in the current rage for transgenderism, I wonder if these boys might be mistaken for trans girls or if these girls might be viewed as trans boys?

Let's try to get some clarity about terminology.

There is a rare birth defect called intersex (formerly hermaphroditism), in which a baby is born with both, or parts of both, male and female sex organs, or with sex organs that are difficult to categorize. This condition is not synonymous with transgender. Yet in this age at war with convention, some have attempted to lasso birth defects of a sexual nature and use them to redefine sexuality.

A 1993 *New York Times* article by Dr. Anne Fausto-Sterling, "How Many Sexes Are There?," claimed that as many as 1.7 percent of babies are born "intersex," but in most cases, this condition was hidden or modified by doctors and parents.[64] Fausto-Sterling was among the first to advance an argument that quickly gained popular currency: namely, that there are not two but as many as five sexes.[65] But as Dr. Leonard Sax and others convincingly demonstrated, Fausto-Sterling included in her definition of intersex a number of conditions and deformities that are not "sexes" in any meaningful sense. Among the syndromes she listed as new sexes were the familiar chromosomal abnormalities Turner syndrome and Klinefelter syndrome, late-onset congenital adrenal hyperplasia, and vaginal agenesis.

Women with Turner syndrome produce no testosterone and usually display exaggerated feminine traits and interests; to say that they are a separate sex is a strange reach. "In females with vaginal agenesis," Sax explained, "the distal third of the vagina fails to develop and is replaced by about 2 centimeters of fibrous tissue." You could say that doctors "hide" this condition by surgically repairing the vagina. But these women are in all other respects normal females, and many go on to give birth vaginally. According to Sax, "Surgical correction for vaginal agenesis is conceptually no different from surgical correction for cleft palate."[66]

Nor are many of the other conditions that Fausto-Sterling lists truly "intersex." Late-onset congenital adrenal hyperplasia usually causes no symptoms until adulthood. The chief symptom for men is thinning hair, and for women, irregular menstrual periods, excess body hair, infertility, and/or acne.

Klinefelter syndrome men have an extra X chromosome and are sometimes infertile and have other, subtler symptoms. Otherwise, they are hard to distinguish from other men. They have male genitalia and develop secondary male sex characteristics in a normal fashion.

Fausto-Sterling includes men with XYY and women with XXX chromosomes as "intersex." But Dr. Sax reports that those with extra sex chromosomes appear normal and are fertile. Men with XYY chromosomes tend to be tall and may have more learning problems than average men, and women with an extra X chromosome are also taller and may have learning difficulties or seizures. It's hard to credit any of these as a new "sex."

One in 12,500 babies is born with both ovaries and testes, or with both penises and XX chromosomes, but 99.98 percent of humans are born either male or female. True intersex babies have a birth defect, and medical professionals must do what they can to treat them in a fashion that offers the best shot at a normal life. Yet their unfortunate situation sheds no more light on the nature of sexuality than conjoined twins teach us about normal twins.

Transgender people are said to be "males trapped in the bodies of females," or vice versa. Other than the subjects' expressed feelings, does any evidence exist that this might be a biological condition? And wouldn't it be wise to find out before plunging into life-altering medication and surgery for children?

Transgender people are such a tiny percentage of the population that research on them suffers from very small sample sizes. Lawrence S. Mayer, PhD, and Paul R. McHugh, MD, summarized the extant research in a special issue of *The New Atlantis,* the journal of the Center for the Study of Technology and Society (an arm of the think tank with which I am also associated). Mayer and McHugh described a 2011 Spanish study that compared the brain MRIs of eighteen female-to-male transsexuals with those from a control group of twenty-four males and nineteen females. The study found that in three of four brain areas studied, the transgender white matter looked more like the white matter of the male controls than of the female controls.

That's interesting, but far from conclusive, as the sample size was small and the subjects were adults. The problem with examining adult brains is that behavior changes the brain itself, so it's hard to know if years of certain behavior had changed the subjects' brains.

There have been a few other studies regarding transgender people, but they are thin on the ground. This is new territory. One strange experiment tested people's responses to pheromones. Another looked at functional (as opposed to structural) brain images, but had just one subject. A study that compared hormone levels in transgender youth with a control group of gender-conforming people of the same age did not find any differences—that is, everyone had hormone levels consistent with his or her biological sex.[67]

More research is obviously needed, but as Mayer and McHugh caution, when it comes to something as complex as sexuality or behavior, brain imaging is not the Holy Grail:

> It is now widely recognized among psychiatrists and neuroscientists . . . that there are inherent and ineradicable methodological limitations of any neuroimaging study that simply associates a particular trait, such as a certain behavior, with a particular brain morphology. . . . The only definitive way to establish epidemiological causality between a brain feature and a trait (especially one as complex as gender identity) is to conduct prospective, longitudinal, preferably randomly sampled and population-based studies.[68]

That research has not been done. As of this moment, we don't have enough information to know whether transgenderism is a result of different brain patterns for a tiny subset of males and females or whether other factors, such as abuse, neglect, stress, or complications during pregnancy may be implicated.

So, what are we to conclude about the phenomenon that many more people are coming out as transgender than was the case even a couple of decades ago? Is this because the stigma has been largely removed, thus freeing individuals who would have suffered in silence in the past to come forward (analogous to homosexuals)?

Judith Butler and the gender feminists have certainly fostered an intellectual climate in which nonconforming or unusual sexualities are celebrated. And our society's history of racism has made us particularly sensitive to claims of prejudice. As a result, schools and governments across the nation are rushing to accommodate transgender people. In the Fairfax County Public Schools in Virginia, for example, students in sex education classes are taught that some people transition from their "assigned sex" to the sex that conforms with their identity. In Fairfax schools, transgender students are offered access to bathrooms, locker rooms, showers, and sports teams of the sex with which they identify, without regard to the sex on their birth certificates.

A Maryland public high school announced in September 2016 that it would have a "gender-neutral" homecoming court. The *Washington Post* explained that, "those honored at halftime might be two boys, two girls, transgender students or a boy-girl duo." Jacob Rains, the student body president, demonstrated how well he had absorbed the current ethos: "It is really not our job, especially with a gender-neutral and transgender population at Bethesda–Chevy Chase, to tell people that boys have to be kings and girls have to be queens. Who are we to put people into those categories?"[69]

In the United Kingdom, the Gender Identity Research and Education Society estimates that the number of transgender children is doubling every year. Schools in that country are scrambling to accommodate them.[70] In the United States, the percentage of transgender adults was revised from 0.03 percent of the population to 0.06 percent (a doubling) between 2011 and 2016.[71] In Oregon, Medicaid patients are eligible to receive hormone treatments and might even qualify for gender reassignment surgery starting at the age of fifteen.[72]

When North Carolina passed a law requiring individuals to use the restroom that matched the sex listed on their birth certificates, businesses ranging from PayPal to the NBA threatened to pull out of the state.[73] Progressives leaped at the opportunity to display their open-mindedness. Similar "bathroom wars" are now ongoing in a dozen other states, and several more have passed laws forbidding "reparative therapy"—that is, counseling to help youths who feel trapped in the wrong body to align their feelings with their biological sex.

No one wants to withhold sympathy from troubled or tormented people dealing with transgender issues. The question is not whether we feel their pain, but whether we are inadvertently causing additional harm by congratulating ourselves on our freedom from bigotry. Who are progressives serving, the interests of children with gender dysphoria or their own self-regard? True compassion means seeking what is best for the suffering individual.

The problems of children with gender dysphoria are complex, and require careful, sensitive treatment. But not every issue can be reduced to discrimination versus inclusion.

Pity the modern parents who are instructed to reinforce their young children's confused identities. A 2012 *Washington Post* story, "Transgender at Five," depicted "Kathryn," who was transitioning to "Tyler." Her mother reported that "Kathryn" wanted to wear pants, play with swords, and cut her hair short. "'I am a boy,' the child insisted, at just 2 years old." Acknowledging the parents' distress, the *Post* story nevertheless warned that "Parents who ignore or deny these problems can make life miserable for their kids, who can become depressed or suicidal, psychiatrists say."[74]

Where is the common sense about the stages children experience? I recall wishing to be a boy myself, when I was about five or six. I didn't like dresses, I played with trucks and toy trains, and I asked my playmates to call me "Timmy." Looking back, I see that I was a bit of tomboy (even that word seems old-fashioned now). What if my parents had been advised, as parents are today, that if they didn't treat this phase as an indicator of gender dysphoria I might become suicidal? I shudder to think about it.

There are thousands of ways children can be miserable, and probably dozens involve sexuality in some sense. But we should not overlook the possibility that by creating such a warm, supportive cocoon for children whom adults have already started to identify as "trans," we are encouraging some kids to adopt this identity. They may be suffering from something else entirely, or they may be going through a phase, but the gravitational tug of the trans identity might be significant. And once on the path to transitioning, it may be extremely difficult or impossible to change course. Once a young person and his family have asked everyone at home, school, church, and community to call him by a new pronoun, once he has been acting as the other sex for a period of months or years, and especially if he has begun taking hormones to change his body and mind, the process likely becomes self-fulfilling.

This approach is breathtakingly radical, especially considering that as many as 80 to 95 percent of children who express feelings of gender incongruity outgrow it.[75] But what will happen if the "affirmative treatment" model becomes the norm? Children who express a desire to be the other sex, often starting in preschool, will be encouraged to adopt the names, pronouns, clothing, hairstyles, and bathrooms of the opposite sex. This is a prelude to puberty-blocking drugs, cross-sex hormone treatments, and then surgery to remove penises, breasts, Adam's apples, and so forth.

The decision to dress a girl in boys' clothing, cut her hair, and call her a boy, even if reversed later, must play havoc with a child's psyche. Imagine the confrontation between a teenaged girl who has changed her mind after reaching puberty (as the overwhelming majority do) and the parents who raised her as a boy. "Did you not think I was pretty enough to be a girl? Wasn't I feminine enough?" Or imagine a teenaged boy demanding to know whether his father thought he lacked masculinity as a child. It's a psychological minefield.

The Hippocratic Oath commands, "First, do no harm." Yet the mental health establishment is bending in the political wind. The latest edition of the American Psychiatric Association's *Diagnostic and Statistical Manual of Mental Disorders* (DSM-V) no longer lists an incongruence between gender identity and biological sex as a disorder. It is so ranked only if it causes distress. What had been "gender identity disorder" is now called "gender dysphoria." The difference is enormous.

Dr. Michelle Cretella, writing in the *Journal of American Physicians and Surgeons,* notes that in other areas of medical practice, those not touching on sexuality, an incongruence between one's subjective feelings and reality is treated as a mental disorder. Patients with anorexia nervosa believe themselves to be fat even when they are skeletal. Those suffering from body dysmorphic disorder falsely believe themselves to be ugly. Patients with body integrity identity disorder (BIID) are convinced they are disabled, though their bodies are normal and healthy. In none of these cases would sound medical practice include ratifying and reinforcing the patient's false belief (for example, providing liposuction for the anorexic), even if patients requested it.[76]

"Children with [gender dysphoria] do not have a disordered body—even though they feel as if they do," writes Cretella. "Similarly, a child's distress over developing secondary sex characteristics does not mean that puberty should be treated as a disease to be halted, because puberty is not, in fact, a disease."[77]

Yet when sexuality is involved, rationality and evidence are overwhelmed by political pressure. Dr. Kenneth Zucker, an acknowledged leader in the treatment of children with gender identity disorder (and an advocate for gay and transgender rights), was fired from his Toronto clinic because his approach to these patients was no longer politically acceptable. Dr. Zucker believed that the best way to treat prepubertal children with gender identity disorder was to help them align their identity with their anatomical sex.[78]

Instead, at dozens of clinics around the United States, and more in Europe, children are not only encouraged in their delusion but are also dosed with powerful drugs to delay puberty. "These medications arrest bone growth, decrease bone accretion, prevent the sex-steroid-dependent organization and maturation of the adolescent brain, and inhibit fertility by preventing the development of gonadal tissue and mature gametes for the duration of treatment."[79] If the child continues with the treatment and proceeds to "sex reassignment," he or she undergoes multiple surgeries (with attendant risks), is consigned to a lifetime of cross-hormone treatment (whose long-term side effects may include increased risk of heart disease and cancer), and is rendered *permanently sterile*. Adolescents, far less children, are not usually considered competent to make such drastic and irreversible life decisions.

The gender identity movement reveals a great deal about our society and our time. On one hand, it demonstrates the insatiable appetite for embracing and normalizing new categories of nonconformists. But the frenzy for more and more arcane sexual classifications (trans, genderqueer, boi, femme) reflects a severe overemphasis on sexuality that diminishes our full humanity.[80] People speak of gender identity and sexual orientation as if it defines their souls. The search for meaning in sexual identity has become akin to a spiritual quest. Could it be that by denying the traditional contours of male and female, we've lost the comfort and predictability they once provided?

We are all, in the beginning, children born of two people. Our identities as sons or daughters of particular mothers and fathers form us, as do our relationships with brothers and sisters, and then, more broadly, with grandparents and other relatives. Our identities begin as members of families (however unstable or unhappy those families may sometimes be) and then extend outward. We often identify as a member of a religious group, as residents of a state, and as patriotic citizens of a nation (or sometimes as its critics). As we grow, our identities come to encompass our interests—we are environmentalists, musicians, athletes, gourmets, or politicos.

In adulthood, our jobs give us another identity, and then, most important, we marry and have children of our own, and our identities as mothers and fathers become a key part of our adult selves. I've heard that the identity of grandparent is even more rewarding than parent, and I'm looking forward to that.

I believe the most rewarding identities are those that take us out of ourselves and into the realm of giving to others. In *Man's Search for Meaning,* Viktor Frankl said, "Happiness cannot be pursued; it must ensue, and it only does so as the unintended side effect of one's personal dedication to a cause greater than oneself or as the by-product of one's surrender to a person other than oneself."[81]

Too often, it seems that sexual identity is about personal definition—it's about navel-gazing (or groin-gazing)—not about the natural extensions to others that sexuality, knitted into family life, normally entails. Meanwhile, the oppression sweepstakes, the scramble to claim the prestige of marginalized status, now has competitors bumping into one another.

Women's colleges have been struggling with how to handle applicants who are transwomen (i.e., transitioning from male to female) and transmen (transitioning from female to male). Smith College made headlines in 2013 when it denied admission to Calliope Wong, who was born male but was transitioning to female. He received his application fee back in the mail, with a note—the *New York Times* editorial board called it "jarring"—explaining that "Smith is a women's college, which means that undergraduate applicants to Smith must be female at the time of admission." Wong launched a Change.org petition to protest.

Germaine Greer stirred dismay among the avant-garde when she denied that transwomen were "real women." She wasn't suggesting that people be denied the surgery, she explained, but "what I'm saying is it doesn't make them a woman." For this, Greer was labeled a "misogynist" on yet another Change.org petition, which was followed by the now-familiar cascade of protests and speaking invitation withdrawals. Her heterodox views on transgenderism are ironic, considering that the key message of *The Female Eunuch* was that all differences between the sexes "could be otherwise."

A few holdouts at women's colleges briefly took Greer's position. A group called Keep Mount Holyoke, Wellesley, and Smith Single Sex, objected that "Becoming a man and remaining at a women's college is analogous to renouncing your citizenship, yet expecting to maintain the benefits of citizenship."[82]

Timothy Boatwright was born female and applied and was accepted to Wellesley, a women's college, as a woman. But when Boatwright arrived, "he" announced that he was "masculine-of-center genderqueer" and preferred male pronouns. All went well, at least insofar as the Seven Sisters college was concerned, until Boatwright ran for "multicultural affairs coordinator" on campus. "Having men in elected leadership positions undermines the idea of this being a place where women are the leaders," one student told the *New York Times*.[83] The trouble with Boatwright is that he had begun life as a woman but had become a white man, apparently the embodiment of the enemy even if unnaturally reached.

Smith College grappled with the question for a few seasons, and then, like other leading single-sex schools, declared that Smith remained a "women's college" that continued to embrace the mission of educating "women of promise for lives of distinction," but that the concept of what a woman was had changed "in light of society's evolving understanding of women's identity."[84]

You could say it's an evolving understanding, or you could say that our society has become unmoored from reality. "Male" and "female" exist. Masculinity and femininity are not entirely socially constructed, but arise from biology. But the worst part about what feminism has gotten wrong is in perceiving women's natural inclinations to be a burden. They are not. They're a treasure. They make women happy, and they enhance the lives of men and children.

For decades, feminists have urged women to flee from what they love and who they are, and rigidly to copy men. It's terrible life advice. It has confused and confounded us to the point where children are being drugged into simulacrums of the opposite sex and women's colleges don't know how to define womanhood.

CHAPTER 3

SEVERING BONDS

"Before I formed you in the womb, I knew you.
Before you were born, I set you apart."

—Jeremiah 1:5

In the 1980s, Betty Friedan had second thoughts as she surveyed the state of things. She was almost alone among feminists in this. Dismayed at the anti-male, anti-marriage tone the women's movement had adopted, she tried to throw the car into reverse. In *The Second Stage,* she recalled the publicity stunt of feminists throwing bras into a bonfire: "That 'bra-burning' note shocked and outraged us, and we knew it was wrong—personally and politically—though we never said so, then, as loudly as we should have. We were intimidated by the conformities of the women's movement and the reality of 'sisterhood is powerful.' "[1]

Friedan had come to believe that too many women had turned their backs on the "life-serving core of feminine identity." Not only that, but she questioned the analogy she had done so much to promote: that women and blacks were fellow victims. "Woman's situation with respect to man or the family was *not* the same as that of the worker and boss, the black race and the white."[2] At that time in her sixties, Friedan revealed herself to be more grounded than the other "founding mothers" of feminism; she had grown reflective, and even a little conservative: "From the totality of our own experience as women—and our knowledge of psychology, anthropology, biology—many feminists knew all along that the extremist rhetoric of sexual politics defied and denied the profound, complex human reality of the sexual, social, psychological, economic, and yes, biological relationship between woman and man. It denied the reality of woman's own sexuality, her childbearing, her roots and life connection in the family."[3]

"Too soon old, too late smart," the old folk expression goes. I honor Friedan for her willingness to flout feminist orthodoxy and reexamine some of her assumptions. She was redeemed, at least in my eyes, in her later career (believe it or not) by her comfort with femininity. I met her once, a sure signal she was open to talking with women of different persuasions. By that time, she had accepted that most women saw becoming wives and mothers as key life goals, no less important than having a career.

Alas, it is necessary to nail one more thesis to her door. Sadly, Friedan never repented of her abortion absolutism and went to her grave fulminating against "so-called pro-lifers." *Roe v. Wade,* she wrote, secured a "right more fundamental" than many of those mentioned in the Bill of Rights.[4] It is a deep tragedy that she never saw how cruel a thing she embraced by endorsing abortion on demand.

The original feminists and suffragists recoiled from abortion, but modern feminists have made it a sacrament of their secular religion. If you don't endorse abortion, you are not invited to consider yourself a feminist. This repels me, and many others.

I did not come to my views on abortion through the usual route. The family I grew up in was not especially religious. *Roe v. Wade* was decided when I was in high school, but I don't recall if the topic ever came up in our household. The issue gained my attention only in college, when I enrolled in a philosophy course that asked each of us to examine a current legal controversy. The professor assigned abortion to me.

I started the inquiry with a view that abortion was morally acceptable in the early phases of pregnancy but became more problematic as the child got closer to full-term. My casual impression was that abortion became wrong at some point between conception and birth; I just had to find that point. But the more I thought about this logically, the less likely it seemed that any line would not be arbitrary. Everyone agreed that killing a newborn as it emerged into the world was infanticide. Then how could it be moral to kill an unborn baby a few minutes, or days, before its birth? And what about a few weeks or months prior to birth? What is the moral distinction between an eight-month-old fetus and a four-month-old fetus?

I read philosophers on the topic—one famously compared pregnancy with being kidnapped and involuntarily hooked up to a great violinist with kidney failure—but none of the arguments or tortured analogies they advanced seemed satisfactory to me. Another writer stressed that an embryo is tiny at the start, only the size of the period ending this sentence. Well, yes, but with the full complement of genes that make it a unique individual. That minute bundle of DNA will rapidly grow and change. Left undisturbed, that tiny package will, through the miracle of biology, grow into a baby. Is size the key determinant of human dignity? Babies are small too, compared with adults.

Feminists urged that the fetus is totally dependent on its mother. Without support, the fetus will die. Yet this is true of a newborn as well, and it's true of many handicapped people, and some of the elderly. Surely dependence does not determine whether it is justifiable to kill?

Feminists argued that women are often the victims of rape and incest and that "forcing" them to carry babies to term further victimizes the mother. These hard cases are genuinely wrenching, but thankfully they are rare—only 1.5 percent of women list rape or incest as the reason they seek abortions.[5] Still, even in those truly horrifying situations, I found it difficult to justify the extreme "solution" of killing the unborn child.

The only cases of termination that strike me as morally and logically sound are those in which the pregnancy threatens the mother's life. One of the most common pregnancy complications is ectopic pregnancy, when the zygote implants in one of the fallopian tubes instead of in the uterus. These are not ethically hard cases. By definition, an ectopic pregnancy cannot result in a live birth. The only question is whether it will also kill the mother when the fallopian tube bursts. Other medical situations in which the pregnancy may threaten the mother's life involve pulmonary embolisms, but they are unpredictable and therefore cannot be prevented with a therapeutic abortion.

The leading cause of pregnancy-related death for women in the developed world is preeclampsia, which nearly always strikes after twenty weeks' gestation. Anyone who has watched *Downton Abbey* has seen the dramatization of a perfectly healthy young woman who gives birth only to go into convulsions and die. Preeclampsia is a killer, so a woman who is diagnosed with it must end her pregnancy. But how?

Infants born at twenty-six weeks have a 90 percent chance of survival, and those born as early as twenty-three weeks have a 20–35 percent chance of making it. So even though a woman with preeclampsia must terminate the pregnancy, the fetus does not necessarily have to die.

During my college inquiries, I noted how rarely those who spoke and wrote about the life of the mother seemed interested in determining if the child could be delivered early and given the best possible care in an incubator. Surely if the baby has a chance, that chance ought to be offered. And because pregnancies that threaten women's lives are rare, abortion advocates who speak of "life of the mother" exceptions usually add "or health" after "life," introducing a huge loophole, as "health" can be broadly interpreted.

I also noticed a certain brutality in the feminist approach to abortion. In the name of empowering the powerless (i.e., women), feminists were asking women to harden their hearts against the most vulnerable members of the human family. In the name of "reproductive rights," the voice of conscience, of simple sympathy, had to be suppressed.

By the time I was considering the ethics of abortion as a twenty-one-year-old, women were fully in control of their "reproduction" and had been for some time. The choices for avoiding pregnancy are abstaining from sex altogether (a technique with a 100 percent success rate) or being scrupulous about contraception. Birth control, when used conscientiously, also has a near 100 percent success rate. Forty-six percent of women seeking abortions in a Guttmacher Institute study had not used contraception in the month they conceived. Among those who said they used contraception, significant numbers used it inconsistently.[6] Women who are raped do not have a choice about the risk of pregnancy, but the abortion controversy does not center around cases of rape; it focuses on whether killing the unborn for any reason or for no reason ought to be considered "women's reproductive health."

We are told to look away and not consider the lives of the unborn children. Pro-choice advocates declared that the pro-lifers' posters featuring photographs of aborted babies were beyond the pale. Former U.S. representative Patricia Schroeder moved, on "breach of decorum" grounds, that such pictures not be permitted on the floor of the House of Representatives when that body was considering abortion legislation. As the feminist writer Naomi Wolf acknowledged later, after she became a mother herself, you cannot avoid the truth by calling it bad taste.

In the discussion of unwanted pregnancies, the possibility of adoption as a humane and loving alternative to abortion was rarely mentioned, and when it was, it was defamed. Stories of birth mothers haunted by the children they gave up dominated the discussion. Pro-choice feminists didn't acknowledge how difficult it would be to find any adoptees who wished their birth mothers had chosen abortion.

The abortion rights narrative also successfully obscures other realities. The United States has waiting lists of couples hoping to adopt babies. International adoption has surged only because so few American babies have been placed for adoption since 1973, the year *Roe v. Wade* was decided. There are even waiting lists for babies with Down syndrome.

Yet the feminist movement undermined its moral standing in the eyes of millions by making abortion, the killing of an unborn baby, its signature issue. This callousness toward the unborn is not only morally blind, but it betrays the traditional feminine sensitivity to the needs and welfare of children. Mary Wollstonecraft, often cited as the first feminist, regarded abortion with horror, writing in *A Vindication of the Rights of Women* (1792) that women "have not sufficient strength to discharge the first duty of a mother; and sacrificing to lasciviousness the parental affection, that ennobles instinct, either destroy the embryo in the womb, or cast it off when born."[7]

Susan B. Anthony, one of the most influential of the suffragists of the late nineteenth and early twentieth centuries, hoped for a day "when the right of the unborn to be born will not be denied or interfered with."[8] Dolley Madison became a benefactor of the Washington Female Orphans Asylum. Reformers such as Jane Addams, Florence Kelley, Grace Abbott, and Lillian Wald worked assiduously for laws outlawing child labor. They lobbied to reform the treatment of youthful offenders in the courts (the first juvenile courts were established in the early twentieth century), to provide federal help for children (the U.S. Children's Bureau was created in 1912), and to make education compulsory.

Throughout human history, women have sacrificed, bled, and starved themselves for the sake of their children, born and unborn. The Madonna and Child is a defining image of Western art, one that has resonated over thousands of years, not just for its religious content but because the mother–child bond is a universally understood symbol of tenderness and selfless love, a sacred part of the human experience.

Evolving scientific knowledge has invalidated feminist claims about men and women being alike, and medical technology has also stripped bare the feminists' dishonesty about abortion. For decades, feminists clothed their embrace of abortion in euphemisms about the unborn child, denying that the unborn were human beings. It was "the product of conception" or just a "clump of cells." The late congressman Henry Hyde used to reply to this argument by noting that whatever a woman was carrying, "It was not a giraffe."

The rigid feminist orthodoxy about the "right to choose" ignored or denied women's own intuitions about pregnancy as well as the advancing field of embryology. Women looking forward to giving birth can relish Lennart Nilsson's exquisite photographs of developing babies featured in *Life* magazine and books. They can gaze beatifically at ultrasound scans of their unborn baby's feet, hands, and faces. They can learn, to their delight, that newborns can distinguish their mothers' voices from the first moments after birth.

Women can also pore over books such as *What to Expect When You're Expecting* for day-by-day, week-by-week descriptions of what their babies look like and can do at various stages of gestation. At four weeks old, before many women even know they are pregnant, the embryo's heart has begun to beat. Six weeks after conception, the baby's arms and legs are growing, and the eyes become visible. At ten weeks, the fetus's face is recognizable and his fingernails have formed. At twelve weeks after conception, the fetus can squint, frown, grimace, urinate, and sometimes suck his thumb.[9]

Neonatal intensive care units are full of severely premature babies. Doctors and parents make heroic efforts to save children born as early as twenty-four weeks. A friend recently described seeing a child who weighed only one pound at birth and whose body was nearly translucent grow strong enough with intensive care to go home several months later at three pounds. Yet the decision to surgically dismember the developing fetus and flush it out of the womb is treated as a morally neutral act, sanitized as a matter of women's "reproductive rights."

Today, surgeons can remove unborn babies with certain defects from the womb, repair their hearts or other organs, and return the baby to the womb to grow to full-term. It is now possible in the United States for two women pregnant at the same point of gestation to check into medical facilities, one to have life-saving surgery performed on her unborn child and the other to have the unborn child terminated. The difference in the two cases is not medical necessity but only the wishes of the mother. An unborn child who is wanted by the mother is given every chance at a healthy life, whereas one who is not wanted by his birth mother can be terminated. In no other realm do we measure human worth this way.

A website for eager pregnant women describes a fetus at fifteen weeks: "Her legs are growing longer than her arms now, and she can move all of her joints and limbs. Although her eyelids are still fused shut, she can sense light. If you shine a flashlight at your tummy, for instance, she's likely to move away from the beam."[10] One might have thought that tenderness toward the small and weak is one of humanity's better instincts, but feminists have been implacably at war with those impulses for decades. The ideology of "choice" has been corrupting in several ways. The first is dishonesty.

Abortions at any stage of pregnancy are violent acts on a living child, but late-term abortions are particularly disturbing. A friend who was the social-work supervisor at a California hospital told me how incredibly difficult it was to find nurses to assist with late-term abortions. "After they've seen one," she said, "they never want to do it again."

With "D and E" (dilation and evacuation), or partial-birth abortions, the cervix is artificially dilated. The abortionist pulls the baby out of the birth canal up to his or her shoulders. Before the head is pulled through, he inserts the sharp point of scissors into the base of the fetus's skull to make a hole. He then inserts a small hose, vacuums out the brain (collapsing the skull), and pulls the head out.

When Congress debated outlawing this procedure in the early 2000s, groups such as NARAL Pro-Choice America responded with a staggering series of lies and distortions. At first, they said the procedure did not exist. Even as recently as 2016, when the subject was raised during a presidential debate, pro-choice advocates huffed on NARAL's Facebook page that " 'partial-birth abortion' is not a thing." This is semantics. The abortionists who perform these procedures call them "intact dilation and extraction." It's true that pro-lifers coined the term *partial-birth* (and it is evocative), but they were labeling a real procedure. It's one thing to quibble about the name and quite another to create a dispute over terminology in order to pretend that the procedure does not happen.

When the "there's no such thing" line proved untenable, the pro-choice advocates claimed that the anesthesia administered to the mother killed the fetus. The American Society of Anesthesiologists, in an effort not to alarm pregnant women with planned operations, rushed to correct this falsehood, noting that pregnant women safely undergo surgery all the time. Anesthesia does not kill the unborn baby.

Next, the feminists/pro-choice forces conceded that while partial-birth abortions were actually "a thing," they were exceedingly rare and performed only to save the life of the mother. Rep. Carolyn Maloney's comments in a C-SPAN appearance were typical: "That's a procedure that's very rarely used, and it's only to save the life of the mother . . . when a fetus is incompatible with life—they would surely die." What a comforting fiction. Others floated three hundred as the number of partial-birth abortions per year, but that figure was risible. The *Washington Post* found that just one New Jersey clinic had performed more than fifteen hundred such procedures in one year. Nor were they were performed only to save women's lives, as President Bill Clinton dishonestly asserted when he vetoed legislation banning the procedure. Dr.

Martin Haskell, one of the procedure's originators, confirmed that 80 percent of the late-term abortions he performed were "purely elective."

It's incredibly rare for anyone on any side of contentious issues in American politics to acknowledge the lies of his own side. But in 1997, Ron Fitzsimmons, executive director of the National Coalition of Abortion Providers, did just that. He had a crisis of conscience. Regretting his willingness to lie about the frequency of partial-birth abortion, he released a letter (published in *American Medical News*) retracting misstatements he had made on *Nightline*. Though he remained in favor of keeping abortion legal, he wrote, he felt guilty for having "lied through my teeth" when he said the procedure was rare and performed only to preserve the life or health of the mother. He said the lies made him "physically ill" and that partial-birth procedures were common and were usually performed on perfectly healthy mothers and babies.[11] When something you advocate requires such prodigious dishonesty, it may be time to reconsider your position.

Another kind of corruption that abortion advocacy has spawned is mental rigidity. The pro-choice movement has made abortion so sacred as the alpha and omega of women's rights that they seem to have shut down their moral imaginations in the process. All too often, the feminist left has argued not only that a woman has an absolute right to choose, but that a pregnant woman having chosen abortion also has a right to withhold lifesaving care from a child who survives abortion.

Early in the twenty-first century, Republicans introduced federal legislation that forbade the killing of a baby who accidentally survives an abortion. Such cases, though rare, do happen.[12] I have met Gianna Jessen. She is not the sort of person you forget. In 1977, when Jessen's mother was seven and a half months pregnant, she underwent a saline abortion in Los Angeles, but her baby was born alive. Though some abortion survivors are killed outright, or left in trays to die without medical attention, Gianna was saved.

She has cerebral palsy due to birth trauma, but she was placed in foster care and eventually adopted. She has become one of the nation's leading pro-life activists and speakers.

When the Florida legislature was considering a variant of the "Born-Alive Infants Protection Act," which would have required abortionists to provide medical assistance to infants "accidentally" born alive during an abortion, Alisa LaPolt Snow, representing the Florida Alliance of Planned Parenthood Affiliates, testified against the bill. Florida representative Jim Boyd, apparently unsure that he had understood her correctly, asked, "So, um, it is just really hard for me to even ask you this question because I'm almost in disbelief. If a baby is born on a table as a result of a botched abortion, what would Planned Parenthood want to have happen to that child that is struggling for life?"

Snow responded that her organization "believes that any decision that's made should be left up to the woman, her family, and the physician." In short, as the *Weekly Standard* summarized, Florida Planned Parenthood is in favor of "post-birth abortion."

Snow was asked why she didn't support simply transporting a breathing, moving infant to a hospital, where he or she would have the best chance of survival. Snow developed a sudden concern for ambulance convenience: "[T]hose situations where it is in a rural health care setting, the hospital is 45 minutes or an hour away, that's the closest trauma center or emergency room. You know there's just some logistical issues involved that we have some concerns about."[13]

Such transparent drivel gets a pass when the subject is abortion. Presumably, no sentient adult would argue that if a full-term baby arrived at a rural clinic suffering from, say, a head wound, and the nearest trauma center were forty-five minutes away, that "logistical" concerns would dictate letting the baby die. The only possible conclusion is that Florida Planned Parenthood believes that when a mother chooses to end her pregnancy, she is also entitled to know that the baby is dead, no matter what.

In the early 2000s, the state of Illinois considered similar legislation, which would simply have required that any baby born alive during an abortion be afforded the same treatment that any other newborn would receive. State senator Barack Obama was one of the only legislators to oppose the bill. Even NARAL in Illinois demurred. Obama argued that the legislation was "designed to burden the original decision of the woman and the physician to induce labor and perform an abortion."[14]

In 2011, Dr. Kermit Gosnell was convicted of three counts of murder in the deaths of second-trimester babies and one count of involuntary manslaughter in the death of a woman. The three babies were all born alive. Gosnell then used scissors to "snip" their spinal columns. One of his assistants, who pled guilty to third-degree murder, said that such "snippings" were "routine" for late-term abortions, so there were probably many more than three infants killed during Gosnell's tenure.

Gosnell was a ghoul. An ultrasound technician recorded the age of one baby he killed as 29.4 weeks, or about 7.5 months. In Pennsylvania, where Gosnell practiced, abortions are not permitted beyond 24 weeks. In one case, a nurse testified that a baby cried after being born. Gosnell snipped his neck and told the nurse not to worry about the baby as he was placed in a basin on a counter. Another large baby was disposed of in a shoe box, but he was too big and his feet dangled over the sides. In another case, Gosnell reportedly joked with a nurse that a baby was so big "he could have walked to the bus stop."

Gosnell's chilling indifference to life, while extreme, is also evident in others who practice abortion. Once the moral line of killing has been crossed, a certain coarsening of the spirit is inevitable. In a series of undercover videos released in 2015, David Daleiden showed Planned Parenthood doctors and other staff members casually haggling over the price of fetal body parts with investigators who were posing as medical researchers. While sipping wine and eating salad, one doctor spoke of adjusting her abortion techniques to be sure she got intact specimens. "We've been very good at getting heart, lung, liver, because we know that, so I'm not gonna crush that part. I'm gonna basically crush below, I'm gonna crush above, and I'm gonna see if I can get it all intact."[15]

At another point in the video, a staffer at a clinic in Houston, Texas, empties the bodies of that day's work onto a light board so that Daleiden, posing as a buyer, can see what "tissues" are available. One of the cadavers is a twenty-week-old fetus. In another case, the clinician picks over other remains with a tweezer. "Twins," she notes, seemingly without emotion.

Planned Parenthood's logic seems to be that human dignity and membership in the human family depend completely on the feelings of others, specifically mothers. A wanted baby is an epochal event, a celebration, a family milestone. An unwanted one is medical waste. Those ideas are incompatible, and attempting to hold both simultaneously has caused some cognitive dissonance. For instance, we bury our dead pets, yet dispose of unborn babies in the trash. As I've been saying since 1991, when we adopted our son Jonathan, "There is no such thing as an unwanted child."

The party line, articulated by Sen. Elizabeth Warren in 2016, is that abortion is "the most difficult decision a woman will make in her entire life."[16] There's the core dishonesty: If it didn't involve the taking of a life, what would be so difficult about the decision? Does a woman agonize about having her tonsils removed? Is that "the most difficult decision?"

Former senator Barbara Boxer once engaged in an unwise colloquy on the Senate floor with former senator Rick Santorum about when infants deserved to be treated as people. When, he queried, did she believe the baby was a person whose life should be protected? Boxer's reply: "When you take the baby home from the hospital."

Someday our descendants will look back at this and ask how we could have tamely accepted such barbarism. A special obloquy will attach to the Orwellians who call it compassion and to the feminists who made this grisly business their calling card.

Feminists claim that their support for abortion rights is about advancing respect for women. But doesn't full respect require women to be seen as competent moral actors, responsible for their decisions?

Finally, the elevation of abortion as a key feminist principle reveals the moral bankruptcy of the movement. It has severed the ageless bond between mother and child, hardening women against their own weak and utterly defenseless unborn children. The feminist embrace of abortion is also a rejection of femininity itself. The warmth, selflessness, and tenderness babies evoke in women is one of the best parts of us. It signals the moment when we cease living entirely for ourselves and expand our scope to encompass someone else in the most profound way possible.

I didn't always have a perfect relationship with my own mother, but I remember her fierce love with something like awe. She told me when I was a child that she would throw herself in front of a truck if necessary to save my life. When I became a mother, I finally understood that completely. Parents are their children's natural defenders. Abortion cruelly severs that bond.

CHAPTER 4

HOOKUP CULTURE

Sexual intercourse began
In nineteen sixty-three
(which was rather late for me)—
Between the end of the "Chatterley" ban
And the Beatles' first LP.

—Philip Larkin, from "Annus Mirabilis"

Some geniuses at an Old Dominion University frat house rang in the 2015 school year by draping bedsheet banners out the windows during orientation. "Rowdy and Fun, Hope Your Baby Girl Is Ready for a Good Time," read one. "Freshman Daughter Drop Off" and "Go Ahead and Drop Off Mom Too," read another. The banners provoked an outcry, and Old Dominion joined a lengthy list of colleges and universities publicly shamed for sexual misconduct.

As a society, we are struggling to account for the sexual abuse and harassment that women too often experience, on college campuses and off. God knows, women need forceful and courageous advocates. Unfortunately, in this area, as in many others, feminists have failed women by misreading the nature of the problem or by adopting such a combative posture toward men that they over-shoot the mark.

To hear feminists tell it, college campuses are the highest of high crime zones, where 20 percent of women can expect to be sexually assaulted before graduation. A recent Oscar-nominated documentary, *The Hunting Ground,* reflects this perspective. So did Vice President Joe Biden when, in 2014, he repeated the activists' talking points: "We know the numbers: one in five of every one of those young women who is dropped off for that first day of school, before they finish school, will be assaulted in her college years."[1]

Some conservatives say that this talk of "rape culture" is a hoax, or a "moral panic," one that has led universities to railroad inno-cent young men into kangaroo courts while failing to hold women accountable for their behavior. They are right that some young men are being treated unjustly by universities, and those stories are chilling. The tribunals hastily patched together by universities to adjudicate cases of sexual assault represent a profound retreat from the principles that have been bedrocks of American jurisprudence for centuries.

At the same time, I believe it is wrongheaded for conservatives to categorically deny concerns about rape and sexual assault on campuses. Sex crimes are real. A great many women, and not just at universities, are being sexually assaulted, raped, and otherwise badly treated. I find it surprising that more conservatives have not stepped forward to uphold traditional values, because taking rape seriously is one of those values.

Still, to identify the problem as "rape culture," as feminists do, is to suggest that we are raising men to rape with impunity, and that is far from the case, thank God. Yet we are not teaching young men to respect women, either. And in the foggy terrain of hookup culture, we've created the conditions where crude and shabby be-havior is easy and where actual rape is not as rare as it should be.

Figuring out the prevalence of rape is extremely tricky, be-cause, as I'll address in the next chapter, the crime is notoriously difficult to prove, and exaggerated numbers are used as political cudgels. But there is no doubt that something is awry. Social life on campuses has become a minefield, with many women feeling at least dissatisfied and many men in danger of miscarriages of justice. The radioactive word *rape* has shone such a blinding glare in all directions that it's difficult to see clearly what is actually happening.

We cannot understand this mess until we locate the root of the trouble, and that begins by asking what has gone wrong with courtship, dating, and sex. So far, neither the "antirape" activists nor those who advocate for wrongly accused young men have focused on the real problem: the hookup ethic and the sexual revolution that spawned it. Campuses that shun the hookup culture (strict religious schools, for the most part) are not having a rape crisis or anything close to it.[2]

Still, no campus is free of the confusion and mixed signals about sex imparted by our larger culture. A Columbia University resident adviser's advice to incoming freshman reflected the murky terrain young people face. Writing in the student newspaper, the *Spectator,* she said, "There are no rules—no second date rule, no three day rule, no hipsters-only rule. The only rules I have to follow are those I set for myself."[3]

But people need rules, particularly when it comes to sex, and young people clearly find current expectations bewildering. Why else would freshmen turn to their resident adviser for hookup rules? Not only does hooking up have no rules, but in researching this book, I've discovered that hooking up has no exact definition.

It's a sexual encounter, but after that, the word *hookup* can connote anything from kissing and fondling to oral sex to intercourse. Keeping it vague serves the interests of both men and women. The vague claim of having "hooked up" gives men boasting rights, letting their buddies assume whatever they may. For women, the term lets their friends know they have attracted someone's interest, though it doesn't necessarily give them a reputation for sleeping around.

Quite often—and this is true in high schools as well—the men get oral sex from the women. It happens much less frequently in reverse. A 2013 *New York Times* feature on sex at the University of Pennsylvania featured a young woman who explained why her encounters during her freshman and sophomore years often ended with fellatio. She told a reporter that "usually by the time she got back to a guy's room, she was starting to sober up and didn't want to be there anymore, and giving the guy oral sex was an easy way to wrap things up and leave."[4]

The *Times* story suggested (hoped?) that college women were fine with this new sexual atmosphere, but the quotations from the kids, including the one just cited, left plenty of doubt. Some young women said the hookup culture suited their needs because they were too busy with schoolwork and Model UN to make time for relationships. But one female student quoted in the piece admitted that men control the hookup culture, and that women must accommodate. "'The girls adapt a little bit, because they stop expecting that they're going to get a boyfriend—because if that's all you're trying to do, you're going to be miserable. But at the same time, they want to, like, have contact with guys.' So they hook up and 'try not to get attached.'"[5]

"Try not to get attached" is the unwritten code of the hookup. Divorcing sex from love is one thing, but the hookup culture is past that. It's about divorcing sex from *feeling*. Students are expected to attach about as much sentiment to it as they would to a sweaty workout. It's a physical thing. No feelings, thank you. Or, to put it another way, the only feelings you're expected to indulge are appetites. The deeper ones are off-limits.

It's a shame that so many young people are losing the entire phase of glorious anticipation that used to fall between meeting and becoming intimate. "It's no big deal," the kids are indoctrinated to believe. But that is a tragic misconception. Sex is and always will be a big deal.

A psychologist I spoke with described a young woman who

first sought therapy at age sixteen. She was already experienced at giving oral sex to boys. "Whatever" was how she replied to questions about how this made her feel. Only after many years of self-examination was she was able to recognize that servicing boys in this way was not what she wanted.

Even if a hookup is pleasant for both parties (and many are not), no one expects this to be the start of something. If a couple hook up a few times, actually wake up together, and speak when they are sober, they might agree they actually like each other. But the initial sexual contract is absolutely no-strings-attached. "It's just something that I feel like as a college student you're supposed to do," one student explained. "It's so ingrained in college life that if you're not doing it, then you're not getting the full college experience."[6]

In their study of a thousand women undergraduates, Norval Glenn and Elizabeth Marquardt found that 91 percent said that hookups happen very often or fairly often. Among those who participated in hookups, 62 percent of women reported feeling "desirable" afterward, but 64 percent said they felt "disappointed," and 57 percent said they felt "confused."[7]

That's not surprising. People, especially women, are bad at detaching emotions from sex. Arguably, it's somewhat biological. In addition to many other reactions to physical intimacy, all human beings secrete the hormone oxytocin when they have sex.[8] Oxytocin has been called the "bonding hormone." Mothers are awash in it after childbirth and during lactation; it helps them bond with their babies. Some studies suggest it makes men more monogamous.[9] After sex, women get a bigger rush of oxytocin than men. This may explain why women can become highly attached to a man they've slept with even if they were less than smitten beforehand. Some men feel the same.

When I suggested to undergraduates that women, on average, might be less into casual sex than men, some saw this as a strange proposition, one that elicited furrowed brows and tilted chins. Really? One student told me he thought men and women approach romance and love differently "based partly on biology." When I asked him to elaborate (in the presence of two other students), he grew wary. "Well, at least, um, well, the more I think about it the less I'm sure I can give you an answer one way or the other." His friend, a self-described antirape activist, chimed in with the firm declaration "I think it's entirely socialized."

The second young man was expressing today's orthodoxy, but there are good reasons to treat that orthodoxy skeptically. Men and women are distinct sexually, and though we might wish it were otherwise, men are more promiscuous than women in every era and in every culture. Hooking up assumes that casual sex is the norm, and it isn't surprising that women are less enthusiastic about it than men.

A survey of sixteen thousand individuals from fifty-two countries and six continents asked whether respondents would like to have more than one sexual partner in the next month. Twenty-five percent of heterosexual men said yes, and 29 percent of homosexual men said the same. But only 4 percent of heterosexual women said yes, and only 5 percent of lesbians agreed.[10] In their now classic study, *Patterns of Sexual Behavior* (1951), Clellan S. Ford and Frank A. Beach looked at 190 different societies around the globe and found that males almost everywhere are more sexually aggressive and less selective than females.[11] For most men, Woody Allen's joke sums it up: "Pizza is a lot like sex. When it's good, it's really good. When it's bad, it's still pretty good."

That's not true for women. Bad sex can be painful, unpleasant, or disgusting—and possibly degrading and disappointing. Women report the greatest sexual pleasure when they are in a committed relationship. Men think about sex much more frequently than women, and their fantasies focus less on the loved person and more on body parts or sexual activities.[12] As Mark Regnerus and Jeremy Uecker document in their 2011 book *Premarital Sex in America,* men are also more open to sexual variety than women. In the National Health and Social Life Survey conducted in 1992, men found thirteen of fourteen sexual activities more appealing than did women, often by large margins. Dr. Steven Rhoads, author of *Taking Sex Differences Seriously,* notes that "The libidos of perfectly ordinary men, when fully understood by women, seem deformed or disreputable to them. Many women strongly resist an accurate presentation of male sexuality."[13] Of course, men also think about love and relationships, sometimes longingly, but their stronger sex drive makes easy sex more tempting.

The students I spoke with seemed to be navigating the hookup and relationship world—many still do form relationships—using the wrong map. The one they've been issued tells them that men and women are indistinguishable. If they knew the truth—that women are actually more monogamous and more vulnerable—it might help them to understand the epidemic of accusations and counteraccusations that cloud their otherwise carefree college years.

Two of the young men I spoke with believed that women had an easier time finding someone to hook up with than to date. Yet they agreed that men's choices were infinite, from hooking up to steady relationships. It sounds like casual sex has put men in the driver's seat, doesn't it?

One college senior told me that if he met a girl he "liked enough," he would date her, but otherwise he was "happy playing the field." A senior woman told me she was sure there were many more lonely women than men at her school. I don't doubt it.

College women find hooking up unnatural and sometimes unsafe and wish there were more opportunities for light flirting, dating, and romance. When women are expected to be freer with their bodies than they are with their Apple IDs, men's incentives to court them practically disappear.

But men are stumbling in the dark too, often expressing uncertainty and disappointment with the hookup ethic. Many want girlfriends—a number of the young men I spoke with were even open to love—but they are unsure how to approach women outside of drunken encounters.

Hanna Rosin, author of *The End of Men: And the Rise of Women*

(2014), argues that the hookup culture is a victory for women, and that it suits their needs perfectly. In "Boys on the Side," a piece for *The Atlantic,* she wrote:

> Single young women in their sexual prime—that is, their 20s and early 30s . . . —are for the first time in history more successful, on average, than the single young men around them. They are more likely to have a college degree and, in aggregate, they make more money. What makes this remarkable development possible is not just the pill or legal abortion but the whole new landscape of sexual freedom—the ability to delay marriage and have temporary relationships that don't derail education or career. To put it crudely, feminist progress right now largely depends on the existence of the hookup culture.[14]

Rosin also wants to debunk the "myth" of the "weepy woman" who has been "duped by a sexual revolution that persuaded them to trade away the protections of (and from) young men. In return, they were left even more vulnerable and exploited than before." On the contrary, she asserts, women acting like "frat boys" is "empowering," and they "benefit greatly from living in a world where they can have sexual adventure without commitment or all that much shame, and where they can enter into temporary relationships that don't get in the way of future success."[15]

Rosin found some extremely crude female business school students who said it was harder to stay out of relationships than to get into them. They were "blasé about blow jobs and anal sex." Maybe that's true for the women she interviewed, though it sounds like bluster (or possibly denial) to me.

No women I interviewed spoke that way. A few said they were fine with hookup culture, but many more expressed misgivings and even sorrow. One student who had participated in hooking up as a freshman told me, "It took me a while to see that I wasn't sad because there was something wrong with me. I was sad because this isn't a fulfilling thing to be doing and so I should stop."

Lisa Wade, a sociologist at Occidental College who has studied hookups, found that most students were "overwhelmingly disappointed with the sex they were having in hookups." This was true of both men and women, but "was felt more intensely by women." The students participating in the study said that they had arrived in college expecting one of three things from sex: "empowerment, pleasure, and/or meaningfulness." The women "felt that they had inherited a right to express their sexuality from the women's movement of the '60s and '70s," but they were disappointed. "They didn't feel like equals on the sexual playground, more like jungle gyms."

Students of both sexes, according to Wade, felt pressured into having sex, but more women than men said that they had engaged in sex they did not desire, even in the absence of coercion, threats, or incapacitation, because they felt it was their only option.[16]

As for pleasure, a study by Paula England and Jonathan Bearak published in the journal *Demographic Research* compiled data on ten thousand college students and found that 42 percent of men, but only 19 percent of women, said they'd had an orgasm in their latest hookup (though about half said they enjoyed the sex "very much"). When students were asked whether they wished for "more opportunities" to hook up on campus, 48 percent of men, but only 16 percent of women, said yes. England and Bearak found a persistent double standard regarding casual sex. Both men (69 percent) and women (61 percent) reported that they had "less respect" for a woman who had lots of hookups. Only 37 percent of men said they respected a man less if he hooked up a lot, though 67 percent of women said they did. Nearly identical numbers of men and women (69 and 70 percent) said they wished there were more opportunities for "finding someone to have a relationship with at my school."[17]

Ironically, the sexual revolution that was meant to ring in an era of libidinous delights has instead led to more misunderstandings and misery. Rather than uniting the sexes, it has erected walls of mistrust that obscure the fact that both sexes actually want and need tenderness and love. As one college senior told me, "So, we are left scarred, bruised, battered, and not wanting to expose ourselves because we don't want to be hurt again, understandably. But that makes for some very callous lovers."

If we were trying to design a social system that inhibited the development of romance, coarsened young people's attitudes toward others, and facilitated date rape, the hookup culture couldn't be more perfect.

Booze

In *The End of Sex,* Donna Freitas, who has taught at Boston University and Hofstra University, describes the drunkenness that dominates social life on college campuses. She saw young people "at their best and brightest" during the day, but after dark, "I would see students coming home so trashed they could barely walk. On Fridays and Saturdays, in the packed elevators among the screaming, drunken masses, there were always a few couples who were sloppy and making out as if they were alone, pressed against each other and too out of it to notice everyone else or to care. By 3 a.m., a parade of students would be doing their best to make it back to one of their rooms without falling down or throwing up before they arrived."[18]

Binge drinking among women has risen quite dramatically in recent years. "Between 1999 and 2008," reports the *Wall Street Journal,* "the number of young women who showed up in emergency rooms for being dangerously intoxicated rose by 52 percent. The rate for young men, though higher, rose just 9 percent."

Something is making young women turn to alcohol in huge numbers. According to the National Institute on Alcohol Abuse and Alcoholism, four out of five college students drink alcohol and 50 percent engage in binge drinking, meaning they consume four drinks in two hours for a woman or five drinks in two hours for a man.[19] One student I interviewed admitted having downed "six drinks" on several occasions. "I know exactly what it does to me," he explained, "and can make decisions about what is safe."

It's common for young people to "pregame" on a Friday or Saturday night, which means drinking before attending a party. The point is not to relax or even to get a little tipsy. Freitas writes, "There was a pervasive perception among students not only that everyone was drinking, but that everyone was drinking *hard,* that is, drinking to get wasted."[20] When I asked a college freshman where the students got the hard stuff (as nearly all freshmen and sophomores are under the legal drinking age), he explained that the shots are provided by upperclassmen.

The National Institute on Alcohol Abuse and Alcoholism estimates that extreme drinking leads to about 1,800 student deaths per year, 690,000 assaults, 599,000 injuries, and approximately 97,000 sexual assaults.[21] Freitas found that 90 percent of unwanted sex (of all kinds, including rape) took place during a hookup, and excessive drinking was involved in 76 percent of cases.[22] The hookup culture is fueled and enabled by booze. It could not exist without it.

Students whom I spoke with did not contest the levels of drinking on campus, and they offered theories to explain it, such as "It's a relief from the pressure we're under" or "It's the forbidden-fruit phenomenon." But are college students really experiencing such a burden of pressure? Some have tough courses, it's true, and many have extracurricular activities, including sports. The economy has been indolent for the past decade or so, and students may feel anxiety about their chances of landing a job after graduation. But let's face it, college is one of the least pressured times of life. Students at residential colleges don't have to worry about food or shelter. They enjoy access to first-rate gyms, pools, and other recreational options, and multiple opportunities to enjoy theater, music, and the arts. In addition, they are surrounded by people just like them and, beyond their curriculum's requirements, are free to study anything that catches their imagination.[23]

Still, many of them get so plastered they often cannot remember what they did the previous evening. This is not pleasure; it's anesthesia. I suspect that hookup culture is causing the drinking, and vice versa. Students may find hooking up so uncomfortable, so odd, so dehumanizing that they use alcohol to dull their senses and diminish their natural (and healthy) inhibitions. They'd probably never get into bed with strangers (at least, most women wouldn't) if they weren't smashed.

Bring Back the Date

Nothing captures the essential hollowness of hookup culture better than the simple offer of an alternative.

When Professor Kerry Cronin of Boston College discovered a decade ago that most students in her senior seminar on the great books had never dated, she decided to make asking someone out on a date part of the curriculum. The rules were that students had to make the request in person, not via text or Facebook. The person they invited had to be a true romantic interest, not just a friend. The two were not to see a movie, which could preclude conversation, and they were not to drink alcohol during the date. The person who did the asking, male or female, was to pay for the date. The outing could take place during the afternoon or evening, but it had to be over by 10:00 p.m.[24]

The response Cronin got the first time she presented this assignment became typical of what she found in the following years. The students were nervous but also intrigued—so much so that they seemed starved for opportunities to talk about it. "We shy away from talking to them about relationships," Cronin told me, "but they know the hookup culture is messed up, and they crave adult guidance."

Cronin has since spoken on at least eighty campuses and has become a relationship guru for the students at Boston College. Even students not taking her course on philosophy and theology some-times drop by her office to seek advice. Class discussions about dat-ing are lively. "We spend a lot of time on the Ask," Cronin reports. "It's a matter of courage—both the courage to make yourself vul-nerable and the courage to say, 'I'm stepping away from hookup culture.'" The kids "root for each other" and for romance.[25]

One student devised a way to frame the invitation that was both practical and romantic: "I have this assignment to go out on a date, but I've been wanting to ask you out for a long time anyway." Is there any decent person, of either sex, who would not prefer that invitation to a drunken hookup?

Romance and love, two of life's greatest joys, must begin with interest in the whole person. To be the object of a crush, to be ap-preciated for your unique qualities, such as your sense of humor, your interests, or your fabulous guitar skills—isn't that what most people hope for? Doesn't that make the heart beat a little faster? Yet all that seems a world away from hookup culture, where everyone is reduced to "bed-able or not bed-able" (to put it politely).

One senior I spoke with was in a long-term relationship, and he agreed emphatically that dating was a dying art on his campus. He was contemptuous of "guys who are clueless" about how to approach women anywhere outside booze-infused parties. "These guys are wusses," he lamented. "I mean, come on, hang out while you're sober. Get lunch. Get coffee. That's way too uncommon."

Okay, but maybe they're not timid or selfish. Maybe they're flailing because of all the confusion about love and romance in our time, and because, as Kerry Cronin notes, the big institutions of our society have relinquished their moral authority, leaving kids adrift. The dating template is on life support.

Anna Bahr, an antirape activist, told *New York* magazine, "Rape culture is an attitude toward women in particular, but not even just to women—to treating all people as sexual objects, noth-ing more than an opportunity for sex." But what she's describing is not rape culture; it's the hookup culture that grew out of the sexual revolution. And Bahr is right: it's bleak.

In the Claremont McKenna College student newspaper, Jordan Bosiljevac published an article in which she argued that sometimes even "yes can mean no." This drew contemptuous commentary about the craziness surrounding the antirape hysteria on campus. But I don't think she's crazy. As Bosiljevac wrote, "Sometimes, for me, there was obligation from already having gone back to someone's room, not wanting to ruin a good friendship, loneliness, worry that no one else would ever be interested, a fear that if I did say no, they might not stop, the influence of alcohol, and an understanding that hookups are 'supposed' to be fun."[26]

Bosiljevac presents a compelling argument against the sexual revolution and hookup culture (though, of course, she would have a difficult time lodging a rape complaint against a man to whom she had said yes). Sadly, she has only the vocabulary of postmodernism with which to express her dissatisfaction, and her article degenerates into a clichéd rant weighted with dull jargon: "[W]e have to realize that all oppression is connected, and all rape is racist, classist, ableist, patriarchal, hetero and cissexist. We cannot make consent available to all if we are not simultaneously disrupting these structures."

The terms she's familiar with are *oppression, racism, sexism,* and so on, but it seems to me that she is feeling the things girls and women have always felt. They don't want to be rushed. They don't want to be told their reticence is illegitimate, or that they just need to relax. They also don't want anyone to make them feel that they *owe* sex to men. They want control over their bodies and their feelings.

I wonder how she would react to a sincere invitation to dinner and a long walk?

If every college and university in America made dating a part of the curriculum, it might be a start toward reforming the dehumanizing hookup culture. If the faculty and staff made it their business to instill mutual respect and new norms of social life (which is to say, old ones), it might have an impact. A male freshman I spoke with at a New England university stressed how "susceptible we are to influence" in the first couple of months of college life. "It's a critical period," he said. "You don't really know who you are, and you're vulnerable to whatever the cultural signals are."

Universities have a lot to answer for. They've been cheerleaders for the sexual revolution, and they cannot escape responsibility for encouraging the insensitive and boorish behavior they're attempting so unsuccessfully to cope with now. There's a joke that a college president's job is to "provide football for the alumni, sex for the undergraduates, and parking for the faculty." That's close to the mark. Colleges and universities are businesses, after all, and they want the applications to keep coming. Their financial interest is in showing the kids a good time, particularly those who can throw a football or dunk a basketball.

Wesleyan University advertises one of its housing options to potential students with this pitch: "Open House is a safe space for Lesbian, Gay, Bisexual, Transgender, Transsexual, Queer, Questioning, Flexual, Asexual, Genderfuck, Polyamorous, Bondage/Disciple, Dominance/Submission, Sadism/Masochism (LGBT-TQQFAGPBDSM) communities and for people of sexually or gender dissident communities. The goals of Open House include generating interest in a celebration of queer life from the social to the political to the academic. Open House works to create a Wesleyan community that appreciates the variety and vivacity of gender, sex and sexuality." *Vivacity* is not a word I associate with "Sadism/Masochism," but they're certainly enthusiastic.

Every American college and university features orientation sessions on the subject of sex and sexual assault, in addition to discussions of contraception and safe-sex practices. In case anyone misses the message, baskets filled with colorful condoms are on display in dorms and student centers. I know a middle-aged mother who was visiting her son's school and reached into a basket expecting to pull out a piece of wrapped candy. Mother and son both were embarrassed.

These orientations usually include warnings about sexual assault and rape—the dos and don'ts of hookup culture. As one student described it to me, "The skit we were all required to watch was called 'Sex on a Saturday Night,' and it dealt with every possible sexual activity and orientation. The clear message was that it was expected that everyone was going to be engaging in the hookup culture, and that if you weren't, you were out of things."

The message that libidinous behavior is expected doesn't start with universities, of course; but orientation programs set a tone. Imagine if schools offered guidance on how to handle drugs in the same way—with a wink and humorous skits about getting high on a Saturday night and warnings about overdoses. The message would be clear that everyone was expected to take drugs.

Schools are careful to let freshmen know that sexuality and sexual identity are part of a "spectrum." A freshman at Princeton described the special "information meeting" he was required to attend. Held in a small classroom, it featured a presentation from a representative of the LGBT center. The student introduced himself as a "homo-romantic demi-sexual," and proceeded to explain what that meant.

The new vocabulary of sex and gender is considered a key component of orientation. Most students I spoke to told me that having the right attitude about sexuality (e.g., understanding the difference between "gender identity" and "gender expression") was more important than any cautions about drinking.

Many schools now instruct students on the proper use of pronouns. At Vanderbilt, for example, students and faculty are encouraged to introduce themselves with their names and preferred pronouns even with "familiar colleagues and students." The acceptable parlance is "I'm Laura. I'm a cisgender woman and I prefer she/her/hers" or "I'm Steve. I'm transitioning and I prefer they/them/theirs."

A few colleges, scorched by recent rape cases, have begun to address their drinking problem. Dartmouth has joined Bowdoin, Bates, and Colby in banning hard liquor from campus, but skeptics note that such rules have been ineffective at schools such as Penn State, Stanford, and Swarthmore, all of which have adopted modified bans.[27]

Nearly all colleges (with the exception of some religious schools and Michigan's Hillsdale College, which is conservative culturally as well as politically) play a role in creating and perpetuating the hookup culture. (Hillsdale, by the way, has had no recorded sexual assaults or rapes in the past ten years.)

Nathan Harden, in his memoir *Sex and God at Yale,* described "Sex Week at Yale": "The campus is flooded with banners and posters announcing 'Sex Week! Sex Week! Sex Week!' Students are barraged with emails announcing each day's proceedings and encouraged to attend the week's 'educational' programs . . . ranging from a porn-star look-alike contest (judged by a real-life porn film director), to safe sex workshops, to lectures on the female orgasm."[28]

Most colleges present their sexual cheerleading as a health matter. "Safe sex" debuted as the reigning orthodoxy in the 1980s, in response to the AIDS epidemic. But the implicit encouragement goes far beyond "safety." Boston University features "Frisky February: 28 Days of Stimulation," courtesy of the Student Health, Wellness, and Prevention Services. In 2015, it kicked off with a "Sexploration Workshop" (a sex toy party). Students were later invited to KISS Bingo (for "Keeping It Sexy and Safe"); an "Aphrodisiac Cooking Class"; a queer-sex workshop hosted by the Center for Gender, Sexuality, and Activism; and an evening with You-Tube personality and MTV star Laci Green, who gave a talk titled "Best Sex Ever!" on the science behind love and relationships. (At least she mentioned relationships.)

Not to be outdone, Harvard has inaugurated its own Sex Week. A recent workshop, sponsored by a local "sex-positive" store called Good Vibrations, located in Brookline, Massachusetts, was titled "What's What in the Butt?" The point of the program (aside from giving the store free advertising) was, according to the *Huffington Post,* "to help college students practice healthy and pleasurable anal sex."[29] The website *The College Fix* listed some of the other offerings during Harvard's Sex Week:

> "Brown Girlz Do it Well: A Queer Diaspora Remix," a workshop
> that will "situate our personal narratives within broader systems
> of racism, casteism, classism, islamophobia, and imperialism." Sex
> Ed 101 promises to teach students the ins and outs of safer sex, in-
> cluding the proper use of dental dams. "Losing Your (Concept of)
> Virginity" will question whether virginity matters. And "Fifty
> Shades of False: Kink, Fantasy, and Fetish" is expected to delve
> into how the bestselling book apparently got BDSM all wrong.[30]

A Northwestern University professor who teaches a popular course, "Human Sexuality," featured a special after-class, live demonstration of a naked woman being sexually stimulated by a sex toy called a "fuck saw."[31] When the story received bug-eyed publicity in the national press, Professor J. Michael Bailey shrugged it off by saying, "Sticks and stones may break your bones, but watching naked people on stage doing pleasurable things will never hurt you."[32]

The University of New Mexico's Sex Week sported titles for sessions such as "Negotiating Successful Threesomes," and "How to Be a Gentleman *and* Get Laid." The events were organized by the university's Women's Resource Center and its Graduate and Professional Students Association, along with Albuquerque's Self Serve Sexuality Resource Center.[33] The university issued an apology for the sensational titles but has not announced plans to discontinue Sex Week.

Conservative students have offered some pushback. Under-graduates for a Better Yale, an antihookup student group, issued the following statement about their university's Sex Week:

> Tell Yale that a pornographic culture does not create respect but
> degrades, does not build up relationships but undermines them,
> promotes not consent but the ugliest form of pressure, does not

stop sexual harassment and the objectification of one another's bodies but makes us numb, blind, and indifferent to how we actually look at and treat others. Tell Yale that you want a campus marked by respect and love, full of flourishing friendships based on the acknowledgment of each person's integral value, relationships based on true love between partners—not transient lust—and a sense of familial trust between all students. Tell Yale to say "No" to Sex Week and all it stands for, because Yale can do so much better.[34]

The hookup culture enables the worst kind of insensitivity and boorishness. Though it gets less attention than rape and sexual assault, a tremendous amount of gross behavior happens on college campuses too. One young woman at an East Coast college told me she'd been groped at least forty times at parties, and a stranger once reached inside her pants. And while some jackasses have always boasted of their sexual conquests, the advent of smartphones has allowed the smarmier types to record such encounters and then share them.

The sexual revolution obliterated so many guardrails. Even when I was an undergraduate, if some guy put his hands on you at a party, he could expect to be slapped away, and he would be shamed.

Early feminists embraced the fashionable view that "sex is no big deal" and boasted about being just as randy as men. But now they have no idea how to handle male sexual predation that is even more unbridled than it used to be. Perhaps it was a mistake to condemn chivalry as a mark of the patriarchy?

There is a deep incompatibility between casual sex and women's best interests. You cannot really understand why rape is worse than other violent crimes without acknowledging that sex is a profound thing. If a drunk young man were to punch another man in the nose, would that be grounds for expulsion? Probably not. Certainly not for a first offense.

But what if he punched a *woman* in the nose? That would be

more serious because our sense of women's greater vulnerability has not been entirely bleached from our psyches. Still, even then, it's not likely the young man would be expelled for that crime or even that the woman would necessarily demand expulsion. But if he raped her, that would be considered a terrible, profound violation.

Why? Because the sexual revolutionaries were wrong: Sex *is* a big deal. Bodies have minds and souls attached.

CHAPTER 5

THE CAMPUS RAPE MESS

Free love is like a free lunch. There's no such thing.

—"Valerie Goldberg" (pseudonym) of Yale's first coed class, 1971

Emma Sulkowicz, a Columbia University student, carried a mattress around the New York City campus for a full year. It was an extra-long twin with a blue cover weighing about fifty pounds. Other students, male and female, often helped her manage the unwieldy thing. The bed lugging was a piece of performance art called *Carry That Weight,* and the university, which had disappointed Sulkowicz in other ways, obligingly gave her course credit for the stunt.

The blue mattress made Sulkowicz a symbol and a media star. Her story (or, at least, her version of it), that she had "survived" a campus rape and her attacker skated free, appeared in 2014 in the *New York Times, New York* magazine, and the *New York Post,* among other publications. Artnet.com called Sulkowicz's performance "one of the most important art works of the year." She was honored by the National Organization for Women and the Feminist Majority Foundation. She attended President Obama's 2015 State of the Union address as the guest of Sen. Kirsten Gillibrand of New York. Roberta Smith, the *Times* art critic, compared *Carry*

That Weight to the Stations of the Cross and Sulkowicz to Hester Prynne, and predicted a great artistic career for Sulkowicz, suggesting that the piece "will also earn her a niche in the history of intensely personal yet aggressively political performance art."[1]

Sulkowicz caught a wave and surfed that blue mattress on a national craze regarding campus sexual assault. Universities across the nation are embroiled in high-profile lawsuits and protests over sexual harassment, sexual assault, and the so-called rape culture. They are revising their policies and hiring regiments of counselors.

Blue mattresses now pop up on other campuses. The sight of them carries tremendous emotional resonance, even when the story on which the symbol is based is in doubt. The Obama administration listened, and announced the "It's on Us" and the "Not Alone" campaigns, which the president explained were intended to "fight the nightmare" of campus sexual assault. A White House task force released a report on campus sexual assault, and before an audience of activists, President Obama repeated the mantra: "An estimated one in five women has been sexually assaulted during her college years—*one in five*. Of those assaults, only 12 percent are reported, and of those reported assaults, only a fraction of the offenders are punished." He continued: "For anybody whose once-normal, everyday life was suddenly shattered by an act of sexual violence, the trauma, the terror can shadow you long after one horrible attack."[2]

With unerring fealty to a leftist interpretation of any issue, Obama embraced the view espoused by feminists and others that campus rape is pervasive, that it arises from a "rape culture," and that women (rather than their attackers) are the ones most often shamed or blamed.

Jessica Valenti, a contributor to *The Nation* magazine and coeditor of the anthology *Yes Means Yes,* argues that "Rape is a standard result of a culture mired in misogyny . . . for whatever reason—denial, self-preservation, sexism—Americans bend over backwards to make excuses for male violence."[3]

The most spectacular and lurid tale about campus rape, "A

Rape on Campus," *Rolling Stone*'s account of a gang rape that supposedly took place at the University of Virginia, fell apart within days of publication on November 19, 2014, and was totally retracted on April 5, 2015. But the sheer number of stories, along with the Obama administration's extremely aggressive moves to limit protections for the accused, created the strong impression that the nation was in the grip of an epidemic of campus rapes. New York senator Kirsten Gillibrand and Missouri senator Claire McCaskill, among many others, soon joined President Obama on the barricades.

Some colleges are creating "special victims units" to deal with campus sexual complaints. At the same time, dozens of young men have sued colleges and universities, claiming that their rights were violated by unjust, one-sided tribunals. The state of California has now legislated that "affirmative consent" be obtained by each party before every sexual act. A contributor to the website *Inside Higher Ed,* in reference to the law, pointed out that "when one sexual partner claims in a student discipline context that the other did not have affirmative consent to engage in any challenged sexual activity, the burden will shift to the initiator of the sexual activity to offer objective evidence of consent."[4]

Many colleges (e.g., Grinnell, Dartmouth, Yale, the University of California) already require this. "Affirmative consent must be ongoing throughout a sexual activity and can be revoked at any time,"[5] Sofie Karasek, an advocate for the law, told the *San Jose Mercury News.* Karasek said the legislation would "change the cultural perception of what rape is. There's this pervasive idea that if it's not super violent then it doesn't really count."[6]

Perhaps. But it may also change the perception of sex. Couples, or what used to be known as lovers, are not automatons. People communicate in a thousand subtle ways, especially when it comes to love and sex. A glance, the lift of a shoulder, the closing of eyes, can convey as much as or more than words. When Antioch College introduced an affirmative consent rule in the 1990s, the ridicule rang from coast to coast, and the concept was parodied on *Saturday Night Live*. Today, it is California law as well as policy at dozens of universities. Sex will be regulated, like trans fats and high-fructose corn syrup.

California colleges will now be required to add the new "yes means yes" directives to the programs already mandated by the Department of Education. *Inside Higher Ed* limned the new rules: "Consent can be revoked at any time, and must be renewed as sexual activity escalates. . . . He or she cannot claim confusion, or that his or her sexual partner did not establish boundaries. If there was no clear invitation to proceed, the college or university must conclude there was no affirmative consent."[7]

That should go well.

Lawmakers in ten states are proposing legislation to permit students to carry handguns. "Some lawmakers see it as way to protect the one in four college women who survive college sexual assault," explained Marina Lopes in a 2015 report for the *PBS NewsHour,* repeating another statistic that is often brandished in the current climate.[8]

A Nevada assemblywoman who is sponsoring one of the bills said, "If these young, hot little girls on campus have a firearm, I wonder how many men will want to assault them. The sexual assaults that are occurring would go down once these predators get a bullet in their head."[9]

Three cheers for the sexual revolution!

The Campus Rape Industrial Complex

Following President Obama's lead, the Department of Education shook the academic world and contributed to the atmosphere of crisis in 2011 by having its Office for Civil Rights (OCR) issue new regulations for handling sexual harassment and sexual assault cases.

What became known as the "Dear Colleague" letter decreed that all campus adjudications of sexual harassment *and* sexual assault use a lower standard of proof. Most cases of serious infractions at universities require a "clear and convincing" standard of proof, but the Education Department ruled that students could be found guilty, even of serious crimes such as rape, based merely on the "preponderance of the evidence," which is the lowest standard of proof in law, usually translated as a 50.1 percent likelihood that the offense took place. This means that at nearly all universities today, administrators must clear a higher burden to prove that a student committed plagiarism or cheated on an exam than to prove that he committed rape.

In the normal course of things, rape is a crime handled by local police, prosecutors, and courts. Despite the fevered rhetoric of the feminist left, rape has always been treated in Anglo/American law as the second most serious offense that can be committed. Although rape cases can be difficult to prove due to a lack of witnesses and other evidence, conviction results in long prison sentences. And like other violent crimes, rape is nearly always a state matter.

So why did the Department of Education lump sexual assault, a violent crime, together with sexual harassment? Sexual harassment can be a pattern of off-color jokes, inappropriate attention of a sexual nature, or repeated and intimidating demands for dates. Yet the Obama administration conflated the two. (In 2017, the Trump administration began the process of repealing some of these rules, but they persist because several states have since enacted the guidelines into their laws and a number of universities have vowed that they will stick with the Obama rules.)

The "Dear Colleague" letter spelled out the feminist-influenced, progressive guidelines by stating that "the sexual harassment of students, including sexual violence, interferes with students' right to receive an education free from discrimination and, in the case of sexual violence, is a crime. Title IX of the Education Amendments of 1972 . . . prohibits discrimination on the basis of sex in education programs or activities operated by recipients of Federal financial assistance. Sexual harassment of students, which includes acts of sexual violence, is a form of sex discrimination prohibited by Title IX."[10]

Sexual harassment includes sexual violence? Isn't that like saying that when you smash someone's temple with a hammer, it is a form of insult and ought to be treated under the libel laws? Why would the government make such a leap? One explanation is that it was a straightforward power grab. If sexual assault can be subsumed under the broad definition of sexual harassment, it falls under the purview of Title IX of the Education Amendments of 1972, and it can be regulated by the federal Department of Education. As Sen. McCaskill explained to the *St. Louis Post Dispatch,* "The federal government has no authority to prosecute rape cases, generally." Yet armed with Title IX, universities are taking cases of sexual assault and rape out of the hands of local police, prosecutors, and courts. Serious crimes are now adjudicated by campus administrators under the supervision of Washington officials.

Of course, sexual assault is nothing like sexual harassment. It's a crime that carries a high standard of proof—or it did. Under Education Department guidance, campus tribunals adjudicating serious cases of sexual misconduct have dispensed with sacred rights protecting the accused, including the right to be represented by counsel, the right to confront witnesses, and the presumption of innocence. As of November 2017, the Justice Department had investigated some 450 colleges and universities (among them UCLA, the University of Michigan, Princeton, Emory, Ohio State, and Harvard) for possible violations of the civil rights acts due to their handling of sexual assault and sexual harassment allegations.[11]

Colleges have been scrambling to respond. Lawrence Wright, vice president and general counsel of the University of Delaware, told the *Chronicle of Higher Education,* "The surest route to disaster is for the Office for Civil Rights to find out we hadn't done training."[12] So they train. Harvard University employs fifty-four Title IX compliance officers.[13] "Gender-based misconduct" officials are in high demand, and sexual misconduct boards, abuse counselors, and offices of "student conflict" resolution have proliferated. If you are looking for a job and can market yourself as having expertise in this area, it's a seller's market these days.[14]

Feminists have supported the creation of this bureaucratic labyrinth in part because they believe the criminal courts are unfair to women in rape cases. Dahlia Lithwick, writing for *Slate,* quoted Anne Coughlin, who teaches gender at the University of Virginia, as saying, "Women have not complained to the police because they have had good reason to fear that the police would not believe their claims. And, in cases where the survivor had been drinking at the time of the assault, she was likely to be told that her intoxication amounted to consent."[15]

Whether the criminal justice system actually revictimizes women is a matter for debate. Surprisingly, few seem concerned that in bypassing the police and the courts, victims may actually be disadvantaged. If victims are not seen quickly enough by trained investigators and examined at hospitals equipped with rape kits, key evidence can be lost. Forcible rape cases belong in the hands of experienced police and prosecutors, not college ethics panels. Rapists should be jailed, not transferred to another university.

The kangaroo courts erected by universities have shocked even some feminists. As attorney Judith Grossman wrote in the *Wall Street Journal* in 2013, "I am a feminist. I have marched at the barricades, subscribed to *Ms.* magazine, and knocked on many a door in support of progressive candidates committed to women's rights. Until a month ago, I would have expressed unqualified support for Title IX and for the Violence Against Women Act." Then her son, attending a New England college, was accused of sexual assault by a former girlfriend. The accusation came years after the purported events. Nevertheless, "what followed was a nightmare—a fall through Alice's looking-glass into a world that I could not possibly have believed existed, least of all behind the ivy-covered walls thought to protect an ostensible dedication to enlightenment and intellectual betterment."[16] Grossman's son was not permitted to have his lawyer present for the hearing, or even to consult with him outside the room. He was not allowed to call witnesses on his own behalf, though witnesses against him were heard. He was forbidden to question the witnesses or his accuser.

These stories, repeated at a number of schools, were too much for the law faculties of Harvard and the University of Pennsylvania. Twenty-eight members of the Harvard Law School faculty signed an open letter in October 2014 objecting to the rules that Harvard promulgated under federal government pressure, stating that the university's sexual harassment policy was "inconsistent with many of the most basic principles we teach."

Among their many concerns were that "Harvard has adopted procedures for deciding cases of alleged sexual misconduct which lack the most basic elements of fairness and due process, are overwhelmingly stacked against the accused, and are in no way required by Title IX law or regulation." After the professors itemized the procedural and substantive problems with the regulations, they protested that Harvard was "adopting rules governing sexual conduct between students both of whom are impaired or incapacitated, rules which are starkly one-sided as between complainants and respondents, and entirely inadequate to address the complex issues in these unfortunate situations involving extreme use and abuse of alcohol and drugs by our students." The University of Pennsylvania Law School faculty signed a similar letter in February 2015.

This agenda to fuse sexual assault and sexual harassment is congenial to feminists who sincerely believe the two are linked. They see mistreatment of women as a continuum. At bottom are men's negative or patronizing attitudes about women. Next are discrimination and wage differentials. A little farther up is sexual harassment. At the top is rape. All involve varying degrees of hostility by men toward women.

Before we look at why this completely misperceives men and relations between the sexes, let's examine a bit more about the world that progressive feminism has created.

Star Chambers

Students who are adjudicated for rape or assault only by a campus tribunal cannot be sent to prison, but they do face severe consequences. They can be expelled, suspended, or have their movements on campus severely restricted. Many have been publicly branded as criminals, which is a devastating blow. Administrators have become so terrorized about being seen as insufficiently responsive to complaints of sexual assault that some colleges have left the realm of reason altogether. Harvard law professor Janet Halley, writing in the *Harvard Law Review Forum,* described a student at a "small liberal arts university in Oregon"

> [who underwent a month-long investigation into] all his campus relationships, seeking information about his possible sexual misconduct in them (an immense invasion of his and his friends' privacy), and who was ordered to stay away from a fellow student (cutting him off from his housing, his campus job, and educational opportunity)—all because he *reminded her* of the man who had raped her months before and thousands of miles away. He was found to be completely innocent of any sexual misconduct and was informed of the basis of the complaint against him only by accident and off-hand. But the stay-away order remained in place, and was so broadly drawn up that he was at constant risk of violating it and coming under discipline for *that.*
>
> When the duty to prevent a "sexually hostile environment" is interpreted this expansively, it is affirmatively indifferent to the restrained person's complete and total innocence of any misconduct whatsoever.[17]

The Oregon case may be an outlier, but a 50.1 percent standard of proof increases the likelihood that many innocents will be wrongly convicted. Moreover, in cases that are turned over to local prosecutors, the evidence adduced at slanted campus hearings can be used against the accused in criminal proceedings. Since 2011, male students have filed at least 150 lawsuits against colleges, alleging that their rights were trampled in campus proceedings or that *they* were victims of sex discrimination because the tribunals were biased against men.[18]

Counselors, tribunals, lawsuits, rape activists, Title IX coordinators—the whole wobbly edifice is a failure of progressivism to deal honestly with human nature and to respect the traditional guardrails of sexuality.

At Occidental College, an eighteen-year-old freshman was expelled after an investigation found he had engaged in sex with a seventeen-year-old student who was too drunk to give consent. According to the *Los Angeles Times,* the college's investigative report said that "both parties agreed on the following facts: Both had been drinking, she went to his room, took off her shirt while dancing, made out with him and returned to his room later for sex, asking if he had a condom. When friends stopped by the room to ask if she was OK, she told them yes."

When the young woman filed a complaint, the university, in a departure from usual practice, referred the matter to the Los Angeles County district attorney. The DA's investigation concluded that "both parties were drunk but willing participants exercising bad judgment."[19]

The consequences for both students have been harrowing. The female student has dropped out of school for now. Her lawyer reports that she is in therapy and suffering from posttraumatic stress disorder. The male student says he has been physically attacked and called a rapist. He applied to and was accepted at another college, only to find on the day he arrived that his acceptance had been rescinded following an anonymous phone call about his case.[20] "It's been a soul-crushing experience," he said.[21]

The Supreme Court has called cross-examination "the greatest legal engine ever invented for the discovery of truth,"[22] but the Education Department rules have dispensed with it in cases that involve sexual assault. According to its advisory, titled "Questions and Answers on Title IX and Sexual Violence," the "OCR strongly discourages a school from allowing the parties to personally question or cross-examine each other during a hearing on alleged sexual violence. Allowing an alleged perpetrator directly to question an alleged victim may be traumatic or intimidating, thereby possibly escalating or perpetuating a hostile environment."[23]

Colleges also may withhold the identity of accusers and deny the accused an opportunity to be represented by counsel. Some of these rights date back to the Magna Carta, but today they are expendable in the rush to police campus sexual misconduct.

This retreat from cherished norms of justice is justified as a protection for women, who might be "traumatized" by having to answer questions. It is curious that modern feminism can claim that women are infinitely strong, capable, and sturdy (tough enough to serve in combat infantry brigades, lead multinational corporations, and serve as president of the United States) yet are so vulnerable and weak they cannot be questioned about their sexual victimization or even exposed to stories about rape and abuse without receiving "trigger warnings."

Wendy McElroy, a feminist and a rape survivor, is an eloquent defender of individual rights. "As a woman who has been raped," she wrote in *Sexual Correctness,* "I will never downplay the trauma it brings. But being raped was not the worst thing that ever happened to me, and I have recovered from it. Feminists who say otherwise are paying me a disrespect."[24]

These "trigger warnings" and demands for "safe spaces" infantilize women and potentially victimize men. Judith Shapiro, former president of Barnard College, is a rare voice of protest against "safe spaces," writing that "This magnifies the sense of personal danger out of all proportion and interferes with students' appreciation of what it means to be in real peril. It is an obstacle to the development of authentic courage."[25]

Yet in 2011, the federal government endorsed just this kind of infantilization of women. Rules from the Department of Education dictate how the most complex and delicate human interactions are to be evaluated and judged. And woe to the college that fails to treat women as delicate flowers that might be crushed at the mere mention of the word *rape*.

Victim Blaming

Though it would seem obvious to warn students (particularly women, who are 90 percent of rape victims) about the dangers of excessive drinking, political correctness brands this as "victim blaming" or, as some feminists have it, "slut shaming." Darcie Folsom, director of sexual violence prevention and advocacy at Connecticut College, told the *Chronicle of Higher Education*: "The first things we hear are: 'What was she wearing?' and 'How much alcohol did she drink?' But those are not causing a sexual assault to happen. The perpetrator is the problem here."[26]

Any recommendations that young women limit their alcohol intake, maintain awareness of their surroundings, and take other commonsense precautions to protect themselves are greeted with shrill protests. Emily Yoffe of *Slate* ran into a feminist buzz saw when she wrote simply that "The campus culture of binge drinking is toxic, and many rapists prey on drunk young women."[27] The website Feministing called Yoffe's article a "rape denialism manifesto." A college professor objected that Yoffe was echoing "the old Puritan line that women need to restrain and modify their pleasure-seeking behaviors," which represented "a big step backward."[28] Most feminists saw the matter in black-and-white terms: that society needs to "teach men not to rape. Period."[29]

Colleges make violence prevention a key part of freshman orientation, but many avoid any suggestion that women limit their drinking. "What we steer our campuses away from is anything that says someone experienced gender violence because they had been drinking," explained Joan Masters, coordinator of a statewide coalition of colleges in Missouri called Partners in Prevention.[30]

Naturally, there's a government angle as well. Since 1999, the

Department of Justice has offered grants to colleges to implement sexual assault prevention programs. The guidelines specify that programs encouraging sobriety are considered "out of scope." The department advises colleges not to attempt to "change victims' behavior."[31]

Some students arrive on campus wary (due to parental or other influences) and lose their natural common sense in response to the ideology of "rape culture." The *Chronicle of Higher Education* described Ayushi Roy, who said "her parents warned her before her freshman year to be careful about drinking—and she was." But she eventually grew resentful that other people were causing her to watch what she did. "'The cost of any form of self-policing—not walking alone in the dark, watching what you drink and what you wear—is that you live under a self-inflicted form of fear. You are living in this fear that drinking or letting yourself go is a bad thing.'"[32]

Is the goal of the feminist left to strip young women of their natural guardedness and leave them vulnerable? Are ordinary precautions a "self-inflicted form of fear"?

Instead of warning young women (and men) about the dangers of excessive drinking, colleges rely on "task forces" to increase awareness and dispel "myths." The American College Health Association, for example, provides a twenty-four-page "toolkit" chock-full of suggestions, such as:

Develop educational/outreach programming that:
- recognizes that sexual violence is a learned behavior
- teaches bystander intervention techniques
- addresses the role of consent in sexual relationships
- encourages the involvement of men
- addresses alcohol and other drug issues and the connection with sexual violence
- provides concepts that encourage healthy, consensual sexual relationships

- addresses non-stranger sexual violence and dispels traditional beliefs
- Create and codify amnesty policies for underage drinking for victims who report sexual assault.[33]

That is drivel. A program that "addresses non-stranger sexual violence and dispels traditional beliefs"? What traditional beliefs? That men should not expect sex from women before marriage? That men should never take advantage of a drunk woman? Some traditional beliefs clearly protected women.

"Bystander intervention" is the new catchphrase for those who fear being accused of "victim blaming." The government website Notalone.gov also offers resources for preventing sexual violence: "Skills are provided to help when participants see behavior that puts others at risk. Skills include speaking out against rape myths and sexist language, supporting victims, and intervening in potentially violent situations."

Note the assumption that rapists can be detected by "sexist" language. I sincerely doubt this. Former president Bill Clinton said all the right things about feminism and abortion and violence against women, yet large numbers of women accused him of sexual predation, and one even said that he raped her. Serial abuser Harvey Weinstein was a feminist in good standing who contributed to Planned Parenthood and other feminist causes. Doubtless he avoided sexist language. Yet he has been credibly accused of sexual assault and rape.

Perhaps it's a good idea to train "bystanders" to intervene when they see a potentially violent scenario unfolding, but how many rapes feature eyewitnesses? How would it work? Most rapes happen when two drunk students leave a party and stumble back to a dorm room. Will the "intervention" take place earlier, when a couple is fondling each other on the dance floor? Why won't that be interpreted as disrespecting the rights of the students involved?

As for what goes on in dorm rooms, a number of stories that have been reported feature friends inquiring as to whether a woman was okay, and her reassurance, before the sex act, that she was. Many women report being raped by men they'd already hooked up with at least once before, or by friends of long standing. How could a bystander be helpful in those cases?

Encouraging bystander intervention is clumsy and demeaning to women. A grown woman must be the first and best judge of her own safety. Encouraging others to intervene while discouraging the woman from taking sensible precautions is an odd way to respect women and their agency. Feminists worry about victim blaming—that authorities will say she was "asking for it" if a woman had something to drink before she was attacked—but these lines, which can seem so clear in some situations, can be indistinct in others.

Obviously, there is no excuse for rape. It doesn't matter what a woman was wearing or doing. It may be unwise for women to dress provocatively, but that doesn't excuse rape. And a man who takes advantage of a woman's impairment is still a rapist. But when two drunk freshmen remove their clothes and get into bed together, the question of her responsibility is much less clear. Emily Yoffe of *Slate* offered this example from Yale:

> The *Yale Daily News* recently reported on . . . a male and female who were sometime lovers. [They] hooked up one night after she had been drinking and they had been sending flirty texts. (She wrote to him, "Don't let me try to seduce you though. Because that is a distinct possibility.") She eventually invited him to her room, where she says she capitulated to his desire for sex because in the past when she refused him he would scream and cry, which she found overwhelming. His version was that upon arrival she grabbed him, kissed him, they each took off their clothes, and then had sex twice that evening and once in the morning. Although she was sober by the time of the morning encounter, she later told Yale officials that all of the sex was nonconsensual be-

cause she was too drunk during the evening to consent, and in the morning, the *Yale Daily News* reports, "she did not resist because she felt refusal would be too emotionally exhausting." A full year after the encounter, she brought a sexual assault charge against the young man, hoping to get him expelled.[34]

He was found not responsible, but it could easily have gone the other way.

Common sense and about five thousand years of human experience suggest that women should keep themselves as safe as possible, mindful that they are the smaller and weaker sex, that some men are not gentlemen, and that even seemingly nice men can behave badly when drunk. Women might also want to consider that their own judgment will be impaired by alcohol. As Camille Paglia wrote in *Sex, Art, and American Culture: Essays* (1992): "Feminism keeps . . . telling women that they can do anything, go anywhere, say anything, wear anything. No, they can't. Women will always be in sexual danger . . . feminism, with its pie-in-the-sky fantasies about the perfect world, keeps young women from seeing life as it is."[35]

When scientists at North Carolina State invented a nail polish that changed color if a woman ingested a "date rape" drug, feminists responded with anger, not gratitude. Rebecca Nagle, a cofounder of an activist group called FORCE: Upsetting Rape Culture, said, "As a woman, I'm told not to go out alone at night, to watch my drink, to do all of these things. That way, rape isn't just controlling me while I'm actually being assaulted—it controls me 24/7 because it limits my behavior. Solutions like these actually just recreate that. I don't want to f—ing test my drink when I'm at the bar. That's not the world I want to live in."

Maybe not, but it requires fierce ideological rigidity and even imperviousness to reality to say, "That's not the world I want to live in." None of us prefers to live in a world where we must lock our doors, memorize fifty passwords, or stay away from certain neighborhoods after dark, but not taking steps to protect yourself as a matter of principle is juvenile and foolish. Women have never experienced a time when they were perfectly safe because men had been "taught not to rape." Nor have men ever been perfectly safe because men had been "taught not to fight." Both are goals of all good societies, but as Immanuel Kant observed in the eighteenth century, "Out of the crooked timber of humanity, no straight thing was ever made."

The Elusive Numbers

If the "one in five" figure brandished by President Obama and others were true, college campuses could be considered among the most dangerous places for women on the planet. As Heather Mac Donald, of the center-right think tank the Manhattan Institute, observed, "No crime, much less one as serious as rape, has a victimization rate remotely approaching 20 or 25 percent, even over many years. The 2006 violent crime rate in Detroit, one of the most violent cities in America, was 2,400 murders, rapes, robberies, and aggravated assaults per 100,000 inhabitants—a rate of 2.4 percent. The one-in-four statistic would mean that every year, millions of young women graduate who have suffered the most terrifying assault, short of murder, that a woman can experience."[36]

The one-in-five number—some advocates use "one in four"— originated with a *Ms.* magazine survey from the 1980s that asked college women whether they had experienced sexual assault, coercion, or rape. Mary Koss, a researcher from the University of Arizona who designed and conducted the survey, included two questions that clouded the results. One asked: "Have you had a man attempt sexual intercourse (get on top of you, attempt to insert his penis) with you by giving you alcohol or drugs, but intercourse did not occur?" Another asked: "Have you given in to sexual intercourse when you didn't want to because you were overwhelmed by a man's continual arguments and pressure?" A positive response to the first question was counted as "attempted rape," and a positive response to the second was counted as "completed rape."[37]

This was the beginning of rape being downgraded from a violent crime involving forced sexual intercourse or sodomy to sex that results from nagging and "pressure." This radical redefinition of rape is really a cry of pain by women who have been given no other vocabulary to object to sex. Feminists do women no favors by diluting the seriousness of rape. Yet dilution is exactly what happens when forcible rape is lumped in with "psychological" pressure or when the burden falls on the man, as the Obama Department of Education placed it, to establish whether a woman was so intoxicated she was unable to consent. It rarely comes up that he might also have been unable to consent because men almost never complain of rape (at least at the hands of women). If the feminist/progressive dogma that the sexes are just alike is accurate, why should this be so?

Politicians, academics, and activists refer to "many studies" showing that rape, especially campus rape, is endemic, but the numbers are actually hard to come by. One commonly cited source for the one-in-five statistic is the 2007 Campus Sexual Assault Survey conducted by Christopher Krebs. Krebs and his colleagues questioned 5,466 students on two campuses, and concluded that about 25 percent of college women had experienced rape. But as Christina Hoff Sommers of the American Enterprise Institute, Emily Yoffe of *Slate,* and others have objected, the CSA's survey, like the *Ms.* magazine survey of the 1980s, defined sexual assault as everything from nonconsensual sexual intercourse to such unwanted activities as "forced kissing," "fondling," and "rubbing up against you in a sexual way, even if it is over your clothes."

As Sandy Hingston reported in *Philadelphia* magazine, "The survey asked whether students had experienced unwanted sexual contact, defined as forced kissing, grabbing, fondling, touching of private parts, and/or oral, anal or vaginal penetration via finger, mouth, tongue, penis or object. If students checked YES, as 1,073—one in five—did, that was deemed a sexual assault."[38]

Significantly, Hingston continued, "when researchers asked the young women themselves if they considered what happened to them 'rape,' three-quarters of the 'incapacitated' victims did not. Only two percent reported what happened to campus security or police. Asked why they hadn't, the women said they didn't consider the incident serious enough (66 percent) and/or that it wasn't clear a crime or harm was intended (36 percent). Half said they themselves were partially or fully responsible for what had happened."[39]

Christopher Krebs himself told *Slate,* "We don't think one in five is a nationally representative statistic." But that has not stopped it from being repeated thousands of times, including by Sen. Kirsten Gillibrand on her official website and by then–vice president Joe Biden. (Gillibrand later removed the statistic from her website.)

The Justice Department's own numbers contradict the activists' claims. In 2015, the DOJ released the results of an eight-year study called "Rape and Sexual Assault Victimization Among College-Age Females, 1995–2013." The study questioned 100,000 individuals and defined rape and sexual assault to include completed and attempted rape, completed and attempted sexual assault, and threats of rape or sexual assault. The survey included students and nonstudents. The incidence of rape, attempted rape, and sexual assault among college students was found to be 6.1 per thousand, which is 0.6 percent. (It was one and a half times higher among nonstudent women in the same age group.)[40]

The *Washington Post* recently concluded that the one-in-five figure was correct. The *Post* teamed up with the Kaiser Foundation to poll 1,053 young men and women between the ages of seventeen and twenty-six who were now or recently had been undergraduates at four-year institutions. A *Post* headline declared, "Twenty percent of women and five percent of men reported being sexually assaulted by physical force or while incapacitated." But that's not what the survey found.

The poll did shed some light on the sexual ecosystem at American colleges. For example, 56 percent identified alcohol and drugs as a problem, and 37 percent said the same about sexual assault. But far from resolving the question about the prevalence of rape, the poll repeated the sloppiness of earlier surveys. Deep into the *Post*'s coverage, we learn that the *Post*/Kaiser poll defined sexual assault and rape more broadly than the common understanding of those terms. Though the poll included questions about forced vaginal and anal intercourse as well as forced oral sex, it also defined "forced touching of a sexual nature" to include "forced kissing, touching of private parts, grabbing, fondling, rubbing up against you in a sexual way (even if it is over your clothes)."[41]

The poll encouraged students to include under "coercion" situations in which they had sex in response to "verbal . . . promises." These overly broad definitions led to the sort of ambiguities that have yielded excessively high estimates of the prevalence of rape in the past.

"Guys at frat parties were grabby," one undergraduate told me. "There were no boundaries. They'd just put their hands on your ass, on your boobs, whatever." No one should behave that way, but it's not rape or sexual assault.

Crimes

In 1986, Jeanne Clery, a Lehigh University freshman, was raped and murdered in her dorm room. Her parents were distraught to discover that in the three years preceding the attack on Jeanne, thirty-eight violent crimes had occurred at the Pennsylvania school. They pushed for and got federal legislation, the Clery Act, requiring all colleges and universities to publish annual reports of crimes committed on and around their campuses. Among the crimes that must be reported are murder, rape, stalking, robbery, and aggravated assault.

A check of the Clery Act data for some of the universities under investigation by the Department of Justice in recent years does not show an epidemic of sexual violence. The University of California at Los Angeles, for example, had 42,163 students in 2013. A total of 33 forcible sexual assaults (which may or may not have included completed rapes) were reported that year. Brown University had 8,943 students in 2013. The number of "forcible sex offenses" was 21.

No one disputes that some, and perhaps many, rapes and sexual assaults go unreported, but it's simply not possible, or responsible, to guess at the actual numbers, or to project on the basis of one small study, or to assume that a fixed number of rapes is not being counted. I believe many rapes go unreported because of shame, confusion, fear of reprisal, and other concerns, but we cannot know how many. Krebs is currently undertaking a much larger survey, of up to twenty thousand undergraduate students from ten to fifteen schools, and perhaps that will add some needed clarity. Based on my (admittedly unscientific) conversations with undergraduates, I will not be surprised if the numbers are higher than the Clery Act data.

The feminist left will doubtless mine the next study for the most alarming statistics. Barnard College, for example, performed a Campus Climate Survey in 2014 and reported that 20 percent of students had experienced "sexual assault."[42] Yet here again the definition of sexual assault included things such as "Have you given in to sexual play (fondling, kissing, touching, but not intercourse) when you didn't want to because you were overwhelmed by the other person's arguments and/or pressure?"[43] Eighteen percent of students who said they'd been "assaulted" fell into that category. Another 9 percent had engaged in "unwanted sex play or sexual intercourse because you were given alcohol or other substances." Another 7 percent had engaged in "unwanted sex play or sexual intercourse" while under the influence of alcohol. Only 8 percent said they had had sexual intercourse "when they didn't want to" because they were "pressured, forced, or otherwise did not provide consent."[44]

That 8 percent figure requires disaggregation too. One would like to know how many respondents fell into the "pressured" category and how many into the "forced" column. There is a world of difference between being "pressured" to have sex and being "forced" to have sex. The persistent fusing of these two very different things confuses the issue, helps to perpetuate women's self-image as victims, and stokes fear and overreaction.

Between 2001 and 2011, the number of sexual assault complaints reported by colleges increased by 52 percent, to 3,300. But it's impossible to know if the increase in complaints reflects an increase in assaults or if more people are coming forward because of the attention the issue has received. Either way, there's a lot of misery out there.

Sen. Claire McCaskill is certain, based partly on her experience as a prosecutor, that rape is the most underreported crime. That may be true, though child abuse probably ranks higher. We just don't know. But McCaskill seems indifferent to the numbers. "Frankly," she told the *St. Louis Post Dispatch,* "it's irritating that anybody would be distracted by which statistics are accurate."[45] This nonchalance about facts is all too common among activists. It's either "one in five" or it would be one in five if more women reported their victimization. That's not a responsible use of statistics.

Sexual Assault Is Not a Myth

Still, the number of women who tell stories of being groped, abused, and raped is too large to be dismissed as a hoax. A few samples:

- In February 2015, Brock Turner, a male Stanford swimmer, was charged with raping an unconscious woman outside a fraternity party. He was convicted and served three months of a six-month sentence.
- In 2013, four Vanderbilt football players were indicted on

five counts of aggravated rape each, following an attack on an unconscious twenty-one-year-old student. Hallway cameras alerted officials to the crime. Three of the players (so far) have been tried and convicted for the crime. Testimony at trial included the players inserting a water bottle into the victim's rectum while chanting "Squeeze that s——. Squeeze that s——."[46]

- In 2015, two University of Alabama students were arrested for sexually assaulting an incapacitated woman on a Florida beach during spring break. Police discovered the assault when they scanned a cell phone video looking for evidence of a shooting that had happened the same day.[47]

- In 2013, Beau Donaldson, a University of Montana football player, was sentenced to a thirty-year prison term (twenty years suspended) for raping a childhood friend as she slept on his couch.[48]

- Georgetown has expelled two students and suspended six for sexual misconduct since 2012. A *Washington Post* report found similar numbers for the other universities in the Washington, DC, area.

Each year, according to a victims' assistance group at the University of South Florida, about fifty women report being raped. Few attackers are prosecuted. "In general, yes, they're harder to prosecute," chief assistant state attorney for Tallahassee, Georgia Cappleman, told the *Tampa Bay Times*. "Her conduct and guilt, her lack of memory due to alcohol, all of these things contribute."[49]

I interviewed students and recent graduates in 2014 and 2015, and nearly all either knew someone or had heard of someone who had been raped. One lost her religious faith after being assaulted. Two women received training in how to handle sexual assault victims and served as informal student counselors. One told me that over four years at an Ivy League college, she spoke with five women who had been raped or sexually assaulted. She came to know these women not through her work as a counselor but purely at random—they were people she happened to know. Beds were set aside in the health service, she added, for women who did not feel safe in their dorm rooms.

Many students know more than one victim. I heard this from women and men. One male student told me of a young woman he knew well who had gotten a reputation because she was always seen in the company of men early in the morning. But he knew her story. She wasn't promiscuous. She had been raped as a freshman, and she kept company with men she trusted as a form of protection.

Addie Mena, a young journalist working for the Catholic News Agency, knows ten women who were victims of sexual assault over the past seven years. Some were college friends (she graduated in 2012); some are women she's encountered since. What's notable is that she travels in religious circles, and these women were not hooking up or drinking to excess.[50] In some cases, the assault was by boyfriends who simply refused to accept the women's boundaries.

I don't believe all these women were lying or even exaggerating. The true numbers are bad enough, even when it's acknowledged that numbers wielded by activists suffer from definitional vagueness. A recent Columbia University graduate, Luke Foster, a known campus conservative, told me, "I actually disagree with conservatives who try to dispute the scale of the problem. I think the problem is huge." So do I.

Far too many young men behave like pigs. Some even meet the standard definition of rapist and belong in prison. But young women who use principle as an excuse for not taking the most rudimentary steps to protect themselves (such as declining to get blind drunk in the presence of equally drunk and horny young men), then call down the harshest possible judgment upon the men who take advantage of them, undermine their own case. It isn't fair, and it isn't wise, to ask authorities (who inevitably struggle to get at the truth in these cases) to care more about women's safety than the women themselves do.

It's also important to distinguish actual victims from those who use rape as an ideological weapon. Some activists use rape, both real and metaphorical, as a tool to suppress ideas with which they disagree. For example, when Christina Hoff Sommers, author of *Who Stole Feminism,* spoke at Georgetown University in April 2015, protesters offered "safe spaces" in adjoining buildings, as if hearing the views of an American Enterprise Institute scholar and former Clark University philosophy professor would put students in literal danger.[51] The safety they seek is not physical; it's psychic: safety from ideas they find unsettling.

Columbia University is one of the last bastions in academia to hold fast to a "great books" curriculum. Students begin with the Greeks and read many of the pivotal works in the Western canon, including selections from the Bible, Aristotle, Plato, Descartes, Machiavelli, Hobbes, and Locke. To illustrate the lengths to which rape sensitivity is now going, consider this letter to the student newspaper, the *Columbia Spectator,* from four students on the school's Multicultural Affairs Advisory Council:

> During the week spent on Ovid's "Metamorphoses," the class was instructed to read the myths of Persephone and Daphne, both of which include vivid depictions of rape and sexual assault. As a survivor of sexual assault, the student described being triggered while reading such detailed accounts of rape throughout the work. However, the student said her professor focused on the beauty of the language and the splendor of the imagery when lecturing on the text. As a result, the student completely disengaged from the class discussion as a means of self-preservation. She did not feel safe in the class. When she approached her professor after class, the student said she was essentially dismissed, and her concerns were ignored.
>
> Ovid's "Metamorphoses" is a fixture of Lit[erature] Hum[anities], but like so many texts in the Western canon, it contains triggering and offensive material that marginalizes student identities in the classroom. These texts, wrought with his-

tories and narratives of exclusion and oppression, can be difficult
to read and discuss as a survivor, a person of color, or a student
from a low-income background.[52]

If we shun literature that is disturbing or that churns up painful experiences, what will remain? And whose sensitivities are to
govern? If one student in class is a rape survivor, will her feelings
exclude the Bible, Plutarch, and *To Kill a Mockingbird*? If another
student is the descendant of slaves, will *Narrative of the Life of Frederick Douglass* and *Uncle Tom's Cabin* be off-limits? What if some
members of the class have relatives who were murdered in the
Holocaust? Will the works of Elie Wiesel be banned?

This represents a triumph of the therapeutic mindset, in which
feelings reign. But allowing the intensity of feeling, the hegemony
of subjective pain, to govern will mean we have abandoned reason
and descended into a world that cannot support academic freedom.
Harsh personal experiences, properly channeled, can heighten a
student's understanding and interpretation of literature. Literature,
commensurately, can offer a means of understanding and sometimes transcending personal experiences. But whatever the effect
might be on the individual, the current enthusiasm to silence intellectual inquiries altogether in the name of feelings is antithetical
not just to the First Amendment and the academic enterprise but
also to the whole Enlightenment.

Rape is a serious problem on campuses and must be dealt with.
But we're in dangerous territory when feminists are allowed to
hijack it to attack the Western canon, precious legal norms such as
the presumption of innocence, or freedom of thought.

Believing Victims

Feminists assert that our culture doesn't take rape seriously and that
the criminal justice system is unfair to women who report being
assaulted. Rape has always been a touchy matter, but it seems odd

to suggest that it was traditionally taken lightly. Until 1977, when the Supreme Court forbade it,[53] three states still imposed the death penalty for some adult rapes, and five states continued to impose death for child rapes until 2008 when the Supreme Court ruled that punishment unconstitutional.[54] Still today, rape carries the second most severe penalties in the criminal code. It has always been viewed as a heinous act—long before feminism.

Feminists were right to protest that, in the past, women who were raped could be impeached on the stand with questions about their sexual histories. If the woman was shown to be unchaste by the standards of the time, she was less sympathetic as a victim, and her attacker was less likely to be convicted. It's a good thing that, with some exceptions, a rape victim's sexual history is now inadmissible in court. Measures to make the experience of reporting this crime less excruciating are welcome.

But we shouldn't impose rigid categories such as "Believe the women" or "Women don't lie about rape." They sometimes do. The young woman whose story was featured in "A Rape on Campus" in *Rolling Stone* in 2014 lied about nearly every material fact. The woman who accused the Duke lacrosse team of gang rape also lied. It seems highly likely that Emma Sulkowicz was shading the truth. Al Sharpton became a national figure in 1987 when he promoted the story of fifteen-year-old Tawana Brawley, who claimed that six white men had raped her, written "KKK" across her chest, and smeared her with feces. "We have the facts and evidence to prove a district attorney and a state trooper did this," Sharpton declared. It was a hoax. In 2009, a Hofstra University freshman accused five men of gang-raping her in a bathroom. The story fell apart when one of the men produced a cell phone video showing that the sex had been consensual.[55] At Ohio University, a student claimed rape due to incapacitating drunkenness. But a cell phone video of the event (which is another level of offense, just not rape) suggested that it was consensual. A jury found against her. The Justice Department estimates that as many as 8 percent of rape accusations may be unfounded.

Even so, universities across the country teach the "women never lie" dogma. Alan Dershowitz was accused of sexual harassment by a student for even broaching the topic of false rape accusations in the classroom (more evidence of the authoritarian mindset now endemic on campuses).[56] A mandatory University of Montana program called PETSA (Personal Empowerment Through Self Awareness) tells freshmen that one of the "myths" about rape is that women lie. "Believe your friend," they are exhorted; "almost no one lies."

People do lie, and they also differ in how they interpret signals. Some men find themselves accused of rape after genuinely believing their partner was a willing participant. Further, as noted earlier, the Office for Civil Rights essentially presumes that men are guilty in these opaque cases of drunken coupling.

A college student affairs officer published a revealing "open letter" to the Department of Education on *Inside Higher Ed* protesting that the rules did not fit many situations he faced: "In most cases . . . it's the impairment of her judgment—agreeing to have sex with someone who, the next morning, she will regret having had sex with—that causes her friends and supporters and other campus employees to tell her she's been sexually assaulted and needs to file a complaint. This process then begins the long journey down the rabbit hole of OCR-specified response that never ends well."[57]

The website *Minding the Campus* reported that Yale University has broadened the definition of "nonconsensual sex" to include behaviors that no one in civilian life would conceivably define as sexual assault or rape. The university provided this scenario (note the gender-ambiguous names):

Morgan and Kai are friends who begin dancing and kissing at a party. They are both drunk, although not to the point of incapacitation. Together they decide to go to Kai's room. They undress each other and begin touching each other. Morgan moves as if to engage in oral sex and looks up at Kai questioningly. Kai nods in agreement and Morgan proceeds. Subsequently, without pausing to check for further agreement, Kai begins to perform oral sex on Morgan. Morgan lies still for a few minutes, then moves away, saying it is late and they should sleep.[58]

According to Yale, *Minding the Campus* continues, "Kai" is guilty of having had nonconsensual sex—more evidence that the bureaucratic attempt to govern sexual behavior is confusing and opaque.

Some of the most sensational campus rape stories have turned out, upon closer examination, to be questionable. The case of Emma Sulkowicz, of the "blue mattress," is one of them. Even though the student Sulkowicz accused was found "not responsible" by a campus tribunal, he was regarded as a rapist by the university community and much of the world. Cathy Young of the *Daily Beast* has made it her business to let the accused be heard in a number of these cases. She published her findings about Paul Nungesser, Sulkowicz's alleged attacker, in February 2015.[59]

Sulkowicz's version, as told to *New York* magazine, was that, "While they were having consensual sex in her dorm room [Nungesser] suddenly pushed her legs against her chest, choked her, slapped her, and anally penetrated her as she struggled and clearly repeated 'No.'"

Sulkowicz didn't report the incident for six months, when two other women told her stories about Nungesser. After an inquiry that Sulkowicz described as agonizing (one administrator allegedly asked whether Nungesser had used lubricant), her alleged assailant was cleared of rape charges and remained at the university.

Not surprisingly, Nungesser claimed the sex was consensual. He also provided the *Daily Beast* with Facebook messages from Sulkowicz following the encounter that suggest she did not see herself, at the time, as the victim of rape.

On August 29, 2012, two days after the alleged rape, Nungesser messaged Sulkowicz on Facebook to say, "Small shindig in our room tonight—bring cool freshmen." Her response:

lol yusss

Also I feel like we need to have some real time where we can talk about life and thingz

because we still haven't really had a paul-emma chill sesh since summmmerrrr

On September 9, 2012, it was Sulkowicz who initiated the Facebook contact, asking Nungesser if he wanted to "hang out a little bit" before or after the meeting and concluding with:

whatever I want to see yoyououoyou

respond—I'll get the message on ma phone.

Sulkowicz, according to Young, did not dispute the accuracy of the Facebook messages.

Additionally, "on Oct. 3, Sulkowicz's birthday, Nungesser sent her an effusive greeting; she responded the next morning with, "I love you Paul. Where are you?!?!?!?!"

After months of friendly contact with Sulkowicz, Nungesser was stunned to be informed by the Office of Gender-Based and Sexual Misconduct that a complaint had been filed against him. "My first reaction was, 'It has to be a misunderstanding,'" Nungesser told the *Daily Beast*. "Maybe she meant a different guy, or something completely strange happened."

Columbia put Nungesser through a series of long interviews and investigations. He was not permitted to enter the Facebook messages into evidence, yet despite this, and the lower "preponderance of the evidence" standard applied in his case, he was acquitted of rape and sexual misconduct. There were charges of mistreatment by two other women as well, both known to Sulkowicz, but both were found to be without merit.

Nungesser's version of events is also supported by a former Columbia graduate student who was assigned to serve as an adviser during the disciplinary process and who says that when he first heard of the case, he believed that Nungesser was guilty. In 2017, Columbia settled a lawsuit Nungesser had filed against it for an undisclosed sum. The university admitted that "after the conclusion of the investigation, Paul's remaining time at Columbia became very difficult for him and not what Columbia would want any of its students to experience."[60]

Sulkowicz made a bid to become the Rosa Parks for campus sexual assault, but the evidence suggests her motive may have been jealousy or rage at being spurned. Though only two people know what happened in that dorm room, Nungesser shed enough doubt on Sulkowicz's account to make her grandstanding seem suspect.

Something Is Very Wrong: It Must Be Men

Feminists and progressives have become convinced that males are the problem, and that they must be redesigned and reprogrammed. Everything, in their view, is "socially constructed," and if everything is culture, then everything can be changed.

The American College Health Association, in the "toolkit" it provides to college administrators to prevent sexual violence, cites the "pressures exerted upon [young men] by traditional (and often violent) ideas about masculinity" as one of the causes of campus rape.[61] "There is an unfortunate, aggressive sexual norm related to masculinity in our culture," explains Laura Dunn of SurvJustice, a rape survivors advocacy group. "We are asserting our rights now in the face of aggressive, predatory sexuality."

The Obama administration's website Notalone.gov provided links to organizations that promoted "healthy masculinity." One was called Men Can Stop Rape. Among its stated goals was to "Promote an understanding of the ways in which traditional masculinity contributes to sexual assault and other forms of men's violence against women."[62]

The American Association of University Women offers "10 Ways to Fight Against Sexual Assault on Campus." It begins by suggesting contacting "campus resources like counseling centers, advocacy offices, or the police," but among the other suggestions are "Write an op-ed," "Use social media . . . to spread awareness," "Start a conversation on victim blaming," and "Get involved in national campaigns . . . like the Clothesline Project."

The Clothesline Project is bursting with good intentions. On its website, taped messages by young men express views such as "I believe rape will not end until men become part of the solution" and "Because I care about the women in my life" and "Because I recognize that men and women will not be equal until rape ends."[63]

Zerlina Maxwell, an activist who is a rape "survivor" (a term many prefer to "victim"), told Fox News host Sean Hannity, "I don't think that we should be telling women anything . . . If you train men not to grow up to become rapists, you prevent rape."[64]

The Nation magazine identified "Ten Things to End Rape Culture." Among them are "join[ing] organizations working to redefine masculinity."[65] Readers are encouraged to transcend "outdated ideas about women and men's sexuality," "get enthusiastic about enthusiastic consent," and recognize that "rape culture thrives in passive acceptance of female degradation, victim-blaming and hyper-masculinity in our communities, both physical and digital."

And what better way to combat "hypermasculinity" than to put men, particularly soldiers, in women's red high heels? That's what both Arizona State University and Temple University did for their Sexual Assault Awareness Week in 2015. ROTC cadets, in full uniform, were pressured to participate in the "Walk a Mile in Her Shoes" event. Attendance was reportedly mandatory, according to one soldier's online complaint. The cadets wobbled along on red high heels, looking, and doubtless feeling, ridiculous. The army is investigating.[66]

The goal of the organizers of such an event is clearly not just to "raise awareness" but also to humiliate and emasculate men. Rather than make an appeal to what is best in men (their protectiveness toward women, their honor, their ethics), stunts such as

"Walk a Mile in Her Shoes" reflect a deep hostility toward manliness. Not only is this unlikely to reach men's hearts, but it also risks provoking a serious backlash. Contempt toward men is not a wise strategy for enlisting them as allies against sexual assault.

If "traditional masculinity" is the cause of rape, how do progressives explain homosexual rape? No one would argue that homosexual behavior of any kind fits into the "traditionalist" model. Yet the *Post*/Kaiser poll found that 16 percent of students, and 23 percent of men, knew of at least one man who'd been assaulted while in college.[67]

These accounts raise the question of who defines what "traditional masculinity" really means. David Lisak, a psychologist whose small study has been widely cited for its proposition that most college campuses harbor a number of repeat rapists, shares the feminist view that our society encourages rape due to ingrained misogyny. Writing in the journal *Signs,* Lisak endorsed the view that gender is a social construct. "Gender—the division of human qualities into two mutually exclusive categories, each associated with a biological sex—is central . . . to the motivations for rape. . . . [T]his gendering pervades our culture and . . . while it is purported to be founded on biological differences, it is actually a production of culture."[68]

Lisak, like many feminists and progressives, believes our "gender" system, which is not biological but cultural, is responsible for rape and sexual assault. Presumably, if we could eliminate the categories of male and female altogether, as many urge, we'd put a stop to sexual violence. But denying the social, psychological, and, yes, biological differences between the sexes is part of what has brought us to where we are. Progressives survey a flood and prescribe rain.

Depicting "traditional masculinity" as essentially pathological, encouraging disrespect of women and violence against them, is a highly tendentious interpretation of history and culture. While some men have always been violent, it's impossible to think of an era in the West when violence against women was encouraged or celebrated. On the contrary, Western civilization has devoted tremendous effort to constraining male violence (against other men as well as women) and has heaped shame on men who would strike or hurt women.

Today's sexual culture is the creation of some branches of feminism and progressivism. For fifty years, so-called gender feminists have demeaned and disparaged traditional masculine codes of behavior such as chivalry, and now they are shocked to find large numbers of louts who grab and grope and sometimes even rape. There were many aspects of "traditional masculinity" that ought to appeal to those who worry about brutish male behavior toward women. A gentleman considers it his duty to treat every woman with utmost respect.

You can say that many men were not gentlemen, and that's certainly true. *But the model was the right one.* Once you dispense with the ideal, with the informal but powerful mores about what constitutes honorable and, yes, manly behavior, you are left with the unwieldy, capricious, and highly ineffective bureaucracy of sexual assault prevention and punishment. Moreover, if you insult men's natures and insist that the only way to combat sexual assault is to combat manliness, you alienate the whole male sex.

Rape, like murder and theft, has always been a feature of human societies, but the sexual revolution brought about changes in courtship and sexuality (changes eagerly welcomed by feminists) that made women more, not less, vulnerable to shabby treatment by men. In the past, sensible women relied on a man's honor not to take sexual liberties—but only to a point. They were also realistic about a man's much stronger sex drive, and didn't put themselves in sexually tempting situations unless they were prepared for the consequences.

"Just because you go to a guy's room," one undergraduate told me, "it doesn't mean you necessarily want to have sex." No, but it's probably not a good idea, especially if you've both had too much to drink. Most men have enough self-control, and enough basic decency, to stop if you change your mind, but not all, and particularly not now, when the old restraints have been discredited. Even men who are not bad may have trouble interpreting signals. When I was young and single, I was repeatedly taken aback by what young men took to be sexual encouragement when I had intended only politeness.

Rather than acknowledging the real differences between the sexes, and upholding both feminine modesty and masculine honor, feminists were keen to encourage women to become more man-like. That was viewed as the real victory.

Feminists linked arms with progressives and libertines to heap scorn on sexual restraint. The liberationists disparaged modesty as a "hangup," while the feminists dismissed it as a relic of the patriarchy. These are the ideas that discredited traditional sexual codes. These are the ideas that progressives naïvely believed would usher in an era of sexual equality and equitably distributed pleasure.

It has been a dismal failure. It's time to relink sex and love.

CHAPTER 6

FAMILY

It is hard to find a women's liberationist who is not in
some way disaffected by the sound of wedding bells.

—Susan Faludi

A decade ago, Steven Levitt of *Freakonomics* fame pondered the
"paradox" of declining female happiness that I referred to in
the introduction. He was responding to work by Justin Wolfers
and Betsey Stevenson showing that throughout western Europe
and the United States, for the past several decades, women have reported steadily waning rates of happiness. It wasn't just one survey,
either. As Marcus Buckingham has outlined, half a dozen studies
in the United States and Europe have found the same result. The
decades since the 1960s, a period when women achieved most of
the feminist movement's goals, have been characterized by less female happiness.[1]

Levitt considered possible explanations and concluded that two
things were probably at work: women in the 1970s felt tremendous
social pressure to say they were happier than they actually were;
and/or surveys of happiness are hopelessly garbled and shouldn't be
taken too seriously.[2]

Perhaps he's right, but I suspect we should pay attention to what women report. If women really are less happy, it could be because of a lack of security, which is closely bound to women's happiness.

When it comes to voting patterns, women in developed countries favor left-liberal candidates, and these preferences cause gender gaps to be found in nations from Australia to Sweden to Greece. In all these countries and others, women vote for parties that promise generous safety nets. This is particularly true of single women. Women are also less likely than men to vote for radical changes.[3] The 2014 Scottish independence referendum garnered fewer votes from women than men, arguably because women were more sensitive to the risks.

The American Enterprise Institute's Karlyn Bowman has observed that women are consistently more cautious than men. They are more skeptical about using military force, and more likely to express nervousness about the safety of nuclear power. Women report more anxiety about terrorism and health scares such as the Ebola outbreak. When pollsters ask fanciful questions, Bowman noted, such as whether one would accept a ride in a spacecraft, "the gender gap becomes a chasm."[4]

The sexual free-for-all unleashed over the past several decades, combined with the decline of marriage, has left women feeling more vulnerable, exposed, and ill-treated. As cultural bellwethers, let's consider two pop songs from a few decades apart. The first is the 1931 song "As Time Goes By," featured in the movie *Casablanca* (1942). In that iconic film, the character Sam croons that "moonlight and love songs" are "never out of date," and that "woman needs man and man must have his mate." The second is a Bruno Mars song, "That's What I Like" (2017): "Go pop it for a pimp, pop-pop it for me / Turn around and drop it for a pimp, drop-drop it for me."

Feminists probably consider the 1930s the heyday of the patriarchy and therefore a miserable time for women. Yet looking at popular culture of that time, we see that nothing even approaches the level of misogyny and female degradation that is a hallmark of our era. We have slid down a chute from men dropping to one knee to ask their beloved to "make me the happiest man in the world" to women dropping to their knees for other reasons.

Feminists cite this antiwoman, sexist, vulgar tone as the apotheosis of masculinity. They say our culture indoctrinates men to dominate and abuse women, to view them as sex objects, to disrespect their autonomy, and to neglect their needs. There is truth in this, but when did this really begin? Was it traditional mores or post–sexual revolution laxity that created this culture?

My lifetime tracks almost perfectly with the modern feminist movement, and I can testify that the changes wrought by feminism and the sexual revolution have made men more caveman-like than they were before all this "enlightenment." A coarsened culture saturated with vulgar sexuality, the hookup ethic replacing courtship, and the dark undercurrent of pornography—these give the worst men permission to behave in sordid fashion. The casting couch has doubtless been around since the early days of Hollywood, but we are in new territory when a leading producer, Harvey Weinstein, masturbates into a potted plant in a restaurant, or former U.S. representative Anthony Weiner (repeatedly) sends pictures of his penis to women he "met" on Twitter, or Donald Trump boasts of grabbing women by the genitals. The 1960s revolution successfully let it all hang out, and now we're frantically attempting to cope with the consequences.

Today many boys, even as young as middle school, take casual sex for granted. The girls may not like it, but they believe their popularity depends on offering it to the boys. Peggy Orenstein, author of *Girls and Sex,* was dismayed by what she heard from girls between the ages of fifteen and twenty. "Girls are being taught to please their partners without regard to their own desires," she told NPR. "When I would talk to girls, for instance, about oral sex, that was something that they were doing from a pretty young age, and it tended to go one way [and not be reciprocated]."[5]

The feminist and sexual revolutions robbed women of the tools

to keep men's sexual demands at bay. In the past, our culture re-
inforced the limits that girls and women set, and men kept their
expectations more in check. But when we stopped respecting
modesty and reticence, women were cut off from socially enforced
protection. They were left feeling that if they turned aside a man's
sexual demands, it would be considered some kind of insult or,
worse, evidence of an unseemly prudishness. In *A Return to Modesty,* Wendy Shalit argues that girls are naturally reticent, while
at the same time extremely sensitive to popularity and social acceptance. She writes that, without lots of social support for with-
holding sex, "a woman who doesn't want to sleep with a man is
insulting him. Thus, she is perceived as having 'hang-ups,' being
'screwed-up,' or not having 'a healthy attitude toward sex.' "[6]

The actress Sharon Stone was asked what she tells young
women who ask her how to handle pressure for sex: "I tell them
what I believe. Oral sex is a hundred times safer than vaginal or
anal sex. If you're in a situation where you cannot get out of sex,
offer a blow job."[7] Thanks for the tip.

Toxic Masculinity

The feminist project is to redesign the flawed thing feminists call
"toxic masculinity." At a recent "Health Masculinities" conference at Oregon State University, students were taught to "engage
in collective imagining to construct new futures for masculinities,
unrestricted by power, privilege, and oppression."[8]

For a time, feminists denounced "lookism," their jargon-y label
for the human tendency to prefer attractive people. The campaign
against lookism had a tilting-at-windmills quality. People who
judge others solely based on looks are shallow; this is a matter of
character and judgment. But feminists tried to make it, in Orwell's
terms, a "thought crime." As they're discovering, no amount of
social justice conditioning can eradicate men's tendency to think
about sex when they see alluring women. The only thing "soci-

ety" can do is regulate how men behave, not the thoughts that leap unbidden from the hypothalamus.

On that score, young women are often unclear about how to behave sexually. Should they aspire to be sexy as soon as they reach puberty? Is being sexually uninhibited an important part of women's power, as the "sex-positive" feminists argue, even if it makes girls uncomfortable? Popular culture, bolstered by the lucrative business of selling sex, pushes women and girls toward sluttiness. It pays off for the Madonnas and Miley Cyruses and Beyoncés of this world. Yet the common feminist response, rather than upholding standards of behavior for both sexes, is to place the blame entirely on masculinity. So-called Slut Walks, featuring women dressed only in bras, panties, and fishnet stockings, are the feminists' idea of a bold statement against "rape culture." This is intended as a protest of male sexual aggressiveness, but the message is lost when the women themselves embrace lewdness. In the postsexual revolution world, no one is more despised or mocked than the prude, but perhaps it's time to reclaim something like prudishness, or at least to speak up for decent manners.

Even the most wholesome young women get sucked into the vortex of sexual excess. In 2017, gymnast Aly Raisman, an Olympic gold medalist, posed for a semi-topless photo in *Sports Illustrated*. She explained that she was concerned about body image issues and the need for young women to have confidence. "Women don't have to be modest in order to be respected," she said.[9] Raisman is hardly the first female athlete to take this route. Serena Williams posed topless, as did fellow tennis player Genie Bouchard. But the notion that this act is some sort of brave affirmation of female confidence and integrity is laughable. First of all, there's a big paycheck involved from the suits at *Sports Illustrated*. Second, men who look at a photo of a topless gal don't think, "Hey, there's that impressive woman athlete. Isn't it great that she's not embarrassed about her body!" No, ninety-seven men out of one hundred are going to think about sex. The other 3 percent are gay.

Yes, if you want to be respected, it is important to keep your clothes on in public. Posing for nude or semi-nude photographs—the women athletes weren't completely exposed—actively discourages people (all people, not just men) from taking you seriously. Imagine if German chancellor Angela Merkel posed topless. Would it be a positive statement that she is free from "body image issues"? Is she repressed because she never forgets to don a blouse?

Particularly in an era when we're discovering the pervasiveness of sexual harassment and sexual misbehavior of all sorts, the time may have come to renew our appreciation for repression. Human beings have countless inclinations that are best inhibited: toward selfishness, toward violence, toward baseless hatred, toward scapegoating minorities, and toward lust, to name just a few. The Catholic list of seven deadly sins is a handy cheat sheet: pride, greed, lust, envy, gluttony, wrath, and sloth.

The twentieth century (not least due to Freud's influence) was one long striptease of repression shedding. Suppressing desires, Freud's acolytes said, was unhealthy, and expressing them, whatever they were, was authentic and natural (which often became a synonym for good, which it isn't).

The post–sexual revolution era has unbuckled all the seat belts, and feminists played a part. Though feminists made a stab in the 1990s at combating sexual harassment—they were fiercely critical of Republican senator Bob Packwood and Republican Supreme Court justice Clarence Thomas—they reversed course when Democratic president Bill Clinton was credibly accused of far worse. Gloria Steinem penned an op-ed in the *New York Times* during the Monica Lewinsky scandal arguing that Lewinsky was a willing participant, so what was the problem? "Whatever it was, her relationship with President Clinton has never been called unwelcome, coerced or other than something she sought."[10] Well, he was married, for a start. And she was a low-level intern he was disgracefully using.

How different would our culture be if feminists had taken a different approach, one that embraced ethics and self-control?

Our civilization was built on limiting, not encouraging, men's worst tendencies. That's what civilizations do, and ours did it for centuries. Yes, women were expected to "love, honor, and obey" their husbands (at least that was the traditional vow), and the "obey" part sounds like fingernails on a blackboard to our modern ears. But consider the promise that grooms, in the Anglican tradition, made at the same time: "With this ring I thee wed. With my body I thee worship. And with all my worldly goods I thee endow." That's not a terrible bargain if upheld by both parties. The Catholic and Jewish services are similar to the Anglican. Did some husbands cheat on their wives, treat them with contempt, and deny them economic sustenance? Of course. People fall short, but the goal was sound. Gentleness and respect toward women were built into the marriage contract.

In *Coming Apart,* Charles Murray describes the McGuffey Readers in wide circulation in American schools in the nineteenth century. These books, with their moral lessons and emphasis on character development, were almost as popular in nineteenth- and early-twentieth-century America as the Bible. One story featured a boy who "never forgot the lesson of that night; and he came to believe, and to act upon the belief, in after years, that true manliness is in harmony with gentleness, kindness, and self-denial."[11]

William Bennett, the former education secretary, compiled inspiring examples of ideal manliness in his collection titled *The Book of Man.* He quoted James Freeman Clarke (1810–1888), for example, an American theologian and essayist who drew distinctions between true and false manliness:

Truth, courage, conscience, freedom, energy, self-possession, self-control. But it does not exclude gentleness, tenderness, compassion, modesty. A man is not less manly, but more so, because he is gentle . . . The manly spirit shows itself in enterprise, the love of meeting difficulties and overcoming them—the resolution that will not yield . . . A false notion of manliness leads boys astray. All

boys wish to be manly; but they often try to become so by copy-
ing the vices of men rather than their virtues.[12]

The nineteenth century had no monopoly on manliness, and
one of the most enriching portraits in Bennett's book is of David
Gelernter, the computer scientist, Yale professor, artist, and social
critic who was badly wounded by a mail bomb sent by the Una-
bomber. Instead of focusing on his scientific achievements or his
personal courage in overcoming his injuries, Bennett's portrait of
Gelernter stresses his role as husband and father. Gelernter and his
wife, in a countercultural act, raised their sons to be chivalrous
gentlemen. The boys were taught that when they took a girl out
on a date, they were to hold doors for her, pick up the check, treat
her with respect, walk her to her door, and offer her their own
coat if she felt cold. A man's role with respect to women, Gelernter argues, "is to protect, to help, to support, [and] to cherish. . . .
Women have an urge to nurture and cherish children; men don't
have that, but they can substitute an urge to nurture and cherish
women. Men need to turn their sexual interest into something
that goes deeper, emotionally and spiritually."[13]

Bennett also quotes Teddy Roosevelt to show that men were
not always socialized to disparage women and neglect their families: "For unflagging interest and enjoyment, a household of children, if things go reasonably well, certainly makes all other forms
of success and achievement lose their importance by comparison."[14]

Historian Robert Griswold writes that even in the late 1800s,
"all social classes conceived of family relations in affective terms,
placed a premium on emotional fulfillment in the family, considered women's opinions and contributions worthy of respect and
consideration, emphasized male kindness and accommodation,
and assumed that children were special members of the household
in need of love and affection."[15]

Language sheds light on social expectations as well. The phrase
"be a man" or "man up" never gave anyone permission to treat

women harshly. On the contrary, those terms referred to stepping up to life's responsibilities, accepting consequences for one's behavior, and protecting the weak. In Yiddish, the term *mensch* literally means "man," but in common usage, it refers to someone who is good, honest, generous, and upstanding.[16]

The sexual and feminist revolutions have left men unsure of what they're supposed to do or where they fit in. A 2017 Pew poll found that only 53 percent of Americans think people look up to masculine men. And among those who agreed that society looks up to these men, there was a partisan split on whether this was a good or a bad thing. Among Republicans, 78 percent said it was good, but among Democrats, only 49 percent thought so.[17] This dichotomy is hard on good men who want to do what's right.

The new order has also thrown open the door to louts who've leaped at the opportunities to abuse and humiliate women. Among powerful men—as we've seen in the epidemic of sexual harassment reports about movie producers, media figures, politicians, and comedians—swinish behavior toward women seems now to be some sort of entitlement. Creeps have always existed, of course, but until recent decades, if a man descended to scatological language in a woman's presence, or used her for sex, or masturbated in front of her, he would have been regarded as a pig. If we are returning to that standard now, it's long overdue. But let's not confuse this behavior with "traditional masculinity."

As George Gilder so persuasively argued in his 1986 book *Men and Marriage,* "the crucial process of civilization is the subordination of male sexual impulses and biology to the long-term horizons of female sexuality."[18] When feminists reject marriage and sex roles, they abdicate this civilizing role.

All societies must mold the little savages we call children into honorable men and women. They won't get there on their own. Children should be taught that every human being is an end in himself, not a means to an end for someone else. With the correct guidance, boys (with their unruly energy, their fascination with things rather than people, their sexual preoccupations, and their competitive zeal) can become admirable men. That's what mothers and fathers, coaches and teachers, rabbis and ministers and priests, should aim to help them do.

Disparaging masculinity itself is unjust, demoralizing to relations between the sexes, and has, inevitably, provoked a backlash. The so-called manosphere online, an informal network of blogs, forums, and websites that discuss masculinity, is an example of the blowback. It features articles on male superiority, advice on how to become a pickup artist, and tips on how to be cruel to women (claiming that women prefer this). The manosphere is a pathetic bid for authentic manliness. True manliness, however, is not abusive to women, but the reverse. It is the code of the gentleman. It is brave and self-sacrificing. Men also are risk takers and inventors and explorers; surely we don't want to label those traits "toxic."

In 2015, a terrorist attacked a commuter train in France. Six unarmed men (three Americans, two Frenchmen, one Briton) joined together to take on the gunman, and ended up saving many lives. Here's some of what I wrote about it at the time:

> The sound of gunfire awakened three young American tourists: Alek Skarlatos, Spencer Stone, and Anthony Sadler. In a moment evocative of the Flight 93 passengers' courage on 9/11, Skarlatos saw Ayoub El-Khazzani struggling with one of his guns and leapt up, saying simply 'Let's go' to his friends. . . .
>
> There's one more thing to be said of the heroes on the train. They were men. So-called traditional masculinity is a major target of feminists on college campuses and elsewhere. That, they teach, is what creates the "rape culture." The Obama Administration has joined in (naturally).
>
> . . . Men have been defamed and devalued in our society for decades. Their high spirits are punished in schools. Their natural protectiveness has been scorned as sexism. . . . The passengers on that French train are surely grateful that some manliness remains indomitable.[19]

In Aurora, Colorado, in 2012, an assassin opened fire in a crowded movie theater. In the chaos and terror of that night, we know of four young men who pushed their girlfriends to the floor and covered them with their own bodies. Three died, and the fourth took a bullet to the leg but survived. There is more to chivalry than rising from tables when ladies approach and pulling out their chairs for them.[20] That such self-sacrificing protectiveness continues to exist after decades of denigration is testament to the best that men are.

Let's also be realistic about human nature. We cannot build a new generation of men who are more interested in baby care than in getting ahead, indifferent to sexual imagery, and more into shoes than cars. Nor should we want to. We can and should insist that boys civilize their urges—to protect women, not harm them; to support their wives and children, not abandon them; to shun pornography, rather than marinate in it; and to treat every person with respect.

In her moving memoir of infertility, *Motherhood Deferred,* feminist Anne Taylor Fleming looked back at how intoxicated with rage she was against men in her youth, and she acknowledged some of the costs (including waiting too long to attempt conception). She had been lit up by Germaine Greer, Shulamith Firestone, Gloria Steinem, Kate Millett, and the rest of the fury sorority. "In the name of equality," Fleming wrote, "we forfeited a certain protective kindness from men, courtesies that were a lot more fundamental than opening a door and yet, in hindsight, not unlinked.[21]

Yet for every Fleming, there were ten Susan Brownmillers, or so it was portrayed.

Brownmiller's much-hailed *Against Our Will: Men, Women, and Rape,* went far beyond a reasonable critique of the judicial system's handling of rape cases and argued that rape was the template for relations between *all men and all women.* "[Rape is] nothing more or less than a conscious process of intimidation by which all men keep all women in a state of fear." In 1975, *Time* magazine called her book a "convincing and awesome portrait of men's cruelty to women" and made Brownmiller one of twelve "Women of the Year."[22] Rapists, according to Brownmiller, were not rare criminals but "the boy next door."[23]

Gloria Steinem went further and said it wasn't just the boy next door—it was the husband in your home: "The most dangerous situation for a woman is not an unknown man on the street, or even the enemy in wartime, but a husband or lover in the isolation of their own home."[24] Some husbands do batter their wives (and vice versa—in about 2 percent of homes), and domestic violence is a serious problem. But the suggestion that husbands in particular were more dangerous than an enemy in wartime was absurd and did a terrible disservice to the women who believed it, as well as to the men who were defamed.[25]

Hollywood became feminism's mouthpiece, reinforcing the idea that ordinary families might look polite and functional, but underneath, they were seething cauldrons of conflict, abuse, and dark secrets. Movies such as *The Burning Bed, Chinatown,* and (in an imagined dystopian future) *The Handmaid's Tale* paint families as nests of incest and abuse. "Beneath the polished facades of many 'ideal families,'" wrote Stephanie Coontz in *The Way We Never Were: American Families and the Nostalgia Trap,* "suburban as well as urban, was violence, terror, or simply grinding misery that only occasionally came to light."[26]

Coontz's book was published in 1992, by which time the decay in family life that started in the 1960s had begun to take its toll. Her goal, clear from the book's title, was to rebut the notion that anything had been lost in the retreat from family life. Ignore that longing for stable homes and the comforting rituals of family life, she counseled readers. They never existed.

Judith Stacey, a sociology professor at New York University, was downright alarmed in 1994 by a backlash she saw against feminism among liberals. She was aware that many centrist and even left-leaning scholars were worried about the decline of marriage in America. She disdained researchers and critics such as David Popenoe, Barbara Dafoe Whitehead, William Galston, Isabel Sawhill,

Ron Haskins, and Jean Bethke Elshtain, who were associated with liberal think tanks and magazines. Writing in the journal *Social Text,* Stacey condemned the "disturbing" campaign to "restore nuclear family hegemony."[27] If "two parents are generally better than one," she mocked, "three or four might prove better yet." *Time* magazine's Barbara Ehrenreich sounded the same arch note, urging that if fathers were beneficial to children's welfare, women should wed "two, three, many husbands."[28]

Feminists did achieve some necessary reforms in how rape was regarded and prosecuted starting in the 1970s. Rape shield laws ended the practice of cross-examining women accusers about their sexual histories during rape trials. And marital rape became a prosecutable crime. But the focus on husbands as batterers and rapists could not have been more misplaced. Of all men, husbands are the *least* likely to commit these crimes. Boyfriends, strangers, live-in lovers, and, most especially, recently dumped boyfriends are the most common perpetrators.[29]

Justice Department data from 1993 to 2010 showed that the safest women were those married without children. At the bottom of the scale (i.e., those the most likely to be victimized) were never-married, single mothers.[30] Additionally, children are far more likely to be victims, of both physical and sexual abuse, when they live in homes with their biological mother and her boyfriend.[31]

Domestic violence is a bitter thing, but retreating from marriage doesn't diminish it. Quite the opposite. Cohabiting couples are three times more likely to experience domestic violence than married ones.[32]

A Nostalgia Trap?

Feminists in the twenty-first century have stuck to the antitraditional family script. Consult any feminist website, and you'll find jeremiads against traditional marriage. The website Feministing, for example, proclaims that "Monogamy is a concept that has been shoved down our throats (in the unsexiest sense of the phrase) as the only relationship model that works."[33]

Often, the antifamily message is delivered using an airbrushed vocabulary. In the same way that feminists substituted the anodyne word *choice* for *abortion,* they've slid in *patriarchy* for *family.* In an article for *The New Republic,* Stephanie Coontz denied that the purpose of marriage was to ensure that children were raised by a mother and a father: "The most common purpose of marriage in history was not to ensure children access to both their mother and father, but to acquire advantageous in-laws and expand the family labor force. The wishes of the young people being matched up and the well-being of their offspring were frequently subordinated to those goals."[34]

One could just as easily say that parents are valuable to children for *their* labor. If the parents don't provide, the kids don't eat, but that hardly sums up children's feelings toward or relationships with their parents. As for in-laws, well, some, like mine, are terrific, but there must be a reason for mother-in-law jokes.

Of course, many matches have involved property, and still do. The superrich sure seem to marry one another. But rich or poor, love was always a factor too. For centuries, at least in Europe, mutual consent was the rule for marriage. In the twelfth century, Pope Alexander III called marriage "a free union of two hearts" and decreed that parental consent was not necessary to validate a marriage.[35] In *Romeo and Juliet,* the Capulets are determined to force Juliet to marry Paris. Some parents have always been insensitive to their children's needs, sometimes justly, sometimes not; that's what makes the play compelling literature. But Shakespeare made Juliet one of drama's most sympathetic reluctant brides, and in the course of the play, her parents come to regret their insensitivity. Generations of theatergoers have come away feeling that the Capulets were wrong to ignore their daughter's wishes. The play's final couplet tolls the price: "For never was a story of more woe / Than this of Juliet and her Romeo."

Feminist Jessie Bernard regarded marriage as hopelessly exploitative when she wrote in 1972, "To be happy in a relationship which imposes so many impediments on her, as traditional marriage does, a woman must be slightly mentally ill."[36] In *The Future of Marriage,* Bernard argues that it was not a loss for women that it was becoming easier to withdraw from a marriage than from an auto payment plan. Women would be forced to change their expectations. They would learn "that marriage was not the be-all and end-all of their existence." If, she writes, "it is good for men to be saved from normlessness by hemming them in, it is good for women to be forced out of their security."[37]

Feminists felt it was their duty to deny women security that they, the feminists, regarded as fraudulent. Bernard was not alone. Feminists agitated for the reform of divorce laws.[38] David Frum, author of *How We Got Here,* a history of the 1970s, describes how California's divorce laws (later adopted by forty-six other states) were changed in 1969 to erase the distinction between contested and uncontested divorce: "The usual new rule was that an unhappy spouse need only remove himself from the house and wait a few months, . . ." Frum writes. "Nor did the law's tilt against the unwilling spouse halt there. The 1969 California divorce reform put an end to the old bias in favor of maternal custody."[39]

Writing in the 1990s, Susan Faludi cited declining alimony settlements as evidence of a "backlash" against feminism, but as Frum noted, the no-fault divorce laws had handed men a huge bargaining chip. If maternal custody was no longer the norm, ex-husbands could threaten to contest for it. "Enhance the bargaining power of husbands, weaken the bargaining power of wives," Frum wrote, "and smaller settlements are exactly what you can expect."[40]

Feminists saw marriage as men's plan to keep women in servitude, which made divorce a critical tool of women's liberation. Women's magazines in the 1970s, '80s, and '90s featured copious advice about the "courage to divorce" swathed in the language of personal growth and self-expression. Books with titles such as *Our Turn: The Good News About Women and Divorce* and *Learning to*

Leave: A Woman's Guide offered unhappy wives a gentle, or sometimes not-so-gentle, push toward the exits.

Barbara Ehrenreich praised "good divorces," and in 1994, Con-
stance Ahrons argued in a book by that very title, *The Good Divorce,*
that it wasn't divorce per se that was harmful but "stereotypes"
and prejudices against divorce that were causing all the suffering.[41]
Ahrons worried that terms such as *broken family* were stigmatizing, and suggested the term *binuclear family* to replace *single-parent
family.*[42]

I was in high school when the divorce tremors rumbled through
the culture, and I remember what it did to friends and family
members. My gloomy classmates robotically recited the popular
mantra: "It's better to come from a broken home than to live in
one," but experience often belied this soothing bromide. Before
too long, my classmates were seeing their fathers less often, and
then Dad would announce that he had great news: a new wife
whom he was sure they were going to love as much as he did. After
a few excruciatingly awkward outings, those visits would fall off
to nothing.

A friend who was raised by "hippie parents" saw them divorce
when she was six years old. She alternated homes and recalled the
"atavistic, creeped-out" feeling of "seeing your mother in bed with
someone not your father." Adults seemed "emotionally naked" in
a way that made her uneasy, and like many children of the 1970s,
she had a dim sense that grown-ups were no longer playing traditional, protective roles. She wound up fantasizing about having
parents like the "adults in *The Donna Reed Show*: mother with a
string of pearls, father with a pipe."

If divorce was a critical step in women's emancipation, having children outside marriage was a no-brainer. In 2012, Katie
Roiphe, feminist and mother of two children by different fathers,
condemned concerns about single motherhood: "If there is anything that currently oppresses the children, it is the idea of the way
families are 'supposed to be.'"[43]

Explicitly feminist websites such as Jezebel, along with implicitly feminist ones such as the *Huffington Post,* endorse "single mothers by choice" as a great option for "strong-ass bitches."

The Ghost of the Moynihan Report

Feminists presented their "liberation" from old norms about love and family as something new, but by the time they came along, a huge social experiment was already underway in the African American community, where the percentage of single-parent families had been skyrocketing.

Though you would never guess it by its reputation then and since, "The Negro Family: The Case for National Action" (1965), also known as the Moynihan Report, was, as Nick Schulz recalled in *Home Economics,* a deeply humane and sensitive examination of the plight of African Americans.[44] It traced the history of slavery and described the unique persecutions and disadvantages suffered by blacks throughout American history. The report next turned to a trend that was then new: the rapid dissolution of black families. Quoting Harlem Youth Opportunities Unlimited, the report noted that in Harlem and around the nation a "massive deterioration of the fabric of society and its institutions" was underway. "*If this is so, it is the single most important social fact of the United States today*" (emphasis in original). The report continued: "The role of the family in shaping character and ability is so pervasive as to be easily overlooked. The family is the basic social unit of American life; it is the basic socializing unit."[45]

When the Moynihan Report was published, the illegitimacy rate among whites was a little more than 3 percent. The rate among blacks was 23.6 (though it was higher in northeastern cities). Separation and divorce were also much more common among black families, with the result that many African American children spent some part of their childhoods in single-parent homes.

The report closed by quoting E. Franklin Frazier, the first black president of the American Sociological Association:

Because the disorganized family has failed in its function as a socializing agency, it has handicapped the children in their relations
to the institutions in the community. Moreover, family disorganization has been partially responsible for a large amount of juvenile
delinquency and adult crime among Negroes. Since the widespread family disorganization among Negroes has resulted from
the failure of the father to play the role in family life required by
American society, the mitigation of this problem must await those
changes in the Negro and American society which will enable the
Negro father to play the role required of him.[46]

When his report came out, Patrick Moynihan, until then a
liberal in good standing, was denounced as a racist and a sexist. As
Steven F. Hayward recounted in *The Age of Reagan,* "The concern
with family stability, critics said in a now-famous refrain, was an
attempt to impose 'middle-class' values on the poor. In fact, it was
asserted, the black female–headed household is a 'cultural pattern
superior in its vitality to middle-class mores.'" At a White House
conference after the report was issued, the "planners demanded
that the question of 'family stability' be stricken entirely from the
agenda."[47]

Family structure became a taboo subject for decades. Into the
1980s and '90s, anyone who raised the issue of illegitimacy, or
"single-parent households," was accused of "blaming the victim"
and forcing women back into the "kitchen and the bedroom,"
or, as feminist Amanda Marcotte put it, hoping to "restore the
patriarchy to a perceived '50s-era heyday."[48] Meanwhile, the
number of children born to unwed mothers continued to rise. By
2013, 71 percent of black children in America were born to single
women. Among Hispanics, the figure was 53 percent, and among
whites, 36 percent.[49] In other words, the rate among whites in
2013 was thirteen points higher than it was among blacks when
the Moynihan Report was issued.

In the 1990s, when my kids were toddlers, public television
shows such as *Barney* delivered the approved, soothing propaganda.

The children on the show sang about families coming in different sizes and different kinds, "but mine's just right for me." They then gave examples. One boy lived with his mom and dad and a dog and cat. A girl lived with her mom, and her dad lived far away. Though she saw her parents just one at a time, they both loved her every day, and so forth. The show's creators clearly wanted the kids of divorce to feel "normalized," but the message was probably also intended for, and received by, some of the adults. Even if your child sees his parents just one at a time, everything's fine. A family is love.

Of course, if a family is love, how does a child process the news that "Mommy and Daddy fell out of love"? That is irrefutable evidence that *some* loves are impermanent and untrustworthy, and the child must wonder if parents also fall out of love with their children. No matter how often parents reassure their kids that parent-child love is forever, children learn the lesson that it's dangerous to trust.

Family is not just love. It's also commitment and, yes, duty. Family means assuming responsibility for others and keeping your promises.

A Happiness Gap

Feminists were as wrong as they could be about marriage. Their campaign against it was like declaring war on food or water. The vast majority of women want and need the emotional support and physical and financial security that marriage confers. Men want and need the role of provider and protector for wives and children. Obviously these are generalizations. Individuals vary; so do marriages. Also, within the broad parameters just mentioned, there is an almost infinite variety of styles. Some couples are extremely egalitarian, attempting to split everything fifty-fifty. Others prefer to invert the usual division of labor so that the wife is the chief breadwinner while the husband is the principal caretaker.

Many, including my husband and me, choose to feel their way forward without fretting too much about who is doing what. And, of course, the single life is best for some. But for most people, marriage fulfills their fundamental needs. At my wedding, our rabbi quoted from Genesis 2:18: "It is not good for man to be alone." No, nor for woman.

Married adults are more likely to describe themselves as "very happy" (43 percent) than are singles (24 percent).[50] Far from a trap for women, marriage is an essential component of happiness. Though you might not guess it from shows such as *Sex and the City,* married people are much more satisfied with their sex lives than single people. Cohabiting couples fall somewhere in between.[51] This goes for both men and women.

According to a report from the National Marriage Project of the University of Virginia: "Thirty-five percent of single men and cohabiting men report they are 'highly satisfied' with their lives, compared to 52 percent of married men. Likewise, 33 percent of single women and 29 percent of cohabiting women are 'highly satisfied,' compared to 47 percent of married women."[52]

Though the studies on happiness are limited by researchers' inability to see into people's souls, we can glean from the data that married people are much healthier,[53] wealthier, less prone to suicide, less likely to be drug abusers or alcoholics, less likely to be unemployed, and more likely to have broad networks of friends and relatives than single or divorced people. Married people are also less likely to develop Alzheimer's disease and are even more likely to survive a cancer diagnosis or other serious illness.[54]

According to the Institute for American Values, longitudinal research shows that it is not merely that mentally healthy people are more likely to get or stay married. Instead, marriage itself appears to boost mental health. "Remaining unmarried or getting divorced seems to result, on average, in a deterioration in mental well-being."[55]

As someone who has been married for nearly three decades,

I can attest that marriage delivers happiness not just because you find your true love, but because it knits the couple into a kinship and community network, which frequently includes churches and synagogues. We are social creatures who thrive in communities. They provide us with a sense of belonging, perspective, and opportunities to offer charity. Being a part of a community also facilitates access to assistance in hard times, leads for job openings, and support during life crises such as illness and death.

One does not have to be married to be part of a community, religious or otherwise, but attachments of all sorts do seem to rise and fall together. As Charles Murray showed in his landmark book *Coming Apart,* people who marry also tend to be churchgoers, to be employed, and to volunteer in their communities. Marriage is a first step on the ladder of adult commitments and connections, so its precipitous decline is a threat to communities as well as individuals.

Compared with 1960, when the overwhelming majority of adults were married, more adults today remain single.[56] In 2014, unmarried adults became the majority for the first time. Perhaps you've seen TV commercials featuring a single woman buying a home? Companies are adjusting their marketing to the new patterns.[57]

Though the divorce rate has ticked down from its highest point in 1980, which is cause for optimism, the decline doesn't mean that more children are growing up with their married parents. No, another pattern is taking hold: more middle-class Americans are having children before marrying or without marrying at all. About 40 percent of American babies are now born to single women. And even though four out of five of those women are in romantic relationships at the time of the birth and have high hopes for the future of those unions, experience shows that most will break up within just a few years.[58]

The fraying of families is not hitting all segments of American society equally. There is a class element to this. A large majority of college graduates has figured out that the key to a stable and prosperous life is to wait until they are married before having babies. Among those with less than a college degree, the opposite is the case. Among working-class families, moving in together and having babies has become the norm. Children born to these unstable unions tend to have a whole skein of troubles. Anyone concerned about the poor and middle class cannot remain indifferent to the large numbers of children growing up without the order and stability children so badly need. Stable families are the key character-forming institutions of society. Moms and dads show children how to delay gratification, to share, to care for siblings, to stick with their commitments, and to tell right from wrong.

Family breakdown is a bitter legacy of feminism, which defined the ideas that shaped behavior. Feminism sanctioned the sexual revolution, easy divorce, and single parenthood. It heartily endorsed discarding the stigma against unwed childbearing. That stigma was painful in many cases, but it also prevented most women from placing their children at risk, and it shamed men who walked away from their responsibilities.

Sex Wars

About 40 percent of marriages now end in divorce, and though progressives and feminists hailed the divorce revolution as liberating for women, and even an opportunity for new adventures and growth for children, the reality has been painful. As Barbara Dafoe Whitehead documents in *The Divorce Culture* (1998), naïve hopes that easier escape from marriage would reduce the sum total of male-female discord proved completely wrong. Whitehead shows that far from reducing family conflict, divorce can actually intensify it. "Divorce could provoke new hostilities; parental conflict often escalated during and after divorce, creating new kinds of deprivation and loss, even an increased threat of violence and abuse to children."[59]

Maggie Gallagher, author of several books on marriage and divorce, laments that only 12 percent of couples that split up do so amicably. "Fifty percent of middle-class divorced couples engage in bitter, open conflict as 'angry associates,' or worse, 'fiery foes.' Five years afterward, most of these angry divorced people remain mired in hostility. Nearly a third of friendly divorces degenerate into open, angry conflict."[60] In Gallagher's own circle of relatives and friends, she saw "one of the kindest, most generous women I know greet her husband with an unrelenting stream of obscenities for weeks on end; I have known a husband call his wife a whore in front of the kids; I have seen a gentle man with no previous hint of violence savagely beat his departing wife."[61]

Some married couples have severe problems that cannot be solved except by parting, but an estimated *two-thirds* of annual divorces occur among couples who do not have high-conflict relationships, at least not until the divorce process begins.[62] Divorce is also financially devastating. The couple's wealth leaches away to lawyers, mediators, therapists, real estate agents, and accountants. Two residences are more expensive than one. An Ohio State University study found that divorce decreases wealth by an average of 77 percent. Jay Zagorsky, the study's author, counseled, "If you really want to increase your wealth, get married and stay married. On the other hand, divorce can devastate your wealth."[63]

Women are commonly worse off financially after divorce than their ex-husbands. Those who worked before, during, or after their marriages experienced a 20 percent decline in income after divorce, compared with men, whose incomes rose by 30 percent. Part of the reason may be that women are more likely than men to have been out of the workforce while caring for children.[64] After divorce, the woman is therefore more often the one who winds up on public assistance.[65]

Couples who stay married, on the other hand, are the winners. Married couples accumulate more wealth than divorced or never-married people do. A study published by the National Bureau of Economic Research found that the median married couple in their sixties had ten times more wealth than a typical single person.[66] Long-married couples not only invest their money jointly, but they also invest in each other. One might work so the other can attend college or graduate school, for instance. And when one gets sick, the other provides care. Or when one cannot care for a sick child, the other picks up the slack, thus making it less likely that either spouse will lose a job due to time away from the office.

Also, men and women have different and complementary strategies when it comes to investing their savings. Men are risk takers, while women are more conservative. It makes for a good balance. A stable married couple is more likely to receive support from grandparents and other relatives in the form of loans, gifts, and time than divorced or never-married parents.[67]

When divorce becomes common, it has a demoralizing effect on others too. As the University of Virginia's Bradford Wilcox explains, marital happiness *in general* declined between the 1970s, when 70 percent of married men and 67 percent of married women reported being "very happy," and the 1980s, when marital happiness was at 63 percent for men and 62 percent for women. Wilcox reported that "widespread divorce undermined ordinary couples' faith in marital permanency and their ability to invest financially and emotionally in their marriages—ultimately casting clouds of doubt over their relationships."

Wilcox cited a study by economist Betsey Stevenson, who "found that newlywed couples in states that passed no-fault divorce were about 10 percent less likely to support a spouse through college or graduate school and were 6 percent less likely to have a child together. Ironically, then, the widespread availability of easy divorce not only enabled 'bad' marriages to be weeded out, but also made it more difficult for 'good' marriages to take root and flourish."[68]

Whatever the consequences for adults, divorce can be a life-stunting disaster for children. As sociologists Sara McLanahan and Gary Sandefur report in their book, *Growing Up with a Single Parent: What Hurts, What Helps*: "[G]rowing up with only one biological parent frequently deprives children of important economic, parental, and community resources, and . . . these deprivations ultimately undermine their chances of future success." The authors are careful to clarify that family instability is not necessarily devastating, and that it was one factor among many. But they add that "a substantial portion of our nation's youth is at risk."[69]

Except when there is abuse in the home, there is no "good divorce" from a child's point of view. It's all loss—of income, security, time with fathers, and often time with mothers as well. Children of divorce are more likely to live in poverty, take up smoking, get pregnant as teenagers, fall behind in math, get physically sick, get divorced themselves, and even die young.[70]

It is no surprise, then, that divorce takes a toll on children's mental health. Consider youth suicide. A 2001 paper published by the Bureau of Economic Analysis, by David M. Cutler, Edward L. Glaeser, and Karen E. Norberg, found that the rate of teen suicides tripled between 1950 and 1990, and the authors found that depression, suicide attempts, and suicide completions were all closely linked with divorce and family structure. Teens who live with a single parent were twice as likely to attempt suicide as those in two-parent families. "[T]he relationship with one's parents is a very strong determinant of teenage depression," the report said. "Individuals who never knew their fathers are particularly likely to be depressed, even more so than those who know their father but whose father is not home. Note that these coefficients were about the same in the regressions for attempting suicide."[71] As the divorce rate rises, the teen suicide rate rises with it.[72]

Some apologists for the "family is love" paradigm have noted that throughout history, children have commonly lived with step-parents. It used to be death that disrupted families, they say, and now it's divorce. So what's all the fuss about?

Divorce is far harder on children than parental death. Death is recognized as a tragedy, and usually draws survivors closer. As Barbara Dafoe Whitehead explains, a parental death elicits help from friends and relatives, including grandparents. Money may be forthcoming from Social Security or life insurance. The surviving parent and child are united in their bereavement and think back on the late parent with affection. The memory of the lost parent can even be a spur to the child to try to live in such a manner as would make the late parent proud.[73]

After divorce, the custodial parent and child have markedly different feelings about the missing parent, and as Whitehead notes, the nonresidential parent "who remains remote or absent can be a source of continued torment [to the child] in a way that a parent who dies is not."[74] Paternal grandparents may be less likely to pitch in with grandchildren who are living with an ex-wife.[75] And children may feel guilty about longing for a father who is such a source of pain to their mother.

Many divorced fathers lose regular contact with their children. Reporting information from the National Survey of Children, Whitehead reports that "close to half of all children had not seen their nonresidential parent (overwhelmingly the father) in the past year, and only one in six had weekly contact or better."[76] Other studies have found that ten years after a divorce, nearly two-thirds of the children had not seen their fathers for a year.[77] These children can be left with psychic scars. Lots of them, perhaps even the majority, bounce back without lifelong wounds. But a large number (more boys than girls) never do.

Yet fathers are not always or even usually to blame. Mothers sometimes restrict a father's access to his children to gain more financial support or to punish him. This strategy commonly causes fathers to withhold, or further withhold, child support payments, and the cycle of bitterness intensifies. Everyone loses—but no one more than the children.

Even when children of divorce reach college, family breakup continues to haunt them. A 2010 study found that college students with divorced parents received only about a third of the financial contributions that students with married parents received. It wasn't just a matter of single parents having less money. Even students whose parents had remarried and had comparable incomes to the married parents received only half the financial support.[78] There's a fraying of attachments.

Children of divorce also experience more emotional strains in college than students from intact families. They are more likely to experience anxiety, depression, and poor grades than their peers. Controlling for demographics, ACT scores, and other factors, the children of divorce had a significantly lower first-year retention rate, were less likely to graduate, and had more financial problems than others.[79]

Responding to an article in the *New York Times* about the impact of divorce on college students, a commenter called "Amy" described a common predicament:

> Coming from divorced and remarried parents I found myself with no assistance with planning, support for, or financial assistance for college upon graduation from high school. One reason for this was due to the anger between my divorced parents. My father felt as if he no longer had to pay "that woman" child support when I turned 18 and was done. My mother, possibly because of her new husband, would not help either. Her new husband had two children of his own. Their paternal grandparents funded their college from what I understand.[80]

In the 1970s, when feminists were promoting the "courage to divorce," therapists, clergy, and others advised that stepfamilies would solve the problems of single parenthood. An unhappy wife would leave her unsuitable mate and find a better one. A "blended" family would slip seamlessly into the slot and provide children with the stability, male role models, and financial security they would need.

But in the intervening years, we've learned that it isn't so simple to put families back together. In fact, stepfamilies turn out to be no better for children than single-parent ones. Children in stepfamilies actually do worse in some crucial respects, such as school performance, than children whose mothers do not remarry.[81]

Fathers who form new relationships and have children with a new partner become more estranged from the children of their first wife or partner. Mothers who welcome new boyfriends or husbands can become less attentive to their children from the first relationship. Children who live in stepfamilies are more likely to report feeling "sad or blue," to wish for more time with their mothers, and to miss out on having parents participate in school or other activities.[82]

Some mothers with new lovers or husbands are discreet about their sex lives and careful to consider their children's feelings of exclusion and loss. But some become preoccupied with their own romantic lives and neglect their children. "Compared with the affectional environment in households with married parents," Whitehead cautions, "who have usually settled into a more sedate sex life, the climate in these post–nuclear family households may be overheated and eroticized."[83]

In the premodern world, when women commonly died in childbirth, fathers remarried, obliging their children to contend with stepmothers, who probably favored their biological children over their husband's children by a previous wife. Stories of "wicked stepmothers" thus had real resonance for children. But in our time, the wicked stepfather is the more likely threat to enter a child's world.

This is not to suggest that most live-in boyfriends or stepfathers abuse children. Few do, thank God, but when a woman lives in a home with a man who is not the father of her children, those children are at increased risk of both physical and sexual abuse. A study published in the journal *Pediatrics* found that children who live in households with unrelated adults are fifty times more likely to die from inflicted injuries than those living with their biological parents.[84] Children in a household with their mother and her boyfriend are about eleven times more likely to be sexually, physically, or emotionally abused than children living with their married biological parents. Also, they are six times more likely to be physically, emotionally, or educationally neglected than children living with their married biological parents.[85]

The biological tie still matters, though it isn't everything. As an adoptive (and biological) parent myself, I can testify that it is absolutely possible to love an adopted child every bit as much as a biological one. But adoption is a special case. Adoptive parents desperately want to be parents and have usually made peace with infertility or have decided for other reasons to expand their families through adoption. In other words, adoptive parents *want* the child. They want children badly enough to go through the exhaustive and expensive steps to be eligible to adopt, which include medical exams, extensive interviews, recommendations, and home visits by social workers. Stepparenting is different. The adult wants the other adult and gets the kids in the bargain. He or she may or may not have any particular interest in these kids, and may accept them happily, grudgingly, or not at all.

I've painted a dark portrait of divorce and single parenting, so I must emphasize that many single parents do a wonderful job and raise happy and well-adjusted children. I must also repeat that some married couples have severe conflicts that cannot be overcome. But the vast majority of unhappy couples who split might have been happier staying together and working on their relationships, and in most cases, their children would have been better off. A British study of young mothers found that 68 percent of those who stayed in an unhappy union after the birth of a child were happy by the time the child reached the age of eleven.

Though many adults who divorce report being happy with their decision, it's impossible to know how many could have worked out their differences if they'd stuck it out. Happiness, or at least contentment, is often an achievement, the result of hard work and perseverance, not the luck of the draw.

The Institute for American Values compared divorced couples with unhappy couples who stayed married[86] and found that unhappily married adults who divorced were no happier five years after the divorce than were the equally unhappy couples who remained together. And two-thirds of unhappily married people who stayed married reported that they were happy five years later. Even among those who rated their marriages as "very unhappy," nearly 80 percent said they were happily married five years later.[87] These were not bored or dissatisfied whiners. They had endured serious problems, including alcoholism, infidelity, verbal abuse, emotional neglect, depression, illness, and work and money troubles.

Even more surprising, unhappy spouses who divorced actually showed slightly more depressive symptoms five years later than those who didn't. (They did, however, report more personal growth.) And the divorced sample reported a good deal more alcohol consumption than the married group.[88]

The study suggested that if a couple is unhappy, the chances that they will be happily married five years later are 64 percent if they stay together but only 19 percent if they divorce and remarry. (The authors acknowledged that five years is a relatively short period, and many divorced people will eventually remarry, some happily.)

How did the unhappy couples turn their lives around? The study found three principal techniques. The first was endurance. Many couples do not so much solve their problems as transcend them. By pushing through their difficulties, many couples found that time often improved matters. Moreover, these couples maintained a negative view of the effects of divorce. "The grass is always greener," explained one husband, "but it's Astroturf."

The researchers said that others had a "marital work ethic" and arranged for more private time with one another, sought counseling (from clergy or professionals), received help from in-laws or other relatives, or, in some cases, threatened divorce or consulted a divorce lawyer. A third category, "personal happiness seekers," found other ways to improve their overall contentment, even if they could not markedly improve their marital happiness.

The most telling aspect of this research is the light it sheds on the importance of attitudes toward marriage. Those who enter marriage with a dim (some might say accurate) view of divorce and a strong religious or other motivation for avoiding it are not only less likely to divorce; they are also less likely to be unhappy.

Baby Carriage Before Marriage

As bad as divorce often is for kids, being raised by a never-married mother is usually worse. The poverty rate for children raised in two-parent families is 6.8 percent, and these children, on average, get good grades in school, go on vacations with Mom and Dad, and plan for the future with confidence. For kids raised by single mothers, the poverty rate is 37.1 percent. When Harry Truman was president, only about 5 percent of all births were to unwed mothers. By the Nixon years, the rate had doubled to about 10 percent, and then, with an assist from feminism and the sexual revolution, it took off. In 2014, more than 40 percent of all births were to unmarried women. Among mothers under the age of thirty, 64 percent were single.[89] Opinions about what used to be called "illegitimacy" changed with head-snapping speed. In 1974, 62.7 percent of American adults disagreed with the statement "There is no reason single women shouldn't have children." By 1985, only 45.3 percent did.[90]

Again, the African American community was the warning light. Over the past fifty years, the percentage of black families headed by married couples declined from 78 percent to 34 percent.[91] It's hard to prove causation, but this rise in single parenting was accompanied by a steep rise in crime, drug abuse, indiscipline in schools, and unemployment. As then–presidential candidate Barack Obama noted in a Father's Day speech in 2008, "If we are honest with ourselves, we'll admit that too many fathers are . . . missing . . . from too many lives and too many homes. They have abandoned their responsibilities, acting like boys instead of men. And the foundations of our families are weakening because of it."[92]

After crunching the numbers, Sara McLanahan and Cynthia Harper concluded that growing up in a single-parent home is more predictive of involvement with the criminal justice system than any other factor *including race and income.*[93]

Look at what works and what doesn't. The poverty rate among married black couples today is 8 percent, or half the national rate of 16 percent. Among black single mothers, 46 percent live in poverty.[94] The ratios are similar for whites. The poverty rate for married white couples is 3.1 percent,[95] and for single white parents, it's 22 percent.[96]

Many on the left, transfixed by America's original sins of slavery and racism—and I would be the last to deny that those sins were/are real—cannot think clearly about anything that can be construed as criticism of black behavior. And a few on the right point to black family structure with a trace of smugness as if it explains everything that goes wrong in the lives of American blacks. Yet neither side of the family structure wars has assimilated the new reality: Americans of every color and ethnicity have a problem with family structure; blacks just happen to have been the first ones out the matrimonial door.

If Americans of all backgrounds had heeded Moynihan's advice in 1965 and rushed to shore up fatherhood and marriage, many of the self-inflicted wounds we now suffer might have been avoided. Instead, we chose the opposite route. The white rate of out-of-wedlock births rose from 3.1 percent in 1965 to 29.4 percent in 2013. For Hispanics, the rate increased from 26 percent in 1980 to 53.5 percent in 2013. And for blacks, as noted, the 2013 rate was 72.2 percent, compared with 24 percent in 1965.[97]

Isabel Sawhill, of the liberal-leaning Brookings Institution, has concluded that virtually the entire increase in child poverty in the United States since the 1970s can be attributed to family breakdown.[98] In fact, as Kay Hymowitz described it, we have evolved a caste system. At the top are the college graduates, nine out of ten of whom get married before becoming pregnant. At the bottom are poor women of all races and backgrounds who routinely have babies before they marry (if they ever marry).[99]

Scholars have begun to study the things conducive to success beyond socioeconomic status and race. Richard V. Reeves, also of the Brookings Institution, studies the noncognitive traits associated with life success. These include "perseverance, industriousness, grit, resilience, curiosity, application, self-control, future orientation, self-discipline, impulse control, and delay of gratification." He found that these traits track closely with the mother's level of education and whether or not a child has parents who are continuously married. Having married parents was shown to predict these character traits even more than being born to well-off parents.[100] So in other words, if you were a birth mother choosing a family to place your baby with, you'd be better advised to choose a married couple of moderate means rather than a wealthy unmarried couple.

James Heckman of the University of Chicago explains how unmarried, uneducated mothers often fail to cultivate these crucial traits in their children: "[They] talk less to their children and are less likely to read to them daily. Exposure to this type of parenting leads to substantial differences in the verbal skills of disadvantaged children when they start school. Disadvantaged mothers encourage their children less and tend to adopt harsher parenting styles. Disadvantaged parents tend to be less engaged with their children's school work. The environments provided by teenage mothers are particularly adverse."[101]

For many women, the link between marriage and childbearing no longer applies. In a 2009 *Washington Post* story, one unmarried mother explained why she hadn't married the father of her three-year-old: "He's a good dad and a good person, but he's just not right for me." Another offered, "I didn't want to pick the wrong person just to have a kid, so I just decided to go ahead and do it and work on the relationship later."[102] Our culture has clearly not discouraged these women from single parenting. No one told them they might be handicapping their children. Nor did anyone advise the second woman she *might* be lucky enough to find a man who would be a good stepfather, but the child's biological dad has a running start in caring about that particular baby. That's just the way we're designed.

Though some single-parent families do well, the children in many American households are subjected to more stress than children can usually bear. American adults with some college or less have become promiscuous not just about sex but about children. Kids are dragged from one unstable home to another, living first with their own unmarried parents, then with Mom and her new boyfriend, then with Grandma for a few months, then with yet another new boyfriend or husband of their mother's. Along the way, they may acquire half-siblings, or be forced to live with step-siblings and other adults to whom they are not related (the boyfriend's family) but to whom they must nonetheless adjust.

As sociologist Andrew Cherlin notes in *The Marriage-Go-Round,* Americans now hold the dubious distinction of leading the world in chaotic adult relationships. American young adults are quicker to form unions and faster to end them than are adults in any other country. Forty percent of American children will see their parents' arrangement, either marriage or living together, dissolve by the time they reach the age of fifteen. And even more damaging, 47 percent will see a new partner enter their home within three years of their parents' separation.[103] Among cohabiting couples, the breakup rate is 55 percent after five years, the highest among OECD (Organisation for Economic Co-operation and Development) countries. The next highest rate is in Spain, at 42 percent.[104]

In *Hillbilly Elegy,* J. D. Vance describes growing up in just such a household in Ohio. Many times in his early life, his home was so turbulent that he was kept awake all night by terrifying fights between his mother and her latest live-in boyfriend, and he could not concentrate in school at all. For a while, he and his older sister lived by themselves while his mother underwent (another) stint in rehab. They concealed this embarrassing situation as best they could, but they were children—alone. Vance quotes one of his teachers, who did her best with kids who came from anarchic homes like his, as saying, "They want us to be shepherds to these kids. But no one wants to talk about the fact that many of them are raised by wolves."[105]

Lost Men

Now that the Supreme Court has made same-sex marriage the law of the land, I devoutly hope marriage will do for same-sex couples what it has done for heterosexual couples. There just hasn't been enough time to measure if that will be so. I also hope that children raised by same-sex couples will get all the benefits of mother-and-father unions.

Still, same-sex marriage has arrived at a moment when heterosexual marriage is in a rickety state. The social science world continues to debate whether less-educated men remain single because their low earning prospects make them less desirable or whether failing to marry makes them less likely to work hard and get ahead. This same debate raged in the 1980s regarding the African American community. William Julius Wilson famously argued that black women were having children out of wedlock because of fewer marriageable black men. The men were jobless, Wilson argued, due to deindustrialization.

In a direct echo of Wilson's theory about the black underclass, the academic world and popular press has focused recently on the theory that unwed parenting among white working-class Americans has increased because men have been hit hard by the loss of factory jobs. "All the men here are either on drugs or unemployed," a young woman from an industrial region of Ohio told *The Atlantic* in 2017.[106] This is called the "marriageable man" theory, which suggests that women are having children out of wedlock because the men they're sexually involved with are unable to find work. If it's true that declining job opportunities for less-educated men account for the rise in unwed childbearing, shouldn't the opposite be true? If well-paying jobs for men without college degrees suddenly become available, wouldn't marriage increase and unwed childbearing decline?

Melissa Kearney and Riley Wilson, economists at the University of Maryland, decided to test what Kearney described to me as the "reverse marriageable man" hypothesis. Since the late 1990s, a number of regions in the United States have experienced a boom in fracking, which has led to well-paying jobs for people with no more than a high school diploma (average salaries between $70,000 and $80,000 per year). Somewhat to their surprise, Kearney and Wilson found that when working-class wages rose, marriage rates didn't budge. Women had more children with the men who had good-paying jobs, but they were no more likely to marry. The rate of unwed childbearing didn't change at all.[107]

It's impossible to imagine the rise of single parenthood without three things: first, a welfare system that makes it economically possible to raise a child without a husband; second, a disability system that permits many men with only mild impairments to collect benefits; and third (and most important, in my judgment), an anything-goes culture that does not uphold any particular family structure.

Working-class people used to have more conservative social views than other Americans, but that has been changing. In the 1970s, 39 percent of the least-educated adults said that premarital sex is always wrong, compared with 15 percent of the highly educated. By the 2000s, the people at the top had become more socially conservative: 21 percent of the highly educated thought premarital sex was wrong, and among the lesser educated, the number who thought so declined to 28 percent. Even more revealing were data showing that adolescents from homes with highly educated mothers were more likely to be "embarrassed by a teen pregnancy" (76 percent) than teenagers from homes with the least-educated mothers (48 percent).[108]

Yet the effects of being raised by a single mother do seem to discriminate—against boys. Studies have found that father absence in African American homes leads to more mental health and behavioral problems for boys than for girls.[109] Similarly, two MIT economists, David Autor and Melanie Wasserman, found this to be true of all races. They examined brothers and sisters born in Florida between 1992 and 2002. "Growing up in a single-parent home appears to significantly decrease the probability of college attendance for boys, but has no similar effect for girls," they conclude. "Fatherless boys are less ambitious, less hopeful, and more likely to get into trouble at school than fatherless girls."[110] Girls raised by mother-father couples appear no more likely than those raised by mothers alone to be employed as adults. But for boys, being raised without a father decreased their likelihood of being employed as adults by eight to ten points.[111]

When boys raised without fathers grow up—wait. Do they grow up? Some 22 percent of men in their prime (ages twenty-five to fifty-four) are doing no paid work at all. Note, this is a category apart from unemployed men. They are not considered unemployed, because they are not looking for work. Some explain that they are out of the labor force because of disability or chronic pain. Yet when asked, only 14 percent of the nonworkers in 2014 said they were idle because of a lack of job opportunities.[112] Most are low-skilled, never-married, and native-born, and many are African American. The never-married element is key.

African American *husbands* participate in the labor force at higher rates than never-married white men.[113] And married men with high school diplomas are more likely to be employed than single men with some college or even an associate's degree.[114] You wouldn't expect to see those numbers if it were all about the loss of unskilled jobs.

This caste of men who don't work, don't marry, and don't support children is worrying. They spend an average of five and a half hours a day watching TV and movies, and less time caring for household members than either unemployed men or employed women. How do they derive meaning in their lives? How do they gain self-respect?

Meanwhile, women now earn the majority of bachelor's, master's, and PhDs in America.[115] Women tend to prefer to marry men with at least as much education as they have. The Department of Education estimates that by 2023, 47 percent more women than men will obtain college diplomas. That's three women for every two men.[116] The Pew Research Center estimates that about one in four young adults today will never marry.[117]

Among African Americans, these trends are even more stark, as Moynihan warned us. The overwhelming majority of black college graduates are women. Females now account for 66 percent of all bachelor's degrees earned by blacks, and for even higher percentages of advanced degrees. According to an analysis by the Brookings Institution, the percentage of black women college graduates aged twenty-five to thirty-five who have never married is 60 percent, compared to 38 percent for white college-educated women.[118]

And what becomes of communities where large numbers of men are not modeling behaviors of parental responsibility? The atmosphere in neighborhoods with lots of absent fathers has an effect on everyone. Raj Chetty and his colleagues at Harvard found that even children of intact families do worse if their neighborhoods are full of unwed parents.[119]

The Nobel Prize–winning economist George Akerlof, husband of former Federal Reserve chairman Janet Yellen, has said that men "settle down when they get married; if they fail to get married, they fail to settle down."[120] Doubtless causation runs both ways, and a woman might view a man who is an unemployed high school dropout as just another mouth for her to feed. When unmarried people were asked what traits they desired in a potential spouse, 78 percent of women but only 46 percent of men said, "Having a steady job."[121]

Would that unemployed man get a job and hold on to it if he

got married? W. Bradford Wilcox, in a report for the American Enterprise Institute, makes a strong case that marriage motivates men to get and stay employed, noting that married men "work about 400 hours more per year than their single peers with equivalent backgrounds."[122] He also cites a Harvard study showing that married men earned between 10 and 40 percent more than their single peers with similar education and skills and that this pattern was observed not just in the United States but also in Sweden and the United Kingdom.[123] Wilcox described this as "a substantial marriage premium for men," and added that this held true for "black, Hispanic, and less educated men." A 2004 study found that among sets of identical twin men, the married men earned about 26 percent more than their twin brothers who remained single.[124]

The mother-child bond is the strongest in human life. Only in the direst circumstances (war, famine, severe illness) do women abandon their children, and even then, abandonment is rare. The same cannot be said for men. The data on divorced fathers show that when men are alienated from the mothers of their children, they often permit relationships with their children to decay as well.

My intuition is that marriage to a woman, especially to the mother of his children, cements a man's place in the world. For women, becoming pregnant, giving birth, and raising children provides a built-in sense of identity and meaning. No, this is not the only source of women's identity, but it is a powerful one. Nature or God (however you want to view it) has not given that gift to men to the same degree. Perhaps that's why traditional cultures have such elaborate coming-of-age ceremonies for boys but not for girls. Fatherhood must be "socially constructed" to some degree; motherhood is natural. But when women marry and knit the father of their children into the family, men share that solidity.

Women are also naturally better at forming relationships with others, women as well as men. When men marry, they share in their wives' sociability and develop more connections through them. Perhaps that's why married men not only earn more but also drink less, are more law-abiding, are less depressed, and are more likely to take part in community activities. "Why do we coach Little League and attend Back-to-School night?" *National Review* editor Rich Lowry once quipped. "Because our wives tell us to."

Ideally partnered with a nurturing woman, a man brings particular masculine virtues to child rearing. Men are better disciplinarians, more likely to challenge children, and more inclined to engage in the rough-and-tumble play that is so crucial for growing boys. Children who have good relationships with their fathers show better social adjustment and self-esteem than those who lack this influence.[125] David Blankenhorn of the National Fatherhood Initiative summarized the parenting styles of mothers and fathers: Picture a child on a jungle gym at the park. Mom and Dad are watching their daughter. "Be careful!" the mother cautions. "See if you can get to the top!" calls the father.

In 2015, the husband-wife economist team of Angus Deaton and Anne Case published a stunning study that showed a rising death rate among working-class, middle-aged, white Americans, exactly the population that has seen accelerating family breakdown over the past several years.[126] These death rates had been declining for decades as wealth increased. But now deaths from "diseases of despair" (cirrhosis of the liver, suicide, drug overdoses, and alcohol poisoning) are rising so much that life expectancy for this entire group, particularly whites with a high school education or less, is dropping.

In 2017, Case and Deaton published another paper that confirmed their earlier results. They also found that middle-aged, non-Hispanic whites suffer from diseases of despair in higher numbers than other ethnic groups, and significant and rising percentages of these Americans report chronic pain, which is associated with depression and can be a marker for suicide.[127] With this report, Case and Deaton concluded that family patterns, specifically the fragile relationships so common among white high school graduates, are creating a terrible undertow of unhappiness in American life.

In 1987, Saul Bellow published the novel *More Die of Heart-*

break. The title could be the anthem of America's middle class. In 1950, fewer than 10 percent of American households contained only one person. By 2010, nearly 27 percent of households were single-person. People living alone are not necessarily lonely. If they have a buzzing network of friends and family, they may not be. If Grandpa lives alone, but his daughter and grandchildren live across the street, all may be well. But the number of people in America and Europe who report feeling lonely is rising sharply.

A 2010 American Association of Retired Persons (AARP) survey found that one-third of Americans aged forty-five and older reported being chronically lonely. In 2000, only one in five had described feeling that way. In 1985, only 10 percent of Americans said they had no one with whom to discuss important matters, and 15 percent said they had only one confidante. By 2004, 25 percent trusted no one with their intimate matters, and 20 percent had only one person they could talk to. Fully one in five Americans in 2012 said they were unhappy with their lives because of this corrosive sense of isolation.[128]

Social media outlets such as Facebook and Twitter have not helped our national loneliness epidemic, and may be aggravating it if lonely people get the impression that others are leading perfect lives. Professional cuddlers have stepped up to fill the void—some get eighty dollars simply to hold a stranger for an hour.[129] You can also "rent" a friend to go out for dinner or to a movie. A woman who started a cuddling company expecting to cater to elderly widows and widowers was surprised to find clients ranging from their twenties all the way to their eighties.[130]

Loneliness is now viewed as a public health problem. Chronically lonely people have a rate of death twice that of the obese, and higher rates of suicide. In Great Britain, the Silver Line helpline, a call center for people needing to hear the sound of another human voice, serves ten thousand callers per week.[131]

How Do You Know It's Marriage?

Income inequality is increasing. Children are suffering from behavior problems and poor school performance. Suicide rates are
up. Drug abuse and alcohol abuse are rife. A significant number of
unemployed working-age men are not looking for jobs. Women
are less happy than they were decades ago. Loneliness has become an epidemic. "Diseases of despair" blight the lives of many
working-class people. College students have much higher rates of
mental health disorders than in the past.[132]

How do we know this has been caused by the decline of stable
families and not something else? Perhaps it is caused by many other
things.

Yes, perhaps it is the result of deindustrialization and the changing nature of work. But as Nicholas Eberstadt notes in *Men Without Work,* the labor force participation rate of prime-age males has
trended down steadily over the last several decades in periods of
expansion and in times of contraction.[133] The American economy,
whatever its ups and downs—and I do not discount the problems of slow growth and stagnant middle-class wages—is wealthy
enough to permit millions of men to get by without working at
all. It's wealthy enough to support millions of women who choose
to have babies without fathers in the home. To put it crudely, people would not be able to make those choices if the wolf were truly
at the door.

It's true that the changing nature of work, specifically the transition away from manufacturing to service jobs, has suited wom-
en's skills more than men's. But those who point only to economic
rather than cultural explanations must account for why married
men, even those with only a high school diploma, seem to have
managed this transition well. Their employment rates are higher
than those of single men with some college.[134]

In 2015, feminist Amanda Marcotte objected that "The Republican worldview is one where even basic things like love, connection, and other basic human needs are being reclassified as privileges that should only be available to the wealthy."[135] I don't speak for the Republican Party, but it seems to me that feminism has done exactly what Marcotte accuses Republicans of doing. By devaluing marriage and family, *feminists* have turned those basic human needs into luxury goods broadly enjoyed by men and women with college degrees, and made them less and less the norm for everyone else.

All this comes down to a question about what people need in order to flourish. A stable, loving home is the first and most important ingredient of human thriving. The sexual and feminist revolutions made homes less secure. We are paying a heavy price.

About That Clock

Any number of social scientists take pains to say, as the conservative-leaning Institute for American Values put it in their monograph "When Marriage Disappears:" "We cannot (and should not) simply turn the clock back, trying to recreate the social and cultural conditions of some bygone era."[136]

Andrew Cherlin, one of the most perceptive observers of the changing nature of American families, writes movingly about the disorder and dysfunction that characterize so many American lives. But he shrinks from recommending that young people marry before becoming parents. "[T]he message of our political and moral leaders of late has been almost exclusively 'Get married.' . . . But the message isn't particularly effective: The United States has just experienced the most sustained period of pro-marriage rhetoric in a century, and yet little increase in marriage has occurred."[137] Even Barbara Dafoe Whitehead, author of the scorching *The Divorce Culture,* was compelled to deny that her book was "an appeal for a return to an earlier era of American family life."[138]

I'd bet a month's salary that all of them would love to see marriage and divorce rates among all Americans at 1950s levels. The reluctance to say so is, in my judgment, one result of the feminist defamation of the traditional family. The fear may be that endorsing marriage and traditional family life will be perceived as antiwoman. Unless you think that all those college graduates and doctors and lawyers are being oppressed, this prejudice doesn't survive a minute's reflection.

Of course, we cannot re-create all the conditions of the 1950s, and certainly no one would choose to. Who would give up central air conditioning and tiny insulin pumps? The clock has nothing to do with it. Right now, America's college-educated elites are following the "life script" that best leads to happiness and success. They get educated, get married, and then have babies—in that order, and nearly always in that order. Oh, and they tend to stay married.[139]

Cherlin argues that we've experienced an era of "pro-marriage rhetoric." If so, I missed it. Yes, the George W. Bush administration promoted marriage, but this effort made hardly a ripple in the wider culture. It seems to me that most people would rather swallow their tongues than disapprove of unwed childbearing. A man who doesn't marry the mother of his children is no longer stigmatized. In 2012, a grandmother-to-be wrote to the *Washington Post*'s advice column, capturing current mores well:

> My 26-year-old son's girlfriend—of four months—is pregnant. I have very mixed emotions about this, mainly because he just met her, and I do not know her. They work and live across the country. I am disappointed in their behavior. How do I tell my friends the news? I am embarrassed.

Columnist Carolyn Hax set the grandmother straight:

> American adults overwhelmingly choose premarital sex—the Guttmacher Institute says 95 percent, CDC says about 85 to

91 percent. (Amusingly, a few studies peg approval of premarital sex at 60 to 65 percent; being conflicted is a popular pastime.) Plus, birth control isn't perfect, so you have statistical permission not to single this couple out for shaming. It's more productive anyway to shake off any notions of the way things should be and start making room for the way things are.[140]

I think a little shame can be a good thing. Remember the data showing that daughters of well-educated moms were much more likely to be embarrassed by an unplanned pregnancy than others? Yet even leaving that aside, Hax didn't use the word *marriage*. She suggested that Grandma offer assistance "if they plan to raise the baby as a couple."

If? We are living in a culture that does not encourage marriage and instead upholds "choice" and "alternatives."

The family experimentation we've spent the past fifty years indulging in has some roots in America's self-conception. Our nation's founding documents enshrine the "pursuit of happiness." Questing, rugged individualism, and striking out on one's own are built into the American character. Yet family is the essential foundation of happiness and thriving. As Frenchman Alexis de Tocqueville wrote in *Democracy in America* (1835):

> There is certainly no country in the world where the tie of marriage is more respected than in America, or where conjugal happiness is more highly or worthily appreciated. . . . [W]hen the American retires from the turmoil of public life to the bosom of his family, he finds in it the image of order and of peace. There his pleasures are simple and natural, his joys are innocent and calm; and as he finds that an orderly life is the surest path to happiness, he accustoms himself easily to moderate his opinions as well as his tastes. While the European endeavors to forget his domestic troubles by agitating society, the American derives from his own home that love of order which he afterwards carries with him into public affairs.[141]

We've detoured from the warm embrace of family, but nothing is irreversible. Social learning is possible. The divorce rate has declined. Drunk driving and teen pregnancy have dropped sharply due to changing mores. In just a few years, we transformed our society from one in which homosexual sex acts were illegal in many states (though the laws were almost never enforced) to one that has enshrined same-sex marriage. That's the power of a cultural message. Imagine if we applied that same clout to encouraging traditional marriage.

CHAPTER 7

HAVING IT ALL

You can drive nature out with a pitchfork,
but she will still hurry back.

—Horace

In 2012, Anne-Marie Slaughter created a sensation with an *Atlantic* magazine cover story titled "Why Women Still Can't Have It All." Slaughter was the first woman dean of Princeton's Woodrow Wilson School of Public and International Affairs. Later, she was serving as director of the Policy Planning Staff at the State Department when she decided to give up her high-prestige post to spend more time with her two teenaged sons.

"Eighteen months into my job . . . at the State Department, a foreign-policy dream job that traces its origins back to George Kennan," she wrote, "I found myself in New York, at the United Nations' annual assemblage of every foreign minister and head of state in the world. On a Wednesday evening, President and Mrs. Obama hosted a glamorous reception at the American Museum of Natural History. I sipped champagne, greeted foreign dignitaries, and mingled. But I could not stop thinking about my 14-year-old son, who had started eighth grade three weeks earlier and was already resuming what had become his pattern of skipping homework, disrupting classes, failing math, and tuning out any adult who tried to reach him."[1] That night, she decided to give up her distinguished position and spend the next several years at home.

Slaughter is a Democrat, and we would likely disagree on some political topics, but I honor her forthrightness. She didn't frame her decision as a "sacrifice." She didn't rail about the lack of publicly funded, quality child care in America. No, she was listening to her heart. She didn't say she *should* be home (able to attend baseball games, monitor homework, and drive to appointments); she said she *wanted* to be home. Her husband in Princeton had been shouldering most of the parenting responsibilities while she was in Washington, DC. She saw her family only on weekends. Her children weren't neglected, but the separation pained her.

When Slaughter told a female colleague who also had children that she intended to write the article, her friend was "horrified," saying, "You *can't* write that. You, of all people." Slaughter knew what she meant. "Such a statement, coming from a high-profile career woman—a role model—would be a terrible signal to younger generations of women." Slaughter's reflections about "having it all" became one of the most discussed in *The Atlantic*'s history.

But how do we define the "it" in "having it all"? What do we most value?

Like many women, I had looked forward to marriage and children from the get-go, and my experience of infertility made me even more desperate for a baby of my own. When we adopted our first child, the mothering instinct was so powerful it bowled me over like a freight train.

Adoption is a leap of faith. We knew little of Jonathan's birth parents, and as we soon discovered, we had much to learn about ourselves as well. Our journey as parents began in Ohio. It turns out that you cannot simply pick up a baby in one state and move him to another. There are legal hoops to jump through, and that takes a few days.

Bob and I found ourselves in a hotel room in a town we didn't know, with a three-week-old infant, attempting to sterilize formula bottles with just a sink and a microwave. We strapped Jonathan in a carrier, went for long walks, and took turns staring at him to make sure he was still breathing.

I was recently going through my files in preparation for a move, and I came across a letter I had written to the clients of my syndicated column in 1991 requesting a maternity leave: "I am not sure that there is any precedent for syndicated columnists requesting this kind of leave of absence. But perhaps, as one of the very few (any?) women of childbearing years in this field, I represent the wave of the future. I do hope that you will be able to grant this leave. . . . I hope and expect that when I return to my column, my writing will be enhanced by the experience of motherhood."*

Was it ever. Once or twice a year, while the boys were growing up—we welcomed two more sons into our family—I wrote columns about the funny things they said or did, or some of the challenges we faced. Jon was struck by a car at age ten and was in a coma for three days. He then spent a month in rehab. David was diagnosed with type 1 diabetes at age nine. Ben was crisis free, thank God. But those columns received more responses than any others I wrote. I treasure those letters from readers. Having a family of my own knitted me into the human family in ways I wouldn't have been able to predict.

Since the dawn of second-wave feminism, Western societies have been attempting to fit women's lives into a male model, and forever falling short. Despite decades of classroom encouragement, federal initiatives, scholarships, mentorship programs, and affirmative action, women still don't hold 50 percent of CEO positions, or half of all U.S. Senate seats, and they don't own half of all NFL teams. Sexism is indicted for the "fact" that women earn only seventy-seven cents for every dollar a man earns. We hear about the so-called leaky pipeline that fails to deliver enough women

---

* These columns are available at monacharen.com.

into STEM careers. Sheryl Sandberg asks whether "we've become so focused on supporting personal choices that we're failing to encourage women to aspire to leadership."[2]

Let's begin with the seventy-seven cents statistic. It's phony,[3] but it's also been exceedingly hard to kill. It's derived by adding the total earnings of men and comparing them with the total earnings of women, and that's a meaningless comparison. The "wage gap" doesn't account for hours worked, job tenure, skills, or education. Nor does it account for differences between men and women in job specialization. For example, in medicine, women gravitate to specialties such as family medicine, psychiatry, and pediatrics, which offer regular hours but are not as highly compensated as other fields.

Christina Hoff Sommers responded to President Obama's invocation of this seventy-seven cents "datum" in one of his State of the Union addresses with a survey of college majors chosen by men and women that offers insight into pay disparities. Here, in order, are the ten most remunerative majors:

1. Petroleum engineering: 87 percent male;
2. Pharmaceutical sciences and administration: 48 percent male;
3. Mathematics and computer science: 67 percent male;
4. Aerospace engineering: 88 percent male;
5. Chemical engineering: 72 percent male;
6. Electrical engineering: 89 percent male;
7. Naval architecture and marine engineering: 97 percent male;
8. Mechanical engineering: 90 percent male;
9. Metallurgical engineering: 83 percent male; and
10. Mining and mineral engineering: 90 percent male.[4]

The ten least remunerative college majors, with counseling psychology being the least well compensated, are:

1. Counseling psychology: 74 percent female;
2. Early childhood education: 97 percent female;
3. Theology and religious vocations: 34 percent female;
4. Human services and community organization: 81 percent female;
5. Social work: 88 percent female;
6. Drama and theater arts: 60 percent female;
7. Studio arts: 66 percent female;
8. Communication disorders sciences and services: 94 percent female;
9. Visual and performing arts: 77 percent female; and
10. Health and medical preparatory programs: 55 percent female.[5]

Dangerous jobs such as power line installer, logger, and truck driver are held primarily by men, and they pay more because of the risk involved. Men suffer 92 percent of work-related deaths.[6]

Diana Furchtgott-Roth, of the Manhattan Institute, has reported—many times, as this seventy-seven cents figure is the Rasputin of statistics—that males who work full-time tend to put in forty-three hours a week, while females who work full-time average forty-one hours per week. If you compare childless women and men under the age of thirty, not only does the so-called wage gap disappear but women *outearn* men.[7]

When earnings for men and women over the age of thirty with the same education, skills, and job tenure are compared, the differential in wages reduces to between three and seven cents (depending on the study). The only explanation most mainstream commentators can imagine is "lingering discrimination." Well, that's possible. We all know of situations in which men are treated as more authoritative or competent simply because of their sex. But human interactions are complicated, and wage differentials may exist for reasons that can't be quantified. I've been struck by studies showing that women are less likely to ask for raises than men.[8]

We know testosterone boosts both self-confidence and risk taking. Perhaps men are more willing to take risks on the job, a choice that can have high rewards (along with unfortunate outcomes), while women choose to play it safe.

The National Organization for Women waves away these explanations, saying that women are still being "steered" into different training, career paths, and family roles.[9]

The data (as well as my own experience) suggest that this is just not true. The urge to care for children feels hardwired, though women and men don't express it in exactly the same way. Women, who bear and nurse babies, feel a more pressing need to be with them, to touch them, to guard their every moment. Men receive satisfaction in providing for their wives and children. They, too, have a profound desire to nurture, but fathering is different.

My husband was dutiful with babies, but his pleasure in children really kicked into high gear when they were walking and talking. Like most dads, he engaged with them in a more playful way than I did, throwing them in the air (which always made me nervous) and letting them climb on his back as he crawled on all fours. Social science research tells us that these typically paternal behaviors are important for children's brain development, especially for boys' ability to regulate their emotions later in life. In general, fathers stimulate more and mothers soothe more.[10]

I adore babies, and when I was out with mine, I noticed that women melted at the sight of them in a way men did not. Men (the nice ones, anyway) are solicitous of the mother, holding doors and giving up seats and so forth. But women want to see the baby's face, prop the child on a hip, or stroke the infant's soft cheek.

Motherhood Is Not Oppression

The *New York Times*'s Upshot column follows social trends, and in 2017 one of its headlines, "The Gender Pay Gap Is Largely Because of Motherhood," spoke to the effect of choices on long-term compensation. That's a step forward from the nonsense about "seventy-seven cents" on the dollar and "sexist assumptions" we've become accustomed to.

Claire Cain Miller, looking at data from the *American Economic Review* and the National Bureau of Economic Research, notes that young women and men just starting in their careers are "paid pretty much equally," but that "a gender gap soon appears, and it grows significantly over the next two decades." The reason seems to be that women cut back when they have children. "The *American Economic Review* paper, which examined people born around 1970, found that almost all of the pay gap for college graduates came from ages 26 to 33."[11]

Miller clearly finds this distressing. She quotes one researcher as saying, "On every possible front, women are getting the short end of the stick. Whether they're changing jobs or trying to stick with the current employer, the returns are always smaller."[12]

Nearly all mainstream treatment of these matters incorporates this assumption. If women make less money than men, or get fewer promotions, they are the losers. But viewing the world this way misses things. You cannot separate women's success from that of the men and children to whom they're attached. If a mother cuts back at work and is then able to help a son struggling with a learning disability or a daughter with a social crisis at school, isn't the whole family happier and healthier? And when a mom is there for her kids, they have a greater chance of growing up to be more competent and fulfilled adults, ready to step in and help out Mom and Dad when they are aged and in need of care. The family is a web of mutual aid. My husband's and sons' happiness is far more important to my own life satisfaction than the foregone earnings.

Women do face prejudice and discrimination on the grounds of sex, and that must be combated—it has been illegal since 1963— but our obsessive focus on discrimination as the only explanation for differing life paths misses a huge fact of life. Women have different priorities from men—and thank God, for the good of all, they do. Women are the world's primary caregivers, and not just children benefit. In the United States, an estimated 68 percent of caregivers for the elderly or disabled are women.[13] Across all income groups, races, and ages, women volunteers significantly outnumber men.[14]

The feminist narrative places an excessive focus on the burdens rather than the pleasures of femininity, devaluing the best parts of life—and dare I say, the most admirable aspects of our natures? When we care for others, we are expressing the least selfish, warmest aspects of our humanity. We love to see nurturing qualities in men—and many men excel at nurturing—so why not acknowledge that it's also an admirable trait in women?

As someone who certainly chose to prioritize my family over my career, I deny that I "lost" anything. I made trade-offs, as all adults must, but I am infinitely richer for making the decisions I made. I'm grateful that my husband worked as hard as he did to support us, and I also honor his contributions on the home front. Our children were given the gift of a secure upbringing that would not have been possible if my husband and I hadn't been there in our different ways. And we were fortunate to be able to afford to give them everything they needed, including my time. It grieves and worries me greatly that so many kids are being denied the stability and advantages we were able to give ours.

It is commonly asserted these days that two incomes are essential for a middle-class standard of living. But that notion is likely oversold. For many working- and middle-class families, the costs of child care eat up a big portion of a wife's salary. Add to that the costs of commuting, lunches out, work clothing, and other expenses, and many moms of modest incomes conclude that working is just not worth it.[15]

With a mother and father who both worked, I was raised to focus on career and self-actualization, yet I had always known my life would not be complete without children. What I didn't know until our three boys arrived was that the rest of my life would pale in comparison to motherhood. Women who devote a big part of their lives to caring for children are incredibly blessed. Countless mothers have told me the same thing. Watch their faces as they talk about their kids. A mother's love nourishes her children's souls, but also her own. No one asks for your autograph because you're a mom, and you don't get awards or money. Instead, you get the best life has to offer: deep connection, buoyant delight, and knowing you matter so much.

Susan Pinker, in her carefully researched book *The Sexual Paradox,* presents a mountain of data showing that women, on average, are drawn to people. This is reflected in their job and career choices, and in their willingness to spend time raising children.[16]

Men gravitate to jobs that are the highest paying, the most prestigious, and the most powerful. This isn't just because men are alphas; in many cases, they are thinking of their responsibilities as family providers. They are also drawn to mechanical, physical, and technical tasks. Women are more interested in working with people, making a difference as they see it, and having flexible schedules.

Sylvia Ann Hewlett and Carolyn Buck Luce compared 2,443 women holding graduate or professional degrees with men holding identical credentials and found a marked difference in the life choices made by the sexes. One in three women with MBAs chose not to work full-time compared with only one in twenty men. Also, 38 percent of women had turned down a promotion or had deliberately taken a job with lower pay. Eighty-five percent of women said that working with people they respected, being able to "be themselves" at work, and flexible schedules were all more important than salary.[17]

Our opinion leaders fret endlessly that talented women are denied their place at the table. But consider another study, one that followed nearly 2,000 mathematically gifted adolescents over the course of twenty years. When the group reached adulthood, a majority of the men had gone into engineering, math, or computer science. A majority of these women had chosen medicine and other health professions.[18]

Women dominate in the helping professions. As women joined

the workforce in the 1950s, they didn't spread like a wave across all jobs equally. Rather, they gravitated to people-centered or care-centered fields. Veterinary medicine, for example, was never considered "women's work." In the 1960s, only 5 percent of veterinarians were women. But now 61 percent of veterinarians are women, and there is a shortage of large animal vets because most women vets prefer companion animal care. The care of large animals requires long trips to rural areas, and often overnight stays and travel at night. It's also messy.[19]

Today, 60 percent of pediatricians are women, as are 72 percent of psychologists; that compares with 1970, when only 20 percent of psychologists were women. Nursing has always been dominated by females, and remains so, but now, 57 percent of medical scientists are also women.[20]

You rarely see these statistics. Instead, we are invited to gnash our teeth and rend our garments because only 27 percent of chemists and physicists are women. But chemistry and physics do not hold the same appeal for women as medical science does. A talented woman engineer who quit her science job for elementary education told Susan Pinker, "When I started working in engineering I said to myself, 'I don't like this at all. So the electrical current goes from X to Y, from here to there. Who cares?' I was unhappy and didn't want to continue."[21]

The social scientist Patti Hausman, in a presentation at the National Academy of Engineering, answered the question of why more women don't pursue careers in engineering: "Because they don't want to. Wherever you go, you will find females far less likely than males to see what is so fascinating about ohms, carburetors, or quarks. Reinventing the curriculum will not make me more interested in learning how my dishwasher works."[22]

We can see why women are attracted to working with people and animals, but we don't know why women comprise almost 55 percent of financial managers, 59 percent of budget analysts, and 63 percent of insurance underwriters.[23] Perhaps women are drawn to these jobs because they value intellectually challenging work, flexible hours, and agreeable colleagues. Why is the patriarchy and sexism at work when women choose fields such as nursing or teaching, but society gets no credit for fairness when women dominate fields such as veterinary medicine, human resources management, pediatrics, or budget analysis? Maybe women are just following their wishes.

According to British sociologist Catherine Hakim, countries where women (and men) are under economic stress have less sex segregation in job fields than countries where people are freer to choose. China has the lowest level of sexual disparities in employment. Still, we don't envy their situation. Canada, the United Kingdom, Germany, Switzerland, Norway, the United States, and Japan have more gender disparity in careers than Swaziland and Sri Lanka. Clearly more wealth permits more choice, and when women are free to choose the fields they like best, they rarely go for the biggest bucks.[24]

Economists Matthew Wiswall of Arizona State University and Basit Zafar of the New York Federal Reserve, studying the occupational preferences of undergraduate students, found—surprise!—that women valued job security more than opportunities for advancement. It was the opposite for men. Women also expressed a strong desire for flexibility, and a study by the Obama Department of Labor found that women value "family-friendly" workplaces, flexibility, and job security above the opportunity for greater financial returns.[25]

Women students at Yale Law School publish an annual list of the ten most family-friendly law firms. Sheryl Sandberg expressed concern about this focus (though not specifically about the Yale students) arguing that women should not "leave before you leave," forgoing advancement opportunities.[26] She may be right about that. But this list, made in consultation with women lawyers around the country, tells us that women at America's top law schools, who can write their own tickets, professionally speaking, *want* to plan career pauses and other accommodations to family life.

The most affluent women, those with the best options, are more likely than working-class women to define their ideal work situation as one offering part-time or no work when their children are young. Since 1997, the Pew Research Center has been posing the following question: "Considering everything, what would be the ideal situation for you—working full-time, working part-time, or not working at all outside the home?" In 2007, half of women with at least one child under eighteen at home said part-time work would be ideal. In 2012, the percentage dropped to 47 percent, probably reflecting the sluggish economy.[27] Women at the lower end of the income scale were more likely (40 percent) to say that full-time work would be ideal than were women whose family income was above $50,000. Among more affluent women, only 25 percent said they would prefer full-time work. Sixty-seven percent of all mothers said their ideal work situation would be part-time or no work at all. Among married mothers (who tend to have higher gross incomes), the figure was *76 percent.*[28]

A 2013 CBS/*New York Times* survey asked, "If money were no object, and you were free to do whatever you wanted, would you stay at home, work part-time, or work full-time?" Among women with children under eighteen years old, only 27 percent said, "work full-time." Forty-nine percent would prefer part-time work, and 22 percent would prefer no work outside the home. Among men with children under eighteen, 52 percent said they would work full-time even if money were no object, and 30 percent said they'd work part-time. Only 16 percent said they would stay at home.[29]

The press makes a fuss over any study or survey that suggests family roles are changing. In 2013, headlines said that women were now the "breadwinners" in 40 percent of families.[30] But in reality, the percentage of wives earning more than their husbands was only 22.5 percent. The 40 percent figure included all mothers who were not just the primary but also the sole breadwinners in their homes—in other words, all the single moms.[31] Among married couples, the traditional arrangement still holds. Only 7 percent of fathers with children in the home were stay-at-home dads, and 56 percent of them said illness or disability was the reason. Twenty-one percent said they chose to care for home and kids.[32] I celebrate the expansion of choices for men and women, but feminists and other revolutionaries are pushing a boulder uphill if they expect to flip the script entirely.

Social Engineers Strike Out

Feminists and progressives often glorify Europe, and particularly the Nordic countries, as models of egalitarian families and workplaces. Sen. Bernie Sanders often points to Scandinavia as a model for the United States to emulate. Yet on closer examination, even Scandinavian men and women seem resistant to social engineering.

Noting that women were doing the lion's share of child rearing, Norway, Denmark, and Sweden introduced paid paternal leave in the 1970s and '80s. But few fathers took advantage of it. Accordingly, in 1993, Norway introduced a use-it-or-lose-it, nontransferable father's leave of four weeks. Since then, paid paternal leave has been increased several times. The use-it-or-lose-it feature appears to have affected men's take-up of parental leave, which rose from 1 percent of parental leave days in 1993 to 17.8 percent in 2011. Yet a 2010 poll suggested that paid parental leave (unlike maternal leave) lacked public support. A majority of respondents (68 percent) wanted the quota abolished and only one-third supported it.

In 1980, Sweden introduced paid parental leave of eight months for mothers and fathers, for a total of sixteen months per child. Yet mothers and fathers continued to make different choices. In 2008, Swedish mothers were taking 78 percent of leave days, fathers only 22 percent. Clearly frustrated at the recalcitrant fathers, the Swedish government introduced a "gender equality bonus." Couples who shared parental leave equally got the equivalent of $1,900 from the state—basically a bribe to share parenting tasks. Sveriges

Radio, in Sweden, reported that "A year and a half after the bonus was introduced, the verdict—according to a review made by the Swedish Social Insurance Agency—is clear. The bonus has not helped at all."[33]

Good progressives throughout the developed world labor under the same feminist assumptions. The only reason they can imagine for women doing more child care than men is benighted, prefeminist thinking. "I believe in carrots," explained Sweden's then–prime minister Fredrik Reinfeldt, about the gender equality bonus. Opposition leader Mona Sahlin retorted, "It seems that no one really wants to eat these particular carrots, because hardly any have applied for them."[34]

Perhaps the Scandinavians are too backward.

What if we could design a study in which women and men were completely equal; all stereotypes about "women's work" and "men's work" were obliterated; and children were cared for communally? Of course, people are not lab rats, so we can't design such a study. But starting in the early twentieth century, some Jewish settlers in Palestine, later Israel, joined a kibbutz movement of collective farms. These European refugees were committed, as one study described it, to founding "a new type of human being, motivated by communal commitment and uncontaminated by private greed." There, men and women would "do the same work and have the same privileges and obligations."[35] Men would do the same amount of housework as women. Meals would be served communally in a canteen, with everyone sharing the preparation and cleanup. There would be no sex distinctions in tasks. Children would be raised in dormitories.

I remember kibbutz posters in my Hebrew school class in the 1960s. They showed smiling, suntanned women driving tractors and fit young men atop ladders harvesting oranges. We were told that in the evenings, they all participated in folk dances around campfires. Before it all went wrong, several hundred thousand Israelis (about 5 percent of the total population) lived on kibbutzim. It wasn't *all* wrong, of course. Israeli dancing was real. (And a good thing too, in my judgment. My family has heard my views on the benefits of communal dancing for mental health. But I digress.)

Many of the founders of these settlements had escaped night-marish situations in Europe. They overcame difficult terrain, hostile neighbors, and extreme poverty to inaugurate their experiments in socialism. They were idealists. And the kibbutz movement, unlike other socialist ventures, say, in the USSR and China, had no coercive elements. It was voluntary—except, of course, for the children.

One big flaw of kibbutz life was a sense of unfairness. Industrious people eventually resented that shirkers got the same compensation as they did, and productivity lagged when compared with Israel's conventional farms. The lack of privacy also grated. Most of all, though, kibbutzniks, *especially women,* detested the communal child rearing. In most kibbutzim, parents were allowed to spend the late afternoon and early evening hours with their own children. Then they were required to deposit them in the communal dormitories for the night.

The designers of kibbutz life believed this would create a better world. But as Noam Shpancer recalled of his childhood years later, the results were cold, even borderline cruel. "Woken in the middle of the night with a piercing toothache," Shpancer wrote in the *Guardian,* "I stumble out of my room . . . [and] stand in front of the intercom . . . and I call for help: 'Night guard, night guard, please come over.' If this sounds like the memory of a child in an institution, it is in a way. I was a kibbutz child."[36]

Life was good in some respects. Though they had very few toys or other possessions, the kibbutz children were safe, well nourished, and they had each other. But the separation from their parents was painful: "A friend of mine, I found out years later," Shpancer wrote, "used to wake up every night and sneak out the window to go to his parents' room. Every night he would knock on his parents' door and beg to be let in. Every night they would take him back to the children's house. After repeated episodes, the kibbutz's solution was to move his parents to a room farther away."[37] Later, Shpancer learned that another friend, a girl a few years older than him, had been sexually molested by one of the men in charge of the children.

When Lionel Tiger and Joseph Shepher studied the kibbutzim between forty and fifty years after many had gotten started, they discovered that attempts to alter sexual roles had largely failed. Women gravitated to child care and home responsibilities, and men to heavier work and political roles. Tiger and Shepher noted that the women, above all, agitated against the communal child rearing. In this, the researchers concluded, the women acted "against the wishes of the men of their communities, against the principles of their socialization and ideology, against the economic interest of the kibbutzim, in order to be able to devote more time and energy to private maternal activities."[38]

If you ask me, each mother's stomach was in knots at night, wondering if her child was calling pitifully for the "night guard." Eventually, all 240 of the kibbutz settlements abandoned communal child rearing.[39]

Women want to mother their children. They aren't forced to do this by the patriarchy or oppression or false consciousness. They are drawn to it by something much stronger: their own instincts.

The Mommy Track

Efforts to compensate women for the perceived injustice imposed by child care have sometimes backfired. Steven Rhoads, of the University of Virginia, studied behaviors of academics who took time off ostensibly to care for children. "[F]athers on the tenure track," he wrote, "did less infant/toddler care than mothers on the tenure track, even if the men took parental leave after the child's birth and the women did not. Moreover, when new parents were asked who did more when it came to 25 specific infant and toddler care tasks, on average, the spouses of the male professors did all 25 more often, while the female professors did all 25 more often than their spouses."[40]

Some universities stopped the "tenure clock" for professors as a way of not penalizing women who took time off to care for children. But an Institute of Labor Economics study found that these policies actually benefited men. Women who took family leave actually cared for family members. Men who took family leave often used the freedom from teaching responsibilities to do research. A common saying among academics is, "When a woman takes parental leave, she returns with a backlog. When a man takes parental leave, he returns with a book." The ILE study found that gender-neutral parental leave policies led to a nineteen-point increase in the chances a man would get tenure, and a 22 percent drop in a woman's chances.[41]

The Atlantic magazine's informal survey of Northwestern University students who graduated in 1993 two decades later found that 25 percent of the women were staying home to raise children. "I went to a job interview after my first daughter was born and cried the whole way home," ran a typical account.[42]

So if women are drawn to caregiving, especially of their own children, aren't they suffering? Pew Research asked people how happy they were with the trade-offs they'd made between paid work and family time. Married mothers who had made "sacrifices" for their family were the happiest with their decisions.[43] The General Social Survey asked, "On the whole, how satisfied are you with the work you do?" Forty-four percent of those in paid employment reported being very satisfied. Fifty-seven percent of homemakers said they were very satisfied.[44]

Feminists disdain the opt-out narrative—the *Columbia Journalism Review,* for example, called it a "myth," and *Salon* dismissed it as a fad among privileged white women "who are likely to think something entirely different in 10 years."[45]

Returning to work after raising children can be challenging. We have the luxury of long lives today, and even women who have large families will likely have years, even decades, after the kids are launched to fill with some other activity. Sylvia Ann Hewlett, an economist who heads the Center for Talent Innovation, surveyed thousands of women in 2004 and 2009. She found that some women who attempt to reenter the workforce after taking career pauses have difficulty, though her data coincided with a financial crisis, so it's hard to know how much of the effect was attributable to a poor economy. Among the women Hewlett surveyed, 89 percent attempted to return to work, but only 73 percent were successful—at least as of the time of the surveys.[46]

But so much of this attention to the problems of well-off women feels misdirected. Whole libraries seem to have been filled with reflections on what staying home means for women—whether it causes their marriages to slide into prefeminist models, what the impact is on women's promotions and lifetime earnings, and how much trouble women can have transitioning back to work if they dropped out of the paid workforce completely.

Those are real challenges, but the trade-offs of well-educated women (and men) pale in comparison with the difficulties suffered by less well-educated middle-class and poor women who attempt to raise children on their own.

Forty-one percent of babies in America today are born to unmarried women who don't have choices about opting out of work. They either must work, and place their children in day care, or go on welfare. Many live with their baby's father at the time of the birth, but the average cohabiting partnership lasts about fourteen months and rarely leads to marriage.[47] Five years after having a baby, more than 66 percent of women who were unmarried at the time of the birth, and 50 percent of those who were in cohabiting relationships, were no longer linked with the child's father.[48] I experienced great joy raising children, but I cannot imagine coping as a single mother.

One great tragedy of feminism's triumph is how many women are now shouldering all the work of parenting on their own. If they are low-skilled or unskilled, most of what they earn goes to pay for essentials and day care. Their lives are incredibly difficult. They have limited time for the most enjoyable parts of parenthood, and in many cases, their children hardly stand a chance at escaping poverty.[49]

In *Lives on the Edge: Single Mothers and Their Children in the Other America,* Valerie Polakow profiled a number of women in these situations. Sara Thomas, who grew up with her grandmother and an aunt, described herself as never really having had a family. She got pregnant at seventeen, and her boyfriend told her he "didn't care." Her grandmother evicted her six weeks after the baby's birth, and she bounced around, working at odd jobs and permitting her boyfriend, a drug addict, to care for the baby while she was at work. By the time the baby, Des, was two years old, his father was in prison. Sara found a friend who agreed to watch the child for thirty-five dollars a week. She later learned the friend had neglected the baby, leaving him unattended for long stretches. Des began to display such severe behavior problems by age three that three day care centers rejected him. A concerned special education teacher eventually introduced some equilibrium into Des and Sara's life, but it remained incredibly fragile.[50]

The *Los Angeles Times* profiled twenty-seven-year-old Natalie Cole. She and her four children had moved nearly a dozen times in one year and lived on about a thousand dollars a month in public cash assistance and food stamps. Cole has diabetes and high blood pressure, and despite her attempts to instill good habits in her kids ("get an education"), her son has already been arrested for firing a BB gun into a car, and one of her daughters is failing in school.[51]

Any bump in the road (illness, an accident, becoming a crime victim) can begin a downward spiral for women and children in such vulnerable positions. Welfare, food stamps, Medicaid, and housing subsidies are called the "social safety net," and though they do keep people from complete destitution and hunger, they don't provide a decent life for anyone. These programs cannot help children feel safe in a sketchy neighborhood because Dad is home. They cannot offer Mom a respite when she is exhausted or her patience is wearing thin. They cannot sit at the kitchen table and discuss the children's academic or social problems. They cannot toss a football back and forth or model how a man respects his wife.

Poverty activists stress the importance of "affordable child care" for the poor and near-poor. In 2015, President Obama declared that "In today's economy, when having both parents in the workforce is an economic necessity for many families, we need affordable, high-quality childcare more than ever."[52]

I would support government-subsidized universal child care if it could help single mothers raise happy, secure, and healthy children. Sadly, universal day care can never be high quality across the board. Nor is it clear that we ought to subsidize one form of child care (nonparental) while offering nothing to parents who choose to care for their young children themselves.

The press tends to cheerlead studies that show no harm, or even some benefits, from day care while virtually burying contrary evidence. "Study Shows Consistent Benefit of Early Daycare," chirped a Reuters headline in 2010.[53] The story's first sentence betrayed the implicit agenda: "Parents worried about putting very young children into daycare got some reassuring answers . . . children who have high-quality care see academic benefits lasting into high school." Only further into the story do you learn that children who spent the most hours in day care showed greater impulsiveness and risk taking as fifteen-year-olds than those who had spent less time in care. Further, the study's good news was only about high-quality day care settings, and most of America's offerings fall below that level. A study of early child care published in 2006 by the National Institute of Child Health and Human Development found a majority of day care facilities to be fair or poor. Only 10 percent were found to be of high quality.[54]

The New Republic, while describing America's patchwork of day care as "Dickensian," nevertheless endorsed President Obama's proposal for universal pre-K, which they absurdly and optimistically estimated would cost $75 billion over ten years (theoretically financed entirely by cigarette taxes).[55]

High-quality day care can be good for kids, especially those from disadvantaged backgrounds. The problem is one of scale. A couple of preschool programs, such as the HighScope Perry Preschool Project in Michigan during the 1960s and the Carolina Abecedarian Project in the 1970s, are often cited as the gold standard. They were staffed by college graduates and well funded. The children did have better life outcomes in terms of less crime, higher employment rates, and better health.[56] If such programs could be scaled up for the entire nation, or at least for all the disadvantaged children in the country, that would be a blessing. But how realistic is that? With twenty trillion dollars in national debt and strong resistance to increasing taxes on the middle class, it's hard to imagine that a program to spend billions more on subsidized preschool or day care would be politically viable. Nor can we be at all sure that the new programs would be anything close to the Perry Preschool or Abecedarian standard.

Even if there are no problems with a day care facility, sheer time apart from parents seems to matter. A federal study that followed many American children across decades, the Early Child Care Research Network, found worrying effects of long hours spent in day care, especially for very young children. Results published in 2010 found a "dose response" to the time spent in nonmaternal care. Even as late as high school, kids who had spent many hours in preschool day care were found to be more impulsive and likely to take risks. These effects were evident in kids from all backgrounds and income levels. The differences were significant enough, psychologist Jay Belsky said at the time, that they might have contagion effects by the time kids reached adolescence. "The dynamic becomes, 'I dare you to take a risk, you dare me to take a risk.' Nobody knows what the threshold here is, when a little becomes a lot."[57]

Though Belsky is skeptical about the heavy use of day care, he has also cautioned that some children do fine in nonparental care.

In his 2009 review of the literature, he stressed that family factors were more important than anything else. "It appears that what matters to a child most is the kind of family he comes from," he writes; "that is, whether the family is economically viable, parents are partnered, mother is not depressed, and her parenting is itself sensitive to the needs of the child. Knowing these things tells us more about a child's life prospects than does her child care experience."[58]

That said, there are aspects of parental care that we only dimly understand. For example, before doctors realized the importance of skin-to-skin contact between mothers and infants, premature babies were placed in warm incubators (some preemies still are).[59] But studies showed that for all but very unstable preterm infants, incubators were inferior to being held and cared for by their mothers with direct skin-to-skin contact.[60] The babies were better able to control their body temperatures, had better heart and breathing rates, reduction in crying, better nursing, and experienced many other benefits. Even ten years later, an Israeli study found, babies who'd had skin-to-skin contact with their mothers as infants had better cognitive development and more secure attachments to their mothers.[61]

Deciding how much time a baby or toddler should spend in nonparental care will of course be determined by many factors, but parents should not be misled about the trade-offs. For more than three decades, studies and surveys have shown increased aggression and disobedience among kids who experienced day care. The earlier a baby was placed, and the longer he spent in care, the more those traits were in evidence.

At day care centers, the pay is low and turnover is high. Trust is hard to develop when the minders are constantly departing. Caring for young children individually or in groups of two or three is engaging and enchanting. In numbers above that, it becomes crowd control. Mary Eberstadt described it this way: "[I]nfants being packed off to hospital style rows of cribs called 'school,' toddlers who go for institutionalized walks roped together like members of a miniature chain gang."[62]

Advocates insist that if day care were subsidized by the state, children would be given a great start. In 2017, Rep. Nancy Pelosi and Sen. Chuck Schumer introduced a plan to provide "comprehensive child care and early learning legislation that will ensure that every child has access to high-quality early learning and care that will not break the bank for their parents." Nancy Pelosi said, "We view this as children learning, parents earning."[63] (It might also be seen as a gift to the teachers' unions.)

Canada's recent experiment with exactly this kind of policy should serve as a warning. In 1997, the Canadian province of Quebec began offering day care for just five dollars a day to all children ages four and under. The number of families placing their young children in day care jumped by 33 percent, and many more young mothers joined the labor force. But despite best efforts, the quality of care was not great. A study published in the National Bureau of Economic Research in 2015 found that day care children showed a marked increase in anxiety and aggression, traits that did not abate with time. By contrast, some cognitive benefits of day care dissipated by the time the children reached elementary school. Teenagers who had been placed in care were less healthy and less satisfied with life in general than non–day care kids. Most strikingly, the researchers found "a sharp and contemporaneous increase in criminal behavior among the cohorts exposed to the Quebec program, relative to their peers in other provinces."[64]

Time in day care is also associated with increased levels of cortisol, the "fight-or-flight" hormone. In small doses, cortisol keeps us alert. In emergencies, it can save our lives. But when children are subject to prolonged periods of elevated cortisol, it can have lifelong negative effects on learning, behavior, and mental health.[65]

In the Quebec study, boys and girls experienced the stress of day care differently. Boys were more likely to show increased hyperactivity and inattention, while girls showed more emotional distress and separation anxiety.[66]

A pre-K program aimed at disadvantaged four-year-olds in Tennessee produced similarly disappointing results. Three thousand low-income children were randomly divided into experimental and control groups and then followed for several years. The children enrolled in pre-K seemed to benefit at first. In kindergarten, they scored better on literacy and other skills. But the control group kids caught up within a year. By third grade, there was a crossover. The pre-K children actually fell behind those who had not attended.[67] The results were worrying enough that one of the study's authors cautioned against the national rush to implement universal preschool. "You have school systems that are pushing pre-K when they have demonstrably failing K-12 systems," Dale Farran, one of the study's authors, told FiveThirtyEight. "It makes me cringe."[68]

Another aspect of the parent/child bond that we sense intuitively has recently been studied scientifically. As a parent, you can feel when you are challenging or delighting a child—even a baby. A recent study featured in the Proceedings of the National Academy of Scientists found that when parents and babies gaze into each other's eyes, their brain waves align. The researchers confirmed this by fitting the adults and babies with EEG caps. This synchronization of brain waves is also found in successful high school students who are cooperating with peers, and when two adults reach an understanding. Does it harm a baby if no one is locking eyes with him? Who knows, but it seems that staring into a baby's eyes may be one of hundreds of interactions that are important to development.[69]

Of course, if a mother is a drug addict, an alcoholic, depressed, incompetent, or cruel, center-based care might be superior to a mother's care. Seeing parents abuse or neglect their children is heartbreaking. You can make a strong case for removing some children from their parents. That said, the overwhelming majority of mothers and fathers love and adore their children. Let's start there. How can we encourage a culture and government policies that play to those strengths, rather than swimming upstream against them?

Day care is at its best when it is staffed by people living out their natural attraction to babies and toddlers. However, they are giving care and affection to other people's children, not their own. Perhaps if the human race were something other than what it is, we could love all children as much as we love our own. But that is counterfactual, and not a good foundation for social policy.

A day is packed with hundreds or thousands of subtle interactions between mothers and children. In aggregate, they amount to character formation. How do you instill manners? How do you respond to sibling rivalry—overdo it, and you can stoke real hatred between siblings; underdo it, and you are permitting abuse. Being a parent sometimes requires walking a psychological tightrope. How much do you help a child deal with frustration? How do you teach a child to delay gratification? How do you teach honesty, self-reliance, persistence, and kindness?

Nonmaternal care can be safe and dull, but it usually lacks the kind of engagement a parent brings. A stay-at-home mother I know was the product of day care herself. She remembers crying every day when her mother dropped her off. She is now adamant about raising her own kids and notes that the millennial generation is the most anxious in history—and perhaps it's no accident that it is also the first generation to have spent so much time in day care.

My friend learned through experience, as I did, that being a stay-at-home mom doesn't necessarily mean being a stuck-at-home mom. She enrolls in "mommy and me" classes, and swimming, and takes her children to the park daily. Most of the other kids are in the care of nannies "who are always on their phones." She is in more or less constant conversation with her three-year-old, while her younger child plays in the dirt. "The nannies never let the kids get dirty," she observed, "because they don't want the extra work of cleaning them up before the parents get home."

I have another friend who was raised by divorced parents. Unlike me, she had little interest in children or even in marriage. As a teenager, she had mused about getting sterilized when she reached adulthood. But her entire world was turned upside down by marriage, which for her had a spiritual dimension. After the birth of her first daughter, motherhood was too all-encompassing for description. "Once I gave myself permission to love," she confided, the effect was transformational. "We don't know what is good for us," she concluded. "If I had followed my youthful plan—had my tubes tied, abstained from marriage—I would have denied myself the greatest sources of joy in my life. This culture has denatured women." Yes, and shortchanged children.

Children are little conservatives—they like their routines to be steady and unvarying, their teddy bears to be always within reach, and their mothers to be ready with a hug and a Band-Aid to assure them they can weather life's mishaps. If a toddler were asked which he preferred, a well-lit day care center with a dozen other toddlers or being at home with his family (usually his mother), it's not hard to guess which he would choose.

Yet the feminist movement has spent the better part of the last six decades attempting to squelch the greatest source of love and succor that is to be had in this life. Feminists have erected barricades at the nursery door, shooing mothers away from their babies in the name of "empowerment." Maybe power isn't the highest good to strive for?

Being able to bask in your mother's love ought not be a privilege reserved for the upper classes. Anything we can do to revive marriage among all Americans should be an urgent priority. As we know from the choices of affluent women, mothers enjoy raising kids. Providing more opportunities for all mothers to spend more time with their own infants and toddlers would not require a huge new government program or a tax increase. Instead, it would require a cultural shift, a move back toward marriage being the norm.

Human Flourishing

In his important book *Our Kids,* Robert D. Putnam offers compelling evidence about the "parenting gap" that has emerged in America. In the Ohio of his youth, pretty much everyone came from intact families, class differences were more muted, and upward mobility was taken for granted. Today, children from intact families, even at the lower end of the socioeconomic scale, are still thriving, while kids who are raised in chaotic and fragile families are often handicapped for life.

Putnam proposes increasing the earned-income tax credit, boosting the child tax credit, and providing "wraparound" family services. He recommends home visits by social workers to help single mothers learn best practices such as reading to their children every day.

While some of those seem to be good ideas, others may not be achievable. As someone who worries a lot about children in fragile families, I see the word *wraparound* as conjuring great embracing arms to support vulnerable mothers. I picture social workers showing up three times a week to help with nutrition, discipline advice, suggestions for staying out of debt, medical information, and other aids.

But I'm skeptical that government can accomplish any of those goals. Since the 1960s, Great Society programs have failed signally at their goal of eliminating poverty. We've seen that government is remarkably ineffective. The federal government is particularly feeble at encouraging people to do positive things for themselves. Any number of left-leaning sociologists and other social scientists have pointed to the failure of the Healthy Marriage Initiative, funded by the George W. Bush administration, as proof that encouraging marriage is fruitless. It's funny that the marriage effort is the only government program most liberals cite as a failure. I can agree that the results are poor, but they don't surprise me, because attempting to do good through government frequently backfires.

When the government does such a terrible job at providing health care (the Medicaid program is awful), education (public schools in poor neighborhoods are execrable), and housing (Section 8 housing is often miserable), why would we think that government could competently help single women raise their children?

Moreover, when the government steps in to provide services and supports for people, it denies others the role that brings self-respect, dignity, and meaning to their lives. I'm torn whenever I hear a call to "do more" for single mothers. There is no question that they are in great need, but if government steps into the breach, doesn't it make it that much less urgent for the fathers of those children to step up?

Yet to say that government is better at creating problems than at solving them is not the same thing as throwing up our hands. We need to experiment with different approaches to changing behavior. And the best way to start is through civil society: churches, synagogues, charities, nonprofits, foundations, think tanks, schools, and clubs. These independent actors can work in a hundred different ways to support single parents, teach them parenting techniques, get them skills training or education, and provide play groups for kids. When government makes a mistake, or does something that turns out to be counterproductive, it is extremely difficult to reverse course. Accountability is negligible. Results are not measured, and constituencies build up for existing programs. As Ronald Reagan once quipped, "Government programs, once launched, never disappear. Actually, a government bureau is the closest thing to eternal life we'll ever see on this earth!"[70] Private philanthropies can be far more creative, flexible, and responsive to results.

Even more crucial than providing assistance to existing single parents is discouraging the establishment of more. Not all disturbing trends continue forever. Within just the past few decades, the divorce rate skyrocketed, reaching a peak in 1980, but then slowed and declined. The rate of unwed childbearing, after spiking for a number of decades, peaked in 2008 and has been drifting down since then.[71] The best thing we can do for our kids and our future is to accelerate this trend if we possibly can.

Private philanthropies are already addressing this challenge. The Philanthropy Roundtable recently inaugurated the Culture of Freedom Initiative, a privately funded cross-country partnership designed to strengthen families. As Heather Wilhelm reported for *Philanthropy* magazine, "Live the Life spearheaded a community marriage initiative in Leon County, Florida, which harnessed the resources of 85 churches, the county commission, the chief of police, and school-board officials. . . . By 2015, the divorce rate in Leon County had dropped 48 percent, more than double the drop in the divorce rate across the rest of the state."[72]

Other efforts will focus on teaching everyone the "success sequence" that well-off families instill in their children: get an education, get married, and then have babies, in that order.[73] We know that children from low-income families do well if their parents are married.[74] As Isabell Sawhill and Ron Haskins of the Brookings Institution reported when they studied Census Bureau records, "If young people finish high school, get a job, and get married before they have children, they have about a 2 percent chance of falling into poverty and nearly a 75 percent chance of joining the middle class."[75]

Efforts such as the Culture of Freedom Initiative are necessary, but they're far from sufficient. The key ingredient for reviving the ethic of marriage is culture. To quote Charles Murray's pithy summation, we need to have elites "preach what they practice." When pop singers, journalists, actors, comedians, and television writers line up to support something, it's rocket fuel. When MADD (Mothers Against Drunk Driving) set out to change social attitudes in 1980, twenty-five thousand people were being killed in drunk driving accidents annually. Driving drunk was so utterly commonplace and winked at that comedians joked about it. There was no such thing as a "designated driver." MADD lobbied to change laws, but more important, it changed mores. It stigmatized driving drunk, and fatalities have dropped by 50 percent.[76]

While liberal social scientists such as Isabel Sawhill of the Brookings Institution and Robert Putnam sound the alarm about unwed parenting and the price children are paying, other public intellectuals of the left resolutely refuse to lend their names to anything that can be labeled "marriage promotion." Feminist Amanda Marcotte, for example, has mocked what she calls the "panic" over single motherhood. *Slate* magazine ran a Mother's Day piece by Marcotte in 2016 rebuking society for stigmatizing single mothers.[77]

Rachel Lehmann-Haupt, who became what she calls a "DIY mom" at age forty, when her biological clock was ticking down, advised that "Our choice can also offer some critical lessons for the ways that politicians, policymakers, and the greater community can support all kinds of single mothers, who are continuously shamed and stigmatized."[78]

When NPR's *Talk of the Nation* aired a segment about the struggles of single parents, sociology professor Philip Cohen of the University of Maryland acknowledged that married parents convey many benefits to children, including "security, health insurance, and stable housing." Still, he demurred when asked whether marriage should be encouraged. Instead, he said we should learn how to deliver these desirable goods to children "without worrying about the marital status of the parents."[79] He claimed that staying single was actually a boon to women: "One of the things we should be glad about in the decline of marriage is that there are fewer people who are forced into marriage or compelled into marriage because of economic distress, especially women. So, women's increased earning potential and opportunities have opened up a lot of doors, including not to be married."[80]

This is fantasy, and it's time to move past it. Barack Obama showed the way. Unaccustomed as I am to praising our forty-fourth president, I do think that in this realm he struck the right note, though just a little too infrequently. In 2008, on Father's Day, Obama reflected on the situation of single mothers: "We need to help all the mothers out there who are raising these kids by themselves; the mothers who drop them off at school, go to work, pick them up in the afternoon, work another shift, get dinner, make lunches, pay the bills, fix the house, and all the other things it takes both parents to do. So many of these women are doing a heroic job, but they need support. They need another parent. Their children need another parent. That's what keeps their foundation strong. It's what keeps the foundation of our country strong."

He said, "They need another parent." He didn't say they needed "wraparound" social services, though doubtless he suggested that at other times. He said they needed *fathers*. "I know what it means to have an absent father," he said, and continued: "So I resolved many years ago that it was my obligation to break the cycle, that if I could be anything in life, I would be a good father to my girls; that if I could give them anything, I would give them that rock, that foundation, on which to build their lives. And that would be the greatest gift I could offer."[81]

In 2013, he delivered the same message in a commencement address at Morehouse College, telling young male graduates to "Keep setting an example for what it means to be a man. Be the best husband to your wife, or your boyfriend, or your partner. Be the best father you can be to your children. Because nothing is more important." He praised his "heroic" single mom and his "wonderful" grandparents, but added that "I sure wish I had had a father who was not only present, but involved."[82]

This is the message every young person should be hearing— from presidents, entertainers, teachers, movies, and every other outlet of popular culture. The family is key to everything. It is also the message young men should be hearing from young women with whom they become romantically involved. Far from imagining that they can manage everything on their own, women should convey to these young men that marriage and commitment are important to them and their future children. Women should know that little boys who grow up with their dads are unlikely to get into trouble with the law or drop out of school. They should remember that little girls who live with their fathers feel valued. Girls who grow up with fathers don't feel the need, in adolescence, to go searching for love from random guys. And young adults should know that men who marry become more responsible citizens, earn more money, and live longer than those who remain single.

President Obama didn't say it, but I will: acknowledging the importance of fathers, and of families, is part of reconciling ourselves to life's realities and shedding the feminist illusions we've cultivated for decades. Much of the feminist project of the past half century, with its denial of sex differences and its insistence on stamping out sex roles, was misbegotten. Humans are not "assigned" sexes; we are male and female. Our differences are complementary, not superior or inferior. Decades of war between the sexes have led not to greater happiness but to unspooling ledgers of casualties.

Sexual "liberation" was a fraud that did a disservice to the best instincts of men and the best interests of women. Children are not a burden to be managed but a treasure to be cherished. Any step that reconnects us to lifelong love, commitment, and tenderness will make us personally happier and will move society closer to the ideals we all prize: liberty, equal opportunity, and human flourishing.

Instead of fighting nature, let's be comforted by its contours. The best and most important sources of identity, meaning, and joy, for men and women, are to be found not in the world of work but in our homes and families. If we get that right, the rest will largely take care of itself.

ACKNOWLEDGMENTS

I am deeply grateful to the Ethics and Public Policy Center for being my professional home. I could not ask for more congenial or inspiring colleagues. In particular, I'm indebted to Ed Whelan, president of the EPPC, for suggesting this book's title, and to Sarah Shanoudy and Mark Shanoudy for helping me to navigate the Word labyrinth. (How I miss WordPerfect.)

Jeanne Massey, my research assistant, was tireless in tracking down quotations and half-remembered citations. She lived and breathed this project almost as much as the author. I also had the most prestigious *unofficial* research assistant in the world—retired Harvard professor Stephan Thernstrom, who very kindly pointed me to relevant academic materials.

Daniel E. Troy, Betsy Hart, and Meghan Gurdon read the manuscript and offered extremely helpful comments. Meghan is a beautiful writer and while my prose will never sing as hers does, her wand passing over my words improved them immeasurably. If any adverbs remain in the text, it is not for lack of scolding on Meghan's part (for which I bless her).

I am indebted to my editor, Mary Reynics, who believed in this book from the start and guided it to completion, and to my sub-editor, Henry Ferris Jr., whose organizational sense helped me to produce a more taut final product than would have been possible without his keen eye and good judgment. I also cherish the encouragement of my friend and podcasting partner Jay Nordlinger, a great writer and a great soul.

Lauren Stewart generously made arrangements for a number of student interviews, as did Caitlin La Ruffa. Professor Robert P. George, Matthew Franck, and the Witherspoon Institute were kind enough to host me when I visited Princeton. I also want to thank the students and other young adults there and elsewhere who took the time to talk with me about intimate matters.

I'm grateful to my agent, Glen Hartley, for his advice and unfailing support.

My husband, Robert, and sons, Jonathan, David, and Benjamin, offered suggestions and feedback on the text (especially Ben), but those are not the main reasons I'm mentioning them. They are the inspiration for this book—the source of my deepest joys.

Arlington, Virginia
January 2018

NOTES

Introduction: At What Price?

1. Peter Wehrwein, "Astounding Increase in Antidepressant Use by Americans," *Harvard Health* (blog), Harvard Medical School, Oct. 20, 2011, health.harvard.edu/blog/astounding-increase-in -antidepressant-use-by-americans-201110203624.

2. Mark J. Perry, "'Equal Pay Day' This Year Is April 14: The Next 'Equal Occupational Fatality Day' Will Be on July 29, 2027," *AEIdeas* (blog), April 13, 2015, aei.org/publication/equal-pay-day -this-year-is-april-14-the-next-equal-occupational-fatality-day-will -occur-on-july-29-2027/.

3. "Female High School Football Player in Texas a Game-Changer," CBS News, Sept. 21, 2015, cbsnews.com/news/female-high-school -football-player-in-texas-a-game-changer/.

4. "Boy Allowed to Run for Homecoming Queen After High School Initially Denies Request," WFTV9-ABC, Sept. 21, 2016, wftv .com/news/local/boy-allowed-to-run-for-homecoming-queen-after -high-school-initially-denies-request/448149927.

5. Paul Bedard, "Poll: Women Reject 'Feminist' Label, Call Them 'Too Extreme,' Anti-Men," *Washington Secrets* (blog), *Washington Examiner,* Feb. 24, 2016, washingtonexaminer.com/poll -women-reject-feminist-label-call-them-too-extreme-anti-men /article/2584010.

6. Sarah Kliff, "Only 18 Percent of Americans Consider Themselves Feminists," *Vox,* April 8, 2015, vox.com/2015/4/8/8372417/feminist -gender-equality-poll.

7. "Fraction of Bachelor's Degrees Earned by Women, by Major,

1965–2015" (graph), aps.org/programs/education/statistics/women majors.cfm.

8. W. Bradford Wilcox and Wendy Wang, "The Millennial Success Sequence," AEI and Institute for Family Studies, June 14, 2017, aei .org/publication/millennials-and-the-success-sequence-how-do -education-work-and-marriage-affect-poverty-and-financial-success -among-millennials/.

9. Skye Loyd, "Why Kids Need Their Dads," *Parenting,* parenting .com/article/why-kids-need-their-dads.

10. Bradford W. Wilcox and Kathleen Kovner Kline, *Gender and Parenthood* (New York: Columbia University Press, 2013), 226.

11. Ibid., 227.

Chapter 1: The Feminist Mistake

1. Tara Bahrampour, "'There really isn't anything magical about it.' Why More Millennials Are Avoiding Sex," *Washington Post,* Aug. 2, 2016.

2. Brian Alseth, "Sexting and the Law—Press Send to Turn Teenagers into Registered Sex Offenders," ACLU-Washington, Sept. 24, 2010, aclu-wa.org/blog/sexting-and-law-press-send-turn-teenagers -registered-sex-offenders.

3. Stephanie Hanes, "Singles Nation: Why So Many Americans Are Unmarried," *Christian Science Monitor,* June 14, 2015, csmonitor .com/USA/Society/2015/0614/Singles-nation-Why-so-many -Americans-are-unmarried.

4. Kate Bolick, "All the Single Ladies," *The Atlantic,* Nov. 2011.

5. Mary Wollstonecraft, *A Vindication of the Rights of Women* (1792), Ch. 8, bartleby.com/144/8.html, 103.

6. John Stuart Mill, "The Subjugation of Women," 1869, early moderntexts.com/assets/pdfs/mill1869.pdf.

7. Ibid., 41.

8. Ibid., 42.

9. Ibid., 44.

10. Christina Hoff Sommers, *Freedom Feminism: Its Surprising History and Why It Matters Today* (Washington, DC: AEI Press, 2013), 20.

11. Ibid., 28.

12. Betty Friedan, *The Feminine Mystique* (New York: W. W. Norton, 1963), 461.

13. Gloria Steinem, "After Black Power, Women's Liberation," *New York* magazine, April 4, 1969.

14. Abigail and Stephan Thernstrom, *America in Black and White: One Nation, Indivisible* (New York: Simon and Schuster, 1997), 44.

15. Ibid., 45.

16. Steinem, "After Black Power, Women's Liberation."

17. Ibid.

18. Sara Davidson, "An 'Oppressed Majority' Demands Its Rights," *Life,* Dec. 12, 1969.

19. Quoted in Christine Stolba, *Lying in a Room of One's Own* (Arlington, VA: Independent Women's Forum, 2002), 16.

20. James D. Lutz, "Lest We Forget: A Short History of Housing in the United States," Lawrence Berkeley National Laboratory, aceee .org/files/proceedings/2004/data/papers/SS04_Panel1_Paper17 .pdf.

21. "In the Wealthiest Nation on Earth, 1.6 Million Americans Do Not Have Indoor Plumbing: The Map That Shows Where," *Daily Mail,* April 23, 2014, dailymail.co.uk/news/article-2611602/In -wealthiest-nation-Earth-1-6-million-Americans-dont-indoor -plumbing.html.

22. David Kennedy, *Freedom from Fear: The American People in Depression and War, 1929–1945* (New York: Oxford University Press, 1999), 165.

23. "Rosie the Riveter: 1941–1945," *The Pop History Dig,* pophistory dig.com/topics/rosie-the-riveter-1941-1945/.

24. Ibid.

25. Ibid.

26. Louis Menand, "Books as Bombs," *The New Yorker,* Jan. 24, 2011, newyorker.com/magazine/2011/01/24/books-as-bombs.

27. Ibid.

28. Friedan, *The Feminine Mystique,* 1.

29. Menand, "Books as Bombs."

30. Judith Hennessee, *Betty Friedan: Her Life* (New York: Random House, 1999), 47.

31. Ibid., 64.

32. Ibid., 93.

33. Ibid., 74.

34. Ibid., 8.

35. Friedan, *The Feminine Mystique,* 75.

36. Ibid., 231.

37. E. Fuller Torrey, *Freudian Fraud: The Malignant Effect of Freud's Theory on American Thought and Culture* (New York: HarperCollins, 1992), 128.

38. Lionel Trilling, *The Liberal Imagination* (New York: NYRB Classics, 2008), 226.

39. Friedan, *The Feminine Mystique,* 19.

40. Ibid., 301.

41. Ibid., 37.

42. Joanne Meyerowitz, "Beyond the Feminine Mystique: A Reassessment of Postwar Mass Culture," *Journal of American History* 79, no. 4 (March 1993).

43. Ibid.

44. Ibid.

45. Ibid.

46. Ibid.

47. Quoted in Ashley Fetters, "Four Big Problems with the Feminine Mystique," *The Atlantic,* Feb. 12, 2013.

48. "Percentage of the U.S. Population Who Have Completed Four Years of College or More, from 1940 to 2016, by Gender," Statista: The Statistics Portal, statista.com/statistics/184272/educational -attainment-of-college-diploma-or-higher-by-gender/.

49. Hennessee, *Betty Friedan: Her Life,* 130.

50. Alan Wolfe, "The Mystique of Betty Friedan," *The Atlantic,* Sept. 1999.

51. George Dvorsky, "Why Freud Still Matters, When He Was Wrong About Almost Everything," Aug. 7, 2013, *io9* (blog), Gizmodo, io9 .gizmodo.com/why-freud-still-matters-when-he-was-wrong-about -almost-1055800815.

52. Ibid.

53. Ibid.

54. Frank Newport, "Americans Greatly Overestimate Percent Gay, Lesbian in U.S.," Gallup News, May 21, 2015, news/gallup.com /poll/183383/americans-greatly-overestimate-percent-gay-lesbian .aspx.

55. Caleb Crain, "Alfred Kinsey: Liberator or Pervert?" *New York Times,* Oct. 3, 2004.

56. Dina Spector, "Why Kinsey's Research Remains Even More Controversial than the 'Masters of Sex,'" *Business Insider,* Oct. 18, 2013, businessinsider.com/why-alfred-kinsey-was-controversial-2013-10.

57. Friedan, *The Feminine Mystique,* 365.

58. Ibid., 367.

59. F. Carolyn Graglia, *Domestic Tranquility: A Brief Against Feminism* (Dallas: Spence Publishing, 1998), 118.

60. Daniel Bell, "The Great Back-to-Work Movement," *Fortune,* July 1956 (reprinted in the Sept. 16, 2012, issue).

61. Mitra Toossi, "A Century of Change: The U.S. Labor Force, 1950–2050," *Labor Force Change, 1950–2050,* bls.gov/opub/mlr/2002/05 /art2full.pdf.

62. Theodore Caplow, Louis Hicks, and Ben J. Wattenberg, *The First Measured Century: An Illustrated Guide to Trends in America, 1900–2000* (Washington, DC: AEI Press, 2001), 41.

63. Daniel Walker Howe, *What God Hath Wrought: The Transformation of America, 1815–1848* (New York: Oxford University Press, 2007), 464.

64. Diana Furchtgott-Roth, *Women's Figures: An Illustrated Guide to the Economic Progress of Women in America* (Washington, DC: AEI Press, 2012), 85.

65. Caplow, Hicks, and Wattenberg, *The First Measured Century,* 53.

66. Bell, "The Great Back-to-Work Movement."

67. Daniel Bell, *The Coming of Post-Industrial Society: A Venture in Social Forecasting* (New York: Basic Books, 1973), 127.

68. Alan Petigny, *The Permissive Society: America, 1941–1965* (New York: Cambridge University Press, 2009), 137.

69. Ibid., 137.

70. Wendy Wang, "Mothers and Work: What's 'Ideal,'" Pew Research Center, Fact Tank, Aug. 13, 2013, pewresearch.org/fact-tank/2013 /08/19/mothers-and-work-whats-ideal/.

71. Quoted in Torrey, *Freudian Fraud,* 34.

72. Andrew Carroll, "Canadian Troops Sound Off About the Brits," HistoryNet, Dec. 1, 2010, historynet.com/canadian-troops-sound -off-about-the-brits.htm.

73. Petigny, *The Permissive Society,* 122.

74. David Allyn, *Make Love, Not War: The Sexual Revolution; An Unfettered History* (Boston: Little, Brown, 2000), 21.

75. Helen Gurley Brown, *Sex and the Single Girl* (New York: Bernard Geis Associates, 1962).

76. Nancy Traver, "Celebrating 'Sex and the Single Girl,'" *Chicago Tribune,* July 2, 2003, articles.chicagotribune.com/2003-07-02 /features/0307010395_1_editor-of-cosmopolitan-magazine-single -girl-helen-gurley-brown.

77. Wendy McElroy, *Rape Culture Hysteria* (Seattle, WA: CreateSpace, 2016), 42.

78. Susan Mitchell, *Icons, Saints, and Divas: Intimate Conversations with*

Women Who Changed the World (New York: HarperCollins, 1997), 130.

79. Judith Weintraub, "Germaine Greer—Opinions That May Shock the Faithful," *New York Times,* March 22, 1971.
80. Quoted ibid., 279.
81. Germaine Greer, *The Female Eunuch* (1970; repr., New York: Harper Perennial Modern Classics, 2008), 203.
82. Carmen Winant, "The Meaningful Disappearance of Germaine Greer," *Catastrophe* 57 (Spring 2015), cabinetmagazine.org/issues /57/winant.php.
83. Greer, *The Female Eunuch,* 241.
84. Ibid., 252.
85. Ibid., 358.
86. Ibid., 263.
87. Ibid., 361.
88. Ibid., 368–69.
89. Ibid., 265.
90. Ibid., 364.
91. Winant, "The Meaningful Disappearance of Germaine Greer."
92. Richard Brooks, "Greer Reveals Trauma of Rape, Miscarriage, and IVF," *Times* (London), July 10, 2011.
93. Greer, *The Female Eunuch,* 57.
94. Ibid., 57–58.
95. Ibid., 17.
96. Ibid., 269.
97. Ibid., 275.
98. Ibid., 10.
99. Torrey, *Freudian Fraud,* 23.
100. Ibid., 120.
101. Shulamith Firestone, *The Dialectic of Sex: The Case for Feminist Revolution* (New York: William Morrow, 1970), 48.
102. Ibid., 19.
103. Ibid., 37.
104. Susan Faludi, "Death of a Revolutionary," *The New Yorker,* April 15, 2013, newyorker.com/magazine/2013/04/15/death-of-a -revolutionary.
105. Ibid.
106. Ibid.
107. Ellen Willis, "Toward a Feminist Sexual Revolution," *Social Text,* no. 6 (Autumn 1982), 7.
108. Ibid.

109. Ibid., 18.
110. Edward Erwin, *A Final Accounting: Philosophical and Empirical Issues in Freudian Psychology* (Cambridge, MA: A Bradford Book, MIT Press, 1995), 294.
111. Frederick Crews, *The Memory Wars: Freud's Legacy in Dispute* (New York: New York Review of Books, 1995), 34.
112. Stéphane Courtois et al., *The Black Book of Communism* (Cambridge, MA: Harvard University Press, 1999), x.
113. Kate Millett, *Sexual Politics* (1970; repr., New York: Columbia University Press, 2016), 62.
114. Ibid., 126.
115. Ibid., 119.
116. Ibid., 116.
117. Ibid., 178.
118. Margalit Fox, "Adrienne Rich, Influential Feminist Poet, Dies at 82," *New York Times,* March 28, 2012.
119. Gloria Steinem, "The Moral Disarmament of Betty Coed," *Esquire,* September 1962.
120. Allyn, *Make Love, Not War,* 14.
121. Elizabeth Mehren, "The War over Love Heats Up Again: Author Shere Hite's Third Report on Sexuality Fuels an Old Debate over Her Methodology," *Los Angeles Times,* Oct. 29, 1987, articles.latimes.com/1987-10-29/news/vw-17446_1_hite-report.
122. Ariel Levy, *Female Chauvinist Pigs: Women and the Rise of Raunch Culture* (New York: Free Press, 2005), 56.
123. Barbara Ehrenreich, Elizabeth Hess, and Gloria Jacobs, *Re-Making Love: The Feminization of Sex* (New York: Doubleday, 1986), 195.
124. Willis, "Toward a Feminist Sexual Revolution," 11.
125. Maya Rhodan, "No Satisfaction: Women Are Less Likely to Orgasm During Casual Sex," *Time,* Nov. 11, 2013, healthland.time.com/2013/11/11/no-satisfaction-woman-are-less-likely-to-orgasm-during-casual-sex/.
126. Ibid.
127. Ehrenreich et al., *Re-Making Love,* 193.
128. Allyn, *Make Love, Not War,* 72.
129. Ehrenreich et al., *Re-Making Love,* 72–73.
130. When Robert Rimmer died in 2001, at the age of eighty-four, the *New York Times* obituary noted that he believed in "revolutionizing the institution of marriage," but the article also quoted his wife of sixty years as a skeptic. "I didn't care for that too much," she said. "He was always very liberal-minded."

131. Willis, "Toward a Feminist Sexual Revolution," 6.

132. Quoted in Sara Davidson, "An 'Oppressed Majority' Demands Its Rights."

133. Atkinson was president of the New York chapter of the National Organization for Women, but she left after a dispute over the movement's treatment of Valerie Solanas. Solanas had shot and attempted to kill the artist Andy Warhol. Atkinson wanted NOW to defend her as a "heroine of the feminist movement" and smuggled her manifesto out of prison for her. Solanas founded SCUM: The Society for Cutting Up Men.

134. Carolyn Bronstein, *Battling Pornography: The American Feminist Anti-Pornography Movement, 1976–1986* (New York: Cambridge University Press, 2011), 56.

135. thewrap.com/lena-dunham-coachella-feminist-band-jill-biden-debbie-wasserman-schultz/.

136. Ariel Levy, "The Prisoner of Sex," *New York* magazine, June 6, 2005, nymag.com/nymetro/news/people/features/11907/index3.html.

137. Cathy Young, "The Dworkin Whitewash," *Hit & Run* (blog), Reason.com, April 17, 2005, reason.com/blog/2005/04/17/the-dworkin-whitewash.

138. Quoted in Levy, *Female Chauvinist Pigs,* 49.

139. "The Women's Movement and Women in SDS: Cathy Wilkerson Recalls the Tensions," History Matters: The U.S. History Course on the Web, historymatters.gmu.edu/d/6916/.

140. Ibid.

Chapter 2: Vive la Difference

1. Larry Cahill, "Equal ≠ Same: Sex Differences in the Human Brain," *Cerebrum,* April 2014, dana.org/Cerebrum/2014/Equal_≠_The_Same__Sex_Differences_in_the_Human_Brain/.

2. Ibid.

3. Leonard Sax, *Why Gender Matters: What Parents and Teachers Need to Know About the Emerging Science of Sex Differences* (New York: Doubleday, 2005), 3.

4. Louann Brizendine, *The Female Brain* (New York: Three Rivers Press, 2006), 2.

5. Ibid., 132.

6. Anne Moir and David Jessel, *Brain Sex: The Real Difference Between Men and Women* (Crystal Lake, IL: Delta, 1992), 7.

7. Quoted in Christina Hoff Sommers, *The Science on Women in Science* (Washington, DC: AEI Press, 2009), 2.

8. Stephan Thernstrom, "Harvard's Crucible," *National Review,* April 11, 2005.

9. Nina Teicholz, *Big Fat Surprise: Why Butter, Meat, and Cheese Belong in a Healthy Diet* (New York: Simon and Schuster, 2014).

10. Quoted in Moir and Jessel, *Brain Sex,* 11.

11. Susan Pinker, *The Sexual Paradox: Men, Women, and the Real Gender Gap* (New York: Scribner, 2009), 37.

12. Quoted in "The Science of Gender and Science: Pinker vs. Spelke, a Debate," Edge: The Third Culture, May 16, 2005, edge.org/3rd _culture/debate05/debate05_index.html#p41. Also see Diane F. Halpern, "Preface to the First Edition," *Sex Differences in Cognitive Abilities,* 4th ed. (New York: Psychological Press, 2012), xxi.

13. Steven Pinker, *The Blank Slate: The Modern Denial of Human Nature* (New York: Penguin Books, 2003), 344.

14. Christina Hoff Sommers, "Are There More Girl Geniuses?" AEI, July 1, 2010, aei.org/publication/are-there-more-girl-geniuses/.

15. Simon Baron-Cohen, "It's Not Sexist to Accept That Biology Affects Behaviour," *Guardian,* May 3, 2010, theguardian.com /commentisfree/2010/may/03/biology-sexist-gender-stereotypes.

16. Steven Pinker, *The Blank Slate,* 344.

17. Moir and Jessel, *Brain Sex,* 18.

18. Susan Pinker, *The Sexual Paradox,* 35.

19. Steven Pinker, *The Blank Slate,* 435–39.

20. Steven E. Rhoads, *Taking Sex Differences Seriously* (San Francisco: Encounter Books, 2004), 25.

21. Moir and Jessel, *Brain Sex,* 100.

22. Brizendine, *The Female Brain,* 5.

23. Ibid., 5.

24. Moir and Jessel, *Brain Sex,* 47.

25. Brizendine, *The Female Brain,* 14.

26. Francesca Puoti et al., "Organ Transplantation and Gender Differences: A Paradigmatic Example of Intertwining Between Biological and Sociocultural Determinants," *Biology of Sex Differences* 7, no. 35 (July 2016), ncbi.nlm.nih.gov/pmc/articles/PMC4964018/.

27. Editor's Profile, Biology of Sex Differences, n.d., bsd.biomedcentral .com.

28. Ibid.

29. Cahill, "Equal ≠ Same: Sex Differences in the Human Brain."

30. Brizendine, *The Female Brain,* 26.

31. Rhoads, *Taking Sex Differences Seriously,* 29.

32. Andrew Sullivan, "The He Hormone," *New York Times Magazine,*

April 2, 2000, nytimes.com/2000/04/02/magazine/the-he-hormone .html.

33. Rhoads, *Taking Sex Differences Seriously,* 199.

34. Steven Pinker, *The Blank Slate,* 348.

35. Quoted ibid., 349.

36. Elaine Woo, "David Reimer, 38; After Botched Surgery, He Was Raised as a Girl in Gender Experiment," *Los Angeles Times,* May 13, 2004, articles.latimes.com/2004/may/13/local/me-reimer13/2.

37. Steven Pinker, *The Blank Slate,* 349.

38. Ewen Callaway, "Male Monkeys Prefer Boys' Toys," *New Scientist,* April 4, 2008, newscientist.com/article/dn13596-male-monkeys -prefer-boys-toys/.

39. Sax, *Why Gender Matters,* 61.

40. Simon Baron-Cohen, *The Essential Difference: The Truth About the Male and Female Brain* (New York: Basic Books, 2003), 30.

41. Rhoads, *Taking Sex Differences Seriously,* 145.

42. "Genders Differ Dramatically in Evolved Mate Preferences," *UT News,* Aug. 6, 2015, news.utexas.edu/2015/08/06/genders-differ -dramatically-in-evolved-mate-preferences.

43. Matt Ridley, *The Red Queen: Sex and the Evolution of Human Nature* (New York: Macmillan, 1994), 275.

44. Baron-Cohen, *The Essential Difference,* 36.

45. Susan Pinker, *The Sexual Paradox,* 222.

46. Baron-Cohen, *The Essential Difference,* 35.

47. Sullivan, "The He Hormone."

48. Brizendine, *The Female Brain,* 91.

49. Moir and Jessel, *Brain Sex,* 79.

50. Brizendine, *The Female Brain,* 91.

51. Sax, *Why Gender Matters,* 125.

52. Ibid., 126.

53. Ibid., 125.

54. Letitia Anne Peplau, "Human Sexuality: How Do Men and Women Differ?" *Current Directions in Psychological Science,* 12, no. 2 (April 2003), sites.oxy.edu/clint/physio/article/humansexuality .pdf, 37.

55. Ibid., 37.

56. Rhoads, *Taking Sex Differences Seriously,* 51.

57. Andrew Sullivan, speech at National Review Summit, Washington, DC, January 1993.

58. Mercedes Tappé et al., "Gender Differences in Receptivity to Sex-

ual Offers: A New Research Prototype," *Interpersona* 7, no. 2 (2013), interpersona.psychopen.eu/article/view/121/155.

59. American Psychological Association, *Answers to Your Questions About Transgender People, Gender Identity and Gender Expression* (pamphlet), apa.org/topics/lgbt/transgender.pdf.

60. Quoted in Lawrence S. Mayer and Paul R. McHugh, "Sexuality and Gender," *The New Atlantis,* no. 50 (Fall 2016), 87.

61. Quoted ibid., 88.

62. Quoted in Molly Fischer, "Think Gender Is Performance? You Have Judith Butler to Blame for That," *New York* magazine, June 21, 2016, nymag.com/thecut/2016/06/judith-butler-c-v-r.html.

63. "Dear Colleague Letter on Transgender Students," Archived Information, U.S. Dept. of Justice and U.S. Dept. of Education, May 13, 2016, ed.gov/about/offices/list/ocr/letters/colleague-201605-title -ix-transgender.pdf.

64. Anne Fausto-Sterling, "How Many Sexes Are There?" *New York Times*, March 12, 1993, nytimes.com/1993/03/12/opinion/how -many-sexes-are-there.html.

65. Ibid.

66. Leonard Sax, "How Common Is Intersex?" *Journal of Sex Research* (August 2002), leonardsax.com/how-common-is-intersex-a -response-to-anne-fausto-sterling/.

67. Christopher Wanjek, "Being Transgender Has Nothing to Do with Hormonal Imbalance," LiveScience, July 23, 2015, livescience .com/51652-transgender-youth-dont-have-hormonal-imbalance.html.

68. Mayer and McHugh, "Sexuality and Gender," 103.

69. "Schools Homecoming Strives to Be Inclusive," *Washington Post,* Sept. 28, 2016.

70. "How British Schools Are Adapting to Growing Numbers of Transgender Pupils," *The Economist,* May 4, 2017, economist.com/news /britain/21717739-new-efforts-accommodate-transgender-students -contrast-sharply-controversy.

71. Jan Hoffman, "Estimate of U.S. Transgender Population Doubles to 1.4 Million Adults," *New York Times,* June 30, 2016, nytimes .com/2016/07/01/health/transgender-population.html.

72. Mark Hemingway, "In Oregon, 15-Year-Olds Can Get Taxpayer-Funded Sex Changes Without Parental Consent," *Weekly Standard,* June 17, 2015, weeklystandard.com/in-oregon-15-year-olds -can-get-taxpayer-funded-sex-changes-without-parental-consent /article/973130.

73. Amber Phillips, "These States Are Opening the Doors to Bathroom Wars," *Washington Post,* Jan. 24, 2017, washingtonpost.com/news /the-fix/wp/2017/01/24/new-fronts-emerge-in-the-bathroom -wars.

74. Petula Dvorak, "Transgender at Five," *Washington Post*, May 19, 2012, washingtonpost.com/local/transgender-at-five/2012/05/19 /gIQABfFkbU_story.html.

75. Michelle Cretella, "Gender Dysphoria in Children and the Suppression of Debate," *Journal of American Physicians and Surgeons* 21, no. 4 (Summer 2016).

76. Ibid.

77. Ibid.

78. Jesse Singal, "How the Fight over Transgender Kids Got a Leading Sex Researcher Fired," *The Cut,* Feb. 7, 2016, thecut.com/2016/02 /fight-over-trans-kids-got-a-researcher-fired.html.

79. Ibid.

80. Ariel Levy, *Female Chauvinist Pigs: Women and the Rise of Raunch Culture* (New York: Free Press, 2005), 124.

81. Viktor E. Frankl, *Man's Search for Meaning* (1946; repr., Boston: Beacon Press, 2006).

82. Katy Waldman, "The Wellesley Man," *Slate,* June 2014, slate .com/articles/double_x/doublex/2014/06/transgender_students_at _women_s_colleges_wellesley_smith_and_others_confront.html.

83. Katherine Timpf, "Wellesley College Students Are Okay with Him on Campus, but Not in a Leadership Position," *National Review,* Oct. 15, 2014, nationalreview.com/article/390425/students -transgender-woman-cant-be-diversity-officer-because-shes-white -man-now.

84. Daniel Reynolds, "Smith College Now Admits Trans Women," *Advocate,* May 2, 2015, advocate.com/politics/transgender/2015/05 /02/smith-college-now-admits-trans-students.

Chapter 3: Severing Bonds

1. Betty Friedan, *The Second Stage* (New York: Simon and Schuster, 1981), 35.

2. Ibid., 35.

3. Ibid., 39.

4. Ibid., 5.

5. "Table 2: Percentage of Women Reporting That Specific Reasons Contributed to Their Decision to Have an Abortion, 2004 and 1987," in Lawrence B. Finer et al., "Reasons U.S. Women Have

Abortions: Quantitative and Qualitative Perspectives," *Perspectives on Sexual and Reproductive Health* 37, no. 3 (Sept. 2005), guttmacher .org/sites/default/files/pdfs/tables/370305/3711005t2.pdf.

6. Rachel K. Jones, Jacqueline E. Darroch, and Stanley K. Henshaw, "Contraceptive Use Among U.S. Women Having Abortions in 2000–2001," *Perspectives on Sexual and Reproductive Health* 34, no. 6 (Nov./Dec. 2002), guttmacher.org/journals/psrh/2002/11 /contraceptive-use-among-us-women-having-abortions-2000-2001.

7. Mary Wollstonecraft, *A Vindication of the Rights of Woman* (1792), Ch. 8, bartleby.com/144/8.html.

8. Marjorie Dannenfelser, "Pro-Life Feminists Are Old School," *National Review,* Jan. 20, 2017, nationalreview.com/article/444050/snl -susan-b-anthony-early-feminists-opposed-abortion.

9. "14 Weeks Pregnant," BabyCenter, June 2016, babycenter.com/6 _14-weeks-pregnant_1103.bc.

10. "Your Pregnancy: 15 Weeks," BabyCenter, June 2016, babycenter .com/6_your-pregnancy-15-weeks_1104.bc.

11. David Stout, "An Abortion Rights Advocate Says He Lied About Procedure," *New York Times,* Feb. 26, 1997, nytimes.com/1997/02 /26/us/an-abortion-rights-advocate-says-he-lied-about-procedure .html.

12. Find examples at theabortionsurvivors.com.

13. John McCormack, "Planned Parenthood Official Argues for Right to Post-Birth Abortion," *Weekly Standard,* March 29, 2013.

14. Peter Kirsanow, "Clarifying Obama's Vote on Born-Alive," *The Corner* (blog), *National Review,* Feb. 10, 2012, nationalreview.com /corner/290764/clarifying-obamas-vote-born-alive-peter-kirsanow.

15. Mona Charen, "Democratic Vendetta," *National Review,* March 30, 2017, nationalreview.com/article/446284/california-planned-parent hood-david-daleiden-charged-undercover-videos.

16. See youtube.com/watch?v=DeilHs9kZ2g.

Chapter 4: Hookup Culture

1. Glenn Kessler, "One in Five Women in College Assaulted: An Update on This Statistic," *Washington Post,* Dec. 17, 2014, washington post.com/blogs/fact-checker/wp/2014/12/17/one-in-five-women -in-college-sexually-assaulted-an-update/.

2. Amy M. Burdette et al., " 'Hooking Up' at College: Does Religion Make a Difference?" *Journal for the Scientific Study of Religion* 48, no. 3 (Sept. 2009), onlinelibrary.wiley.com/doi/10.1111/j.1468 -5906.2009.01464.x/full.

3. Rachel Chung, "Ask an RA: How to Navigate Hookup Culture," *Columbia Spectator,* Sept. 23, 2014, columbiaspectator.com/spectrum/2014/09/23/ask-ra-how-navigate-hookup-culture.

4. Kate Taylor, "Sex on Campus: She Can Play That Game Too," *New York Times,* July 12, 2013, nytimes.com/2013/07/14/fashion/sex-on-campus-she-can-play-that-game-too.html.

5. Ibid.

6. Donna Freitas, *The End of Sex: How Hookup Culture Is Leaving a Generation Unhappy, Sexually Unfulfilled, and Confused About Intimacy* (New York: Basic Books, 2013), 33.

7. Norval Glenn and Elizabeth Marquardt, *Hooking Up, Hanging Out, and Hoping for Mr. Right: College Women on Dating and Mating Today* (New York: Institute for American Values, 2001), americanvalues.org/catalog/pdfs/hookingup.pdf.

8. Miriam Grossman, *Unprotected: A Campus Psychiatrist Reveals How Political Correctness in Her Profession Endangers Every Student* (New York: Sentinel, 2007), 8.

9. Maia Szalavitz, "How Oxytocin Makes Men (Almost) Monogamous," *Time,* Nov. 27, 2013, healthland.time.com/2013/11/27/how-oxytocin-makes-men-almost-monogamous/.

10. Leonard Sax, *Why Gender Matters: What Parents and Teachers Need to Know About the Emerging Science of Sex Differences* (New York: Doubleday, 2005), 38.

11. George Gilder, *Men and Marriage* (Gretna, LA: Pelican Publishing, 1986), 12.

12. Letitia Anne Peplau, "Human Sexuality: How Do Men and Women Differ?" *Current Directions in Psychological Science* 12, no. 2 (2003), 38, sites.oxy.edu/clint/physio/article/humansexuality.pdf.

13. Steven E. Rhoads, *Taking Sex Differences Seriously* (San Francisco: Encounter Books, 2004).

14. Hanna Rosin, "Boys on the Side," *The Atlantic,* Sept. 2012, theatlantic.com/magazine/archive/2012/09/boys-on-the-side/309062/.

15. Ibid.

16. Lisa Wade, "The Promise and Peril of 'Hookup Culture,'" (lecture, Franklin and Marshall College Lancaster, PA, March 24, 2011), 7.

17. Paula England and Jonathan Bearak, "The Sexual Double Standard and Gender Differences in Attitudes Toward Casual Sex Among U.S. University Students," *Demographic Research* 30, no. 46 (2014), 1331.

18. Freitas, *The End of Sex,* 39–40.

19. "Drinking Levels Defined," National Institute on Alcohol Abuse

and Alcoholism, niaaa.nih.gov/alcohol-health/overview-alcohol
-consumption/moderate-binge-drinking.

20. Freitas, *The End of Sex,* 41.

21. "Alcohol Facts and Statistics," National Institute on Alcohol Abuse
and Alcoholism, n.d., pubs.niaaa.nih.gov/publications/AlcoholFacts
&Stats/AlcoholFacts&Stats.htm.

22. Freitas, *The End of Sex,* 49.

23. Some college students do commit suicide, though it is not clear that
the pressure of academic work is what drives them to such a drastic
act.

24. Freitas, *The End of Sex,* 172.

25. Interview with the author, July 13, 2017.

26. Jordan Bosiljevac, "Why Yes Can Mean No," The Forum, April 30,
2015, cmcforum.com/opinion/04302015-why-yes-can-mean-no.

27. Richard Pérez-Peña, "Dartmouth Cites Student Misconduct in
Its Ban on Hard Liquor," *New York Times,* Jan. 29, 2015, nytimes
.com/2015/01/30/us/in-response-to-student-misconduct-dartmouth
-to-ban-hard-liquor-at-parties.html.

28. Nathan Harden and Christopher Buckley, *Sex and God at Yale: Porn,
Political Correctness, and a Good Education Gone Bad* (New York:
Thomas Dunne Books, St. Martin's Press, 2012), 11.

29. James Nichols, "Harvard University Offers 'What What in the
Butt: Anal Sex 101,'" *Huffington Post,* Feb. 2, 2016, huffingtonpost
.com/2014/11/05/harvard-anal-sex-class_n_6102804.html.

30. Jennifer Kabbany, "Harvard University Workshop to Teach Students How to Have Anal Sex," *The College Fix,* Nov. 3, 2014, the
collegefix.com/post/19952/.

31. "Northwestern University Professor Under Fire After Sex Toy
Demonstration," *Huffington Post,* March 3, 2011, huffingtonpost
.com/2011/03/02/northwestern-university-p_n_830423.html.

32. Ibid.

33. Kaitlin Mulhere, "Red-Faced over Sex Weeks," *Inside Higher Ed,*
Oct. 15, 2014, insidehighered.com/news/2014/10/15/sex-week
-events-draw-criticism-some-campuses.

34. Anna North, "The Real Reason Yale Banned 'Sex Week,'" *Jezebel,*
Nov. 11, 2011, jezebel.com/5858643/why-yale-really-banned-sex
-week.

Chapter 5: The Campus Rape Mess

1. Roberta Smith, "In a Mattress, a Lever for Art and Power," *New
York Times,* Sept. 21, 2014.

2. "President Obama Launches the 'It's on Us' Campaign to End Sexual Assault on Campus," *The White House* (blog), Sept. 19, 2014, obamawhitehouse.archives.gov/blog/2014/09/19/president-obama -launches-its-us-campaign-end-sexual-assault-campus.

3. "Ten Things to End Rape Culture," *The Nation,* Feb. 4, 2013, the nation.com/article/ten-things-end-rape-culture/.

4. Christine Helwick, "Affirmative Consent: The New Standard," *Inside Higher Ed*, Oct. 23, 2014, insidehighered.com/views /2014/10/23/campuses-must-wrestle-affirmative-consent-standard -sexual-assault-essay.

5. "California Enacts the 'Yes Means Yes' Law, Defining Sexual Consent," *The Two-Way* (blog), NPR, Sept. 29, 2014, npr.org/blogs /thetwo-way/2014/09/29/352482932/california-enacts-yes-means -yes-law-defining-sexual-consent.

6. William M. Weich, "California Adopts 'Yes Means Yes' Law," *USA Today,* Aug. 28, 2014, usatoday.com/story/news/usanow/2014/08 /28/california-bill-yes-means-yes-sex-assault/14765665/.

7. Helwick, "Affirmative Consent: The New Standard."

8. Marina Lopes, "Lawmakers Call for Guns on College Campuses to Prevent Rape," *NewsHour,* PBS, Feb. 19, 2015, pbs.org/newshour /rundown/lawmakers-call-guns-college-campuses-prevent-rape/.

9. Ibid.

10. Archived Information, April 4, 2011, U.S. Dept. of Education, Office for Civil Rights, ed.gov/about/offices/list/ocr/letters /colleague-201104.pdf.

11. "Title IX: Tracking Sexual Assault Investigations" (graph), *Chronicle of Higher Education,* at projects.chronicle.com/titleix/.

12. Quoted in Eric Kelderman, "College Lawyers Confront a Thicket of Rules on Sexual Assault," p. 4, in "In Context: Campus Sexual Assault," *Chronicle of Higher Education* (Fall 2014), chronicle.com /items/biz/pdf/sex_assault_brief_fall2014.pdf.

13. "Harvard Names Title IX Officer," *Harvard Gazette,* April 5, 2017, news.harvard.edu/gazette/story/2017/04/harvard-names-new-title -ix-officer-and-director-of-office-for-dispute-resolution.

14. Kelderman, "College Lawyers Confront a Thicket of Rules on Sexual Assault."

15. Dahlia Lithwick, "The University of Virginia Finally Confronts Its Rape Problem," *Slate,* Nov. 24, 2014, slate.com/articles/news _and_politics/jurisprudence/2014/11/university_of_virginia_gang _rape_investigation_rolling_stone_reveals_limits.2.html.

16. Judith E. Grossman, "Judith Grossman: A Mother, a Feminist,

Aghast," *Wall Street Journal,* April 16, 2013, wsj.com/articles/SB100 01424127887324600704578405280211043510.

17. Janet Halley, "Trading the Megaphone for the Gavel in Title IX Enforcement," *Harvard Law Review* 128 (2015), 116, dash.harvard .edu/bitstream/handle/1/16073958/vol118_Halley_REVISED_2.17 .pdf.

18. "Expelled for Sex Assault, Young Men Are Filing More Lawsuits to Clear Their Names," *Washington Post,* April 28, 2017, washingtonpost .com/local/education/expelled-for-sex-assault-young-men-are -filing-more-lawsuits-to-clear-their-names/2017/04/27/c2cfb1d2 -0d89-11e7-9b0d-d27c98455440_story.html.

19. Teresa Watanabe, "More College Men Are Fighting Back Against Sexual Misconduct Cases," *Los Angeles Times,* June 7, 2014, latimes .com/local/la-me-sexual-assault-legal-20140608-story.html.

20. Ibid.

21. Ibid.

22. Hans Bader, "White House Attacks Due Process and Cross- Examination Rights in Campus Sexual Assault Push," May 3, 2014, College Insurrection, collegeinsurrection.com/2014/05/white -house-attacks-due-process-and-cross-examination-rights-in-campus -sexual-assault-push/.

23. "Questions and Answers on Title IX and Sexual Violence," U.S. Dept. of Education, Office of Civil Rights, April 29, 2014, ed.gov /about/offices/list/ocr/docs/qa-201404-title-ix.pdf.

24. Wendy McElroy, *Sexual Correctness: The Gender-Feminist Attack on Women* (Jefferson, NC: McFarland, 1996), 34.

25. Judith Shapiro, "From Strength to Strength," *Inside Higher Ed,* Dec. 15, 2015, insidehighered.com/views/2014/12/15/essay -importance-not-trying-protect-students-everything-may-upset -them.

26. Robin Wilson, "Why Campuses Can't Talk About Alcohol When It Comes to Sexual Assault," *Chronicle of Higher Education,* Sept. 4, 2014, chronicle.com/article/Why-Campuses-Can-t-Talk/148615.

27. Emily Yoffe, "Emily Yoffe Responds to Her Critics," *Slate,* Oct. 18, 2013, slate.com/blogs/xx_factor/2013/10/18/rape_culture _and_binge_drinking_emily_yoffe_responds_to_her_critics.html.

28. Lorie Adelman, "'Dear Prudence' Columnist Publishes Rape Denialism Manifesto Advising Women to 'Stop Getting Drunk,'" Feministing, Oct. 16, 2013, feministing.com/2013/10/16/emily -yoffe-aka-dear-prudence-publishes-rape-denialism-manifesto -tells-women-point-blank-to-stop-getting-drunk-to-avoid-rape/.

29. Wilson, "Why Campuses Can't Talk About Alcohol When It Comes to Sexual Attack."

30. Ibid.

31. Ibid.

32. Robin Wilson, "Why Campuses Can't Talk About Alcohol When It Comes to Sexual Assault," *Chronicle of Higher Education*, Sept. 4, 2014, chronicle.com/article/Why-Campuses-Can-t-Talk/148615.

33. American College Health Association, "Shifting the Paradigm: Primary Prevention of Sexual Violence Toolkit" (August 2008), acha.org/documents/resources/ACHA_PSV_toolkit.pdf.

34. Emily Yoffe, "The College Rape Overcorrection," *Slate,* Dec. 7, 2014, slate.com/articles/double_x/doublex/2014/12/college_rape _campus_sexual_assault_is_a_serious_problem_but_the_efforts .html.

35. Quoted in McElroy, *Sexual Correctness,* 33.

36. Heather Mac Donald, "The Campus Rape Myth," *City Journal* (Winter 2008), city-journal.org/2008/18_1_campus_rape.html.

37. Neil Gilbert, "Realities and Mythologies of Rape," *Society* 35, no. 2 (Jan./Feb. 1998), 356–62, d.umn.edu/cla/faculty/jhamlin /3925/MythsGilbert.htm.

38. Sandy Hingston, "The New Rules of College Sex," *Philadelphia,* Aug. 22, 2011, phillymag.com/articles/the-new-rules-of-college -sex/.

39. Ibid.

40. Department of Justice, Bureau of Justice Statistics, "Rape and Sexual Assault Victimization Among College Age Females, 1995– 2013," Dec. 2014, bjs.gov/content/pub/pdf/rsavcaf9513.pdf.

41. Nick Anderson and Scott Clement, "1 in 5 College Women Say They Were Violated," *Washington Post,* June 12, 2015, washington post.com/sf/local/2015/06/12/1-in-5-women-say-they-were -violated/.

42. "Spring 2014 Barnard Campus Climate Survey Results," at barnard .edu/sites/default/files/campus_climate_survey_report_final.pdf.

43. Ibid.

44. Ibid.

45. Chuck Raasch, "Campus Sexual Assault Under Fresh Scrutiny After New Survey Shows Lower Incidence," *St. Louis Post-Dispatch,* Dec. 26, 2014, stltoday.com/news/local/govt-and-politics/gateway -to-dc/campus-sexual-assault-under-fresh-scrutiny-after-new -survey-shows/article_8ea64e9d-5dbc-532f-b04d-39465ee20aa5 .html.

46. Stacey Barchenger and Joey Garrison, "Vanderbilt Rape Trial: Defendants Found Guilty on All Charges," *USAToday,* Jan. 28, 2015, usatoday.com/story/sports/ncaaf/sec/2015/01/27/vanderbilt-players-verdict-guilty-rape-vandenburg-batey/22430567/.

47. AnneClaire Stapleton, "Students Accused in Spring Break Gang Rape in Panama City," CNN, April 11, 2015, cnn.com/2015/04/10/us/panama-city-spring-break-gang-rape-case/index.html.

48. Gwen Florio, "Former Griz Beau Donaldson Sentenced to Prison for Rape," *Missoulian,* Jan. 13, 2013, missoulian.com/news/local/former-griz-beau-donaldson-sentenced-to-prison-for-rape/article_1c1b49fa-5c2b-11e2-998c-001a4bcf887a.html.

49. Caitlin Johnston, "In Campus Rape Cases, Victim Often Blamed for Failure to Prosecute," *Tampa Bay Times,* Sept. 22, 2014, tampabay.com/news/education/college/in-campus-rape-cases-victim-often-blamed-for-failure-to-prosecute/2198683.

50. Interview with Addie Mena, May 8, 2015.

51. Laurel Conrad, "'Safe Spaces' Are Unsafe for the Free Exchange of Ideas," *Legal Insurrection,* April 21, 2015, legalinsurrection.com/2015/04/safe-spaces-are-unsafe-for-free-exchange-of-ideas/.

52. "The Canon on Campus," Notable and Quotable, *Wall Street Journal,* May 8, 2015, wsj.com/articles/notable-quotable-1431124660.

53. Coker v. Georgia, 433 U.S. 584 (1977). caselaw.findlaw.com/us-supreme-court/433/584.html.

54. Kennedy v. Louisiana, 554 U.S. 407 (2008). deathpenaltyinfo.org/kennedy-v-louisiana-no-07-343.

55. Emily Bazelon, "Smeary Lines," *Slate,* Sept. 21, 2009, slate.com/articles/news_and_politics/jurisprudence/2009/09/smeary_lines.html.

56. Frank S. Zepezauer, "Believe Her! The Woman Never Lies Myth," *IPT* 6 (1994), ipt-forensics.com/journal/volume6/j6_2_4.htm.

57. Anonymous, "An Open Letter to OCR," *Inside Higher Ed,* Oct. 28, 2011, insidehighered.com/views/2011/10/28/essay-ocr-guidelines-sexual-assault-hurt-colleges-and-students.

58. "The Anti-Male Craze at Yale," *Short Takes* (blog), Minding the Campus, Sept. 11, 2013, mindingthecampus.org/2013/09/another_anti-male_move_at_yale/.

59. Cathy Young, "Columbia Student: I Didn't Rape Her," *The Daily Beast,* Feb. 3, 2015, thedailybeast.com/articles/2015/02/03/columbia-student-i-didn-t-rape-her.html.

60. Kate Taylor, "Columbia Settles with Student Cast as a Rapist in Mattress Art Project," *New York Times,* July 14, 2017, nytimes

.com/2017/07/14/nyregion/columbia-settles-with-student-cast-as
-a-rapist-in-mattress-art-project.html.

61. American College Health Association, "Shifting the Paradigm: Primary Prevention of Sexual Violence Toolkit."

62. mencanstoprape.org.

63. clotheslineproject.info.

64. Mary Elizabeth Williams, "Can Men Be Taught Not to Rape?" *Salon,* March 8, 2014, salon.com/2013/03/08/can_men_be_taught_not_to_rape/.

65. "Ten Things to End Rape Culture," *The Nation,* Feb. 4, 2013, the nation.com/article/ten-things-end-rape-culture/.

66. Dan Lamothe, "Army to Review Decision to Have Male Cadets Wear High Heels," *Washington Post,* April 22, 2015, washington post.com/news/checkpoint/wp/2015/04/22/army-to-review -decision-to-have-male-cadets-wear-high-heels/.

67. Ibid.

68. David Lisak, "Sexual Aggression, Masculinity, and Fathers, *Signs* 16, no. 2 (Winter 1991), journals.uchicago.edu/doi/10.1086/494659.

Chapter 6: Family

1. Marcus Buckingham, "What's Happening to Women's Happiness?" bodyandsoulreconnection.com/the-decline-of-womens-happiness -part-i/.

2. Steven D. Levitt, "Why Are Women So Unhappy," *Freakonomics* (blog), Oct. 1, 2007, freakonomics.com/2007/10/01/why-are -women-so-unhappy/.

3. Karlyn Bowman and Jennifer K. Marsico, "The Past, Present, and Future of the Women's Vote," American Enterprise Institute, Oct. 4, 2012, aei.org/publication/the-past-present-and-future-of -the-womens-vote/.

4. Ibid.

5. "'Girls and Sex,' and the Importance of Talking to Young Women About Pleasure," Shots: Health News from NPR, March 29, 2016, npr.org/sections/health-shots/2016/03/29/472211301/girls-sex-and-the -importance-of-talking-to-young-women-about-pleasure.

6. Wendy Shalit, *A Return to Modesty: Discovering the Lost Virtue* (New York: Free Press, 1999), 61.

7. Quoted in Wendy Shalit, *The Good Girl Revolution: Young Rebels with Self-Esteem and High Standards* (New York: Ballantine, 2008), 9.

8. Todd Starnes, "'Toxic Masculinity? Dude, Now America's Univer-

sities Are Turning Men into Women," Fox News Opinion, Jan. 17, 2017, foxnews.com/opinion/2017/01/17/toxic-masculinity-dude-now-americas-universities-are-turning-men-into-women.html.

9. Taylor Maple, "Aly Raisman on Topless Photo Shoot: 'Women Do Not Have to Be Modest in Order to Be Respected,'" ABC News, April 13, 2017, abcnews.go.com/Entertainment/aly-raisman-topless-photo-shoot-women-modest-order/story.

10. Gloria Steinem, "Feminists and the Clinton Question," *New York Times,* March 22, 1998, scribd.com/document/336603458/Feminists-and-the-Clinton-Question-The-New-York-Times.

11. Quoted in Charles Murray, *Coming Apart: The State of White America, 1960–2010* (New York: Crown Forum, 2012), 288.

12. William Bennett, *The Book of Man: Readings on the Path to Manhood* (Nashville: Thomas Nelson, 2011), 392.

13. Ibid., 401–02.

14. Ibid., 380.

15. Quoted in Michael Grossberg, *Governing the Hearth: Law and the Family in Nineteenth-Century America* (Raleigh: University of North Carolina Press, 1988), 9.

16. beamensch.com/what-is-a-mensch/in-our-words/.

17. Kim Parker et al., "Americans See Society Placing More of a Premium on Masculinity than on Femininity," Pew Research Center, Social Trends Report, Dec. 5, 2017, pewsocialtrends.org/2017/12/05/americans-see-society-placing-more-of-a-premium-on-masculinity-than-on-femininity/.

18. George Gilder, *Men and Marriage* (Gretna, LA: Pelican Publishing, 1986), 5.

19. Mona Charen, "Manliness: An Unsung Trait of the Train Heroes," *National Review,* Aug. 25, 2015, nationalreview.com/article/423044/manliness-unsung-trait-train-heroes-mona-charen.

20. Mona Charen, "Heroism in Aurora," *National Review,* July 27, 2012, nationalreview.com/article/312428/heroism-aurora-mona-charen.

21. Anne Taylor Fleming, *Motherhood Deferred* (New York: Putnam, 1994), 154–55.

22. Sascha Cohen, "How a Book Changed the Way We Talk About Rape," *Time,* Oct. 7, 2015, time.com/4062637/against-our-will-40/.

23. Ibid.

24. Quoted in Wendy McElroy, *Sexual Correctness: The Gender-Feminist Attack on Women* (Jefferson, NC: McFarland, 1996), 109.

25. Cathy Young, "Domestic Violence," Independent Women's Forum, iwf.org/files/50c58dda09f16c86b2c652aa047944f6.pdf.

26. Stephanie Coontz, *The Way We Never Were: American Families and the Nostalgia Trap* (1992; repr., New York: Basic Books, 2016), 35.

27. Judith Stacey, "Scents, Scholars, and Stigma: The Revisionist Campaign for Family Values, *Social Text,* no. 40 (Autumn 1994), 54.

28. Quoted ibid., 70.

29. Brad Wilcox and Robin Wilson, "The Best Way to End Violence Against Women: Stop Taking Lovers and Get Married," *Washington Post,* June 10, 2014, washingtonpost.com/posteverything/wp/2014/06/10/the-best-way-to-end-violence-against-women-stop-taking-lovers-and-get-married/.

30. Ibid.

31. Ibid.

32. Linda J. Waite, "The Negative Effects of Cohabitation," *The Responsive Community* 10, no. 1 (Winter 1999/2000), The Communitarian Network, gwu.edu/~ccps/rcq/rcq_negativeeffects_waite.html.

33. B. Sesali, "Fucking with Feministing: Non-Monagamy," Feministing, 2015, feministing.com/2015/05/15/fucking-with-feministing-non-monogamy/.

34. Stephanie Coontz, "The Way We Never Were," *The New Republic,* March 29, 2016, newrepublic.com/article/132001/way-never.

35. James Q. Wilson, *The Marriage Problem: How Our Culture Has Weakened Families* (New York: HarperCollins, 2002), 76.

36. Jessie Bernard, *The Future of Marriage* (London: Souvenir Press, 1972), 51.

37. Quoted in David Frum, *How We Got Here: The 1970s: The Decade That Brought You Modern Life (for Better or Worse)* (New York: Basic Books, 2000), 80.

38. Though in 2010, when New York State was considering adopting no-fault divorce, the New York State chapter of the National Organization for Women opposed it on the grounds that it would disadvantage women.

39. Frum, *How We Got Here,* 78–79.

40. Ibid., 79.

41. Ibid., 75.

42. Quoted on her website, at constanceahrons.com/books-resources/the-good-divorce.

43. Katie Roiphe, "In Defense of Single Motherhood," Sunday Re-

view, *New York Times,* Aug. 11, 2012, nytimes.com/2012/08/12 /opinion/sunday/in-defense-of-single-motherhood.html.

44. Nick Schulz, *Home Economics: The Consequences of Changing Family Structure* (Washington, DC: AEI Press, 2013).

45. "The Moynihan Report (1965)," blackpast.org/primary/moynihan -report-1965.

46. Ibid.

47. Quoted in Schulz, *Home Economics,* 63–64.

48. Quoted ibid., 8.

49. Nicholas Kristof, "Commentary: Liberals Blew It 50 Years Ago on Moynihan Report," *Columbus Dispatch,* March 14, 2015, dispatch .com/content/stories/editorials/2015/03/14/1-liberals-blew-it-50 -years-ago-on-moynihan-report.html.

50. "Are We Happy Yet?" Pew Research Center, Social Trends Report, Feb. 13, 2006, pewsocialtrends.org/2006/02/13/are-we-happy-yet/.

51. Linda J. Waite and Evelyn L. Lehrer, "The Benefits from Marriage and Religion in the United States: A Comparative Analysis" (2003), ncbi.nlm.nih.gov/pmc/articles/PMC2614329.

52. Kay Hymowitz et al., "Knot Yet: The Benefits and Costs of Delayed Marriage in America," University of Virginia, National Marriage Project, 2013, nationalmarriageproject.org/wp-content/uploads /2013/03/Knot-Yet-FinalForWeb.pdf.

53. "Married Adults Are Healthiest, New CDC Report Shows," Centers for Disease Control and Prevention, Dec. 15, 2004, cdc.gov /nchs/pressroom/04facts/marriedadults.htm.

54. Mona Charen, "What Government Can't Do," Creators .com, May 12, 2016, creators.com/read/mona-charen/05/16/what -government-cant-do.

55. "Marriage and Mental Health in Adults and Children," Research Brief No. 4, Feb. 2007, Center for Marriage and Families, Institute for American Values, americanvalues.org/catalog/pdfs/research brief4.pdf.

56. Institute for American Values, "When Marriage Disappears," *The State of Our Unions* [2010], stateofourunions.org/2010/index.php.

57. E. J. Schultz, "As Single Becomes New Norm, How to Market Without Stigma," AdAge.com, Oct. 11, 2010. adage.com/article /news/advertising-market-singles-stigma/146376/.

58. Sara McLanahan, et al., "The Fragile Families and Childhood Wellbeing Study," fragilefamilies.princeton.edu/sites/fragilefamilies /files/nationalreport.pdf.

59. Barbara Dafoe Whitehead, *The Divorce Culture: Rethinking Our Commitments to Marriage and Family* (New York: Vintage Books, 1998), 97.

60. Maggie Gallagher and Barbara Dafoe Whitehead, "End No-Fault Divorce? A Symposium," First Things, Aug. 1997, firstthings.com /article/1997/08/end-no-fault-divorce.

61. Ibid.

62. W. Bradford Wilcox, "The Evolution of Divorce," *National Affairs* 25, (Fall 2009), nationalaffairs.com/publications/detail/the -evolution-of-divorce.

63. Jay L. Zagorsky, "Marriage and Divorce's Impact on Wealth," *Journal of Sociology* 41, no. 4 (2005), journals.sagepub.com/doi/abs /10.1177/1440783305058478.

64. Darlene Cunha, "The Divorce Gap," *The Atlantic,* April 28, 2016, theatlantic.com/business/archive/2016/04/the-divorce-gap /480333/.

65. National Parents Organization, "Mothers and Children of Divorce More Apt to Live in Poverty," *Our Blog,* n.d., nationalparents organization.org/blog/18807-census-bureau-mothe.

66. Kimberly Bainbridge, "Getting Married Can Be a Wealthy Proposition," CNBC, Feb. 26, 2015, cnbc.com/2015/02/14/getting -married-can-be-a-wealthy-proposition.html

67. Edward Kruk and Barry L. Hall, "The Disengagement of Paternal Grandparents Subsequent to Divorce," *Journal of Divorce and Remarriage* 23, no. 1/2 (1995), 131–47, edwardkruk.com/jdr2.pdf

68. Wilcox, "The Evolution of Divorce."

69. Sara McLanahan and Gary Sandefur, *Growing Up with a Single Parent: What Hurts, What Helps* (Cambridge, MA: Harvard University Press, 1994).

70. Lauren Hansen, "9 Negative Effects Divorce Reportedly Has on Children," *The Week,* March 28, 2013, theweek.com/articles /466107/9-negative-effects-divorce-reportedly-children.

71. David M. Cutler, Edward L. Glaeser, and Karen E. Norberg, "Explaining the Rise in Youth Suicide," in *Risky Behavior Among Youths: An Economic Analysis,* ed. Jonathan Gruber (Chicago: University of Chicago Press, 2001), pp. 219–70), nber.org/chapters/c10690.pdf.

72. Ibid.

73. Whitehead, *The Divorce Culture,* 98.

74. Ibid.

75. Ibid., 174.

76. Ibid., 156.

77. Frank Furstenberg Jr. and Andrew J. Cherlin, *Divided Families: What Happens to Children When Parents Part* (Cambridge, MA: Harvard University Press, 1991), 35.

78. Jennifer Saranow Schultz, "The Financial Impact of Divorce on College Students," *Bucks* (blog), *New York Times,* Dec. 15, 2010, bucks.blogs.nytimes.com/2010/12/15/the-financial-impact-of-divorce-on-college-students/.

79. Krista Soria and Sarah Linder, "Parental Divorce and Undergraduate Students' Success" (2013), University of Minnesota Digital Conservancy, http://hdl.handle.net/11299/161378.

80. J. S. Schultz, "The Financial Impact of Divorce on College Students."

81. Andrew Cherlin, *The Marriage-Go-Round: The State of Marriage and the Family in America Today* (New York: Knopf, 2009), 21.

82. Whitehead, *The Divorce Culture,* 102.

83. Ibid., 162.

84. Associated Press, "Children at Higher Risk in Nontraditional Homes," NBC News, Nov. 18, 2007, nbcnews.com/id/21838575/ns/health-childrens_health/t/children-higher-risk-nontraditional-homes/#.WPfZjVLMyLd.

85. W. Bradford Wilcox, "Suffer the Little Children: Cohabitation and the Abuse of America's Children," *Public Discourse,* April 22, 2011, thepublicdiscourse.com/2011/04/3181/.

86. Linda J. Waite et al., "Does Divorce Make People Happy? Findings from a Study of Unhappy Marriages" (2002), Institute for American Values, americanvalues.org/catalog/pdfs/does/_divorce_/make_/people_happy.pdf.

87. Harry Benson, "Should Couples in Unhappy Marriages Stay Together?" Institute for Family Studies, Feb. 22, 2017, ifstudies.org/blog/should-couples-in-unhappy-marriages-stay-together.

88. Waite et al., "Does Divorce Make People Happy?"

89. All statistics cited here are from cdc.gov/nchs/fastats/unmarried-childbearing.htm.

90. Deanna L. Pagnini and Ronald R. Rindfuss, "The Divorce of Marriage and Childbearing: Changing Attitudes and Behavior in the United States," *Population and Development Review* 19, no. 2 (June 1993), 331–37.

91. Allan C. Brownfeld, "Studies Reflect the Damage of the One-Parent, Fatherless Family," *Communities Digital News,* May 15, 2014, commdiginews.com/life/studies-reflect-the-damage-of-the-one-parent-fatherless-family-17573/.

92. Quoted ibid.

93. onlinelibrary.wiley.com/doi/abs/10.1111/j.1532-7795.2004.00079.x.

94. "Poverty in Black America," Black Demographics, n.d., black demographics.com/households/poverty/.

95. Robert Rector, "Marriage: America's Greatest Weapon Against Child Poverty," The Heritage Foundation, Sept. 16, 2010, heritage .org/poverty-and-inequality/report/marriage-americas-greatest -weapon-against-child-poverty-0.

96. Diane Medved, *Don't Divorce: Powerful Arguments for Saving and Revitalizing Your Marriage* (Washington, DC: Regnery, 2017), 130–31.

97. Child Trends Data Bank, "Births to Unmarried Women: Indicators on Children and Youth," Dec. 2015, childtrends.org/wp-content /uploads/2015/03/75_Births_to_Unmarried_Women.pdf; see also George A. Akerlof and Janet Yellen, "An Analysis of Out-of-Wedlock Births in the United States," (Aug. 1, 1996), Brookings Policy Brief Series, brookings.edu/research/an-analysis-of-out-of -wedlock-births-in-the-united-states/.

98. Isabel V. Sawhill, "Non-Marital Births and Child Poverty in the United States," June 1999 testimony, brookings.edu/testimonies /non-marital-births-and-child-poverty-in-the-united-states/.

99. Kay Hymowitz, *Marriage and Caste in America* (Chicago: Ivan R. Dee, 2006), 17.

100. Richard B. Reeves and Kimberly Howard, "The Marriage Effect: Money or Parenting?" *Brookings Social Mobility Papers,* Sept. 4, 2014, brookings.edu/research/the-marriage-effect-money -or-parenting/.

101. Ibid.

102. Rob Stein and Donna St. George, "Unwed Motherhood Increases Sharply in U.S., Report Shows," *Washington Post,* May 14, 2009, washingtonpost.com/wp-dyn/content/article/2009/05/13 /AR2009051301628.html.

103. Cherlin, *The Marriage-Go-Round,* 207.

104. Ibid., 206.

105. J. D. Vance, *Hillbilly Elegy: A Memoir of a Family and Culture in Crisis* (New York: HarperCollins, 2016), 127.

106. Alana Semuels, "'All the Men Here Are Either on Drugs or Unemployed,'" *The Atlantic,* May 9, 2017, theatlantic.com/business /archive/2017/05/men-women-rust-belt/525888/.

107. Melissa S. Kearney and Riley Wilson, "Male Earnings, Marriageable Men, and Nonmarital Fertility: Evidence from the Fracking Boom," National Bureau of Economic Research, NBER Working Paper No. 23408, May 2017, nber.org/papers/w23408.

108. Institute for American Values, "When Marriage Disappears," 31.

109. W. Bradford Wilcox and Kathleen Kovner Kline, *Gender and Parenthood* (New York: Columbia University Press, 2013), 176.

110. David Autor and Melanie Wasserman, "Wayward Sons: The Emerging Gender Gap in Labor Markets and Education" (2013), Third Way Report, thirdway.org/report/wayward-sons-the-emerging -gender-gap-in-labor-markets-and-education.

111. Thomas B. Edsall, "The Increasing Significance of the Decline of Men," *New York Times,* March 16, 2017.

112. Nicholas Eberstadt, *Men Without Work* (Conshohocken, PA: Templeton Press, 2016), 80.

113. Ibid., 73.

114. Ibid., 74.

115. "Table 318.30: Bachelor's, Master's, and Doctor's Degrees Conferred by Postsecondary Institutions, by Sex of Student and Discipline Division: 2013–14," National Center for Education Statistics, nces.ed.gov/programs/digest/d15/tables/dt15_318.30.asp.

116. Vice Staff, "It's Not Your Imagination, Single Women: There Literally Aren't Enough Men Out There," Vice.com, Sept. 28, 2015, vice.com/en_se/article/youre-single-because-there-arent-enough -men-253.

117. Wendy Wang and Kim Parker, "Record Share of Americans Have Never Married," Pew Research Center, Social Trends Report, Sept. 14, 2014, pewsocialtrends.org/2014/09/24/record-share-of -americans-have-never-married/st-2014-09-24-never-married-08/.

118. Richard V. Reeves and Edward Rodrigue, "Single Black Female BA Seeks Educated Husband: Race, Assortative Mating, and Inequality" (April 9, 2015), Brookings Social Mobility Papers, brookings.edu/research/single-black-female-ba-seeks-educated -husband-race-assortative-mating-and-inequality/.

119. W. Bradford Wilcox, "Family Matters," *Slate,* Jan. 22, 2014, slate .com/articles/double_x/doublex/2014/01/new_harvard_study_ where_is_the_land_of_opportunity_finds_broken_families.html.

120. Quoted in W. Bradford Wilcox, "Don't Be a Bachelor: Why Married Men Work Harder, Smarter, and Make More Money," *Washington Post,* April 2, 2015, washingtonpost.com/news/inspired -life/wp/2015/04/02/dont-be-a-bachelor-why-married-men-work -harder-and-smarter-and-make-more-money/.

121. Wang and Parker, "Record Share of Americans Have Never Married."

122. Wilcox, "Don't Be a Bachelor."

123. Elizabeth H. Gorman, "Bringing Home the Bacon," *Journal of Marriage and Family* 61, no. 1 (Feb. 1999).

124. Kate Antonovics and Robert Town, "Are All the Good Men Married? Uncovering the Sources of the Marital Wage Premium" *American Economic Review* 94, no. 2 (May 2004), jstor.org/stable /3592902.

125. Wilcox and Kline, *Gender and Parenthood,* 226.

126. Anne Case and Angus Deaton, "Rising Morbidity and Mortality in Midlife Among White Non-Hispanic Americans in the 21st Century," *Proceedings of the National Academy of the Sciences of the United States of America* 112, no. 49 (Dec. 2015), princeton.edu/faculty -research/research/item/rising-morbidity-and-mortality-midlife -among-white-non-hispanic.

127. Anne Case and Angus Deaton, "Mortality and Morbidity in the 21st Century" (March 23, 2017), Brookings Papers on Economic Activity, brookings.edu/wp-content/uploads/2017/08/casetextsp17bpea .pdf.

128. Steve Marche, "Is Facebook Making Us Lonely?" *The Atlantic,* May 2012.

129. Olga Oksman, "The Calm, Gentle Rise of Snugglers for Hire," *The Atlantic,* Dec. 3, 2015, theatlantic.com/business/archive/2015/12 /why-isnt-there-a-starbucks-for-hugs/418332/.

130. Ibid.

131. Katie Hafner, "Researchers Confront an Epidemic of Loneliness," *New York Times,* Sept. 5, 2016, nytimes.com/2016/09/06/health /lonliness-aging-health-effects.html.

132. Ally Holterman, "Mental Health Problems for College Students Are Increasing," *Healthline News,* Aug. 25, 2016, healthline.com /health-news/mental-health-problems-for-college-students-are -increasing-071715#1.

133. Nicholas Eberstadt, *Men Without Work: America's Invisible Crisis* (West Conshohocken, PA: Templeton Foundation, 2016), 100.

134. Thomas B. Edsall, "The Increasing Significance of the Decline of Men," *New York Times,* March 16, 2017.

135. Amanda Marcotte, "Paul Ryan's Family Values Are That Only Elite Families Have Value," Alternet, Oct. 22, 2015, alternet.org/news -amp-politics/paul-ryans-family-values-are-only-elite-families -have-value.

136. Institute for American Values, "When Marriage Disappears," 58.

137. Cherlin, *The Marriage-Go-Round,* 193.

138. Whitehead, *The Divorce Culture,* 9.

139. Wendy Wang, "The Link Between a College Education and a Lasting Marriage," Pew Research Center, Fact Tank, Dec. 4, 2015, pewresearch.org/fact-tank/2015/12/04/education-and-marriage/.

140. Carolyn Hax, "A Baby and a Grandmother-to-Be's Disappointment," *Washington Post,* Jan. 24, 2012, washingtonpost.com/lifestyle /style/carolyn-hax-a-baby-and-a-grandmother-to-bes-disappointment /2012/01/10/gIQALqlqLQ_story.html.

141. Alexis de Tocqueville, "Principal Causes Which Tend to Maintain the Democratic Republic in the United States," chap. 17 in *Democracy in America,* vol. 1 (1835), trans. Francis Bowen (New York: Vintage Books, 1959), 315.

Chapter 7: Having It All

1. Anne-Marie Slaughter, "Why Women Still Can't Have It All," *The Atlantic,* July/Aug. 2012, theatlantic.com/magazine/archive /2012/07/why-women-still-cant-have-it-all/309020/.

2. Sheryl Sandberg, *Lean In: Women, Work, and the Will to Lead* (New York: Knopf, 2013), 159.

3. Diana Furchtgott-Roth, "Sorry, Elizabeth Warren, Women Already Have Equal Pay," E21, July 27, 2016, economics21.org/html /sorry-elizabeth-warren-women-already-have-equal-pay-1979 .html; Christina Hoff Sommers, "No, Women Don't Make Less Money than Men," *Daily Beast,* Feb. 1, 2014, thedailybeast.com /articles/2014/02/01/no-women-don-t-make-less-money-than -men.

4. Sommers, "No, Women Don't Make Less Money than Men."

5. Ibid.

6. "The Return of the Stay-at-Home Mother," *The Economist,* April 19, 2014, economist.com/news/united-states/21600998-after -falling-years-proportion-mums-who-stay-home-rising-return.

7. Furchtgott-Roth, "Sorry, Elizabeth Warren, Women Already Have Equal Pay."

8. Catherine Hakim, *Feminist Myths and Magic Medicine: The Flawed Thinking Behind Calls for Further Equality Legislation,* (London: Centre for Policy Studies, 2011), LSE Research Online, eprints.lse. ac.uk/36488/.

9. Sommers, "No, Women Don't Make Less Money than Men."

10. W. Bradford Wilcox and Kathleen Kovner Kline, *Gender and Parenthood* (New York: Columbia University Press, 2013), 8.

11. Claire Cain Miller, "The Gender Pay Gap Is Largely Because of Motherhood," *New York Times,* May 13, 2017, nytimes

.com/2017/05/13/upshot/the-gender-pay-gap-is-largely-because-of
-motherhood.html.

12. Ibid.
13. "Who Are Family Caregivers?" American Psychological Association, n.d., apa.org/pi/about/publications/caregivers/faq/statistics
.aspx.
14. Bureau of Labor Statistics, U.S. Dept. of Labor, "Volunteering in
the United States, 2015," Economic News Release, Feb. 25, 2016,
bls.gov/news.release/volun.nr0.htm.
15. Jessica Dickler, "Moms: 'I Can't Afford to Work,'" CNN Money,
April 20, 2012, money.cnn.com/2012/04/18/pf/moms-work/index
.htm.
16. Susan Pinker, *The Sexual Paradox: Men, Women, and the Real Gender
Gap* (New York: Scribner, 2009).
17. Ibid., 94.
18. Ibid., 76.
19. Amanda Ames, "Shortage of Large Animal Veterinarians Threatens
Health of Arizona Livestock Industry," Cronkite News, Arizona
PBS, March 7, 2016, cronkitenews.azpbs.org/2016/03/07/shortage
-of-large-animal-veterinarians-threatens-health-of-arizona-live
stock-industry/.
20. Jenna Goudreau, "20 Surprising Jobs Women Are Taking
Over," *Forbes,* March 7, 2011, forbes.com/sites/jennagoudreau
/2011/03/07/20-surprising-jobs-women-are-taking-over/#4b915
4bc728f.
21. Quoted in Susan Pinker, *The Sexual Paradox,* 83.
22. Quoted in Steven Pinker, *The Blank Slate: The Modern Denial of
Human Nature* (New York: Penguin Books, 2003), 352.
23. Goudreau, "20 Surprising Jobs Women Are Taking Over."
24. Susan Pinker, *The Sexual Paradox,* 71–73.
25. Mark J. Perry, "No Surprise Here: New Study Finds Gender Differences in Preferences for Higher Earnings vs. Other Job Attributes," AEI, June 8, 2016, aei.org/publication/new-study-finds
-gender-differences-in-preferences-for-higher-earnings-vs-other
-job-attributes/.
26. Sandberg, *Lean In,* 93.
27. Wendy Wang, "Mothers and Work: What's Ideal?" Pew Research Center, Fact Tank, Aug. 19, 2013, pewresearch.org/fact
-tank/2013/08/19/mothers-and-work-whats-ideal/.
28. Ibid.

29. Charlotte Rampell, "Working Parents Wanting Fewer Hours," *New York Times,* July 10, 2013.

30. Cathy Payne, "Moms Are Primary Breadwinners in 40% of U.S. Households," *USA Today,* May 29, 2013, usatoday.com /story/money/personalfinance/2013/05/29/breadwinner-moms -families/2364191/.

31. Mona Charen, "Breadwinner Moms," Creators.com, May 31, 2013, creators.com/read/mona-charen/05/13/breadwinner-moms-.

32. Kim Parker and Gretchen Livingston, "6 Facts About American Fathers," Pew Research Center, Fact Tank, June 15, 2017, pew research.org/fact-tank/2016/06/16/fathers-day-facts/.

33. sverigesradio.se/sida/artikel.aspx.

34. Ibid.

35. Lionel Tiger and Joseph Shepher, *Women in the Kibbutz* (San Diego: Harcourt Brace Jovanovich, 1975), 4.

36. Noam Shpancer, "Child of the Collective," *Guardian,* Feb. 18, 2011, theguardian.com/lifeandstyle/2011/feb/19/kibbutz-child-noam -shpancer.

37. Ibid.

38. Brigitte Berger, review of *Women in the Kibbutz,* by Lionel Tiger and Joseph Shepher, *Worldview* 19, no. 4 (April 1976), 48–51, Carn- egie Council for Ethics in International Affairs, worldview.carnegie council.org/archive/worldview/1976/04/2671.html.

39. "A Society of Misfits? The Kibbutz Experience," Jan. 1, 2009, mainstreamparenting.wordpress.com/2009/01/01/a-society-of-misfits -the-kibbutz-experience/.

40. Steven E. Rhoads, "Lean In's Biggest Hurdle: What Moms Most Want," IFS Family Studies, March 16, 2017, ifstudies.org/blog/lean -ins-biggest-hurdle-what-most-moms-want.

41. Justin Wolfers, "A Family-Friendly Policy That's Friendliest to Male Professors," *The Upshot* (blog), *New York Times,* June 24, 2016, nytimes.com/2016/06/26/business/tenure-extension-policies-that -put-women-at-a-disadvantage.html.

42. Hana Schank and Elizabeth Wallace, "When Women Choose Children over a Career," *The Atlantic,* Dec. 19, 2016, theatlantic .com/business/archive/2016/12/opting-out/500018/.

43. W. Bradford Wilcox, "Moms Who Cut Back at Work Are Happi- est," *The Atlantic,* Dec. 18, 2013.

44. Charles Murray, *Coming Apart: The State of White America, 1960– 2010* (New York: Crown Forum, 2012), 258.

45. E. J. Graff, "The Opt-Out Myth," *Columbia Journalism Review* (March/April 2007), archives.cjr.org/essay/the_optout_myth.php.

46. Judith Warner, "The Opt-Out Generation Wants Back In," *New York Times,* Aug. 7, 2013, nytimes.com/2013/08/11/magazine/the -opt-out-generation-wants-back-in.html.

47. Robert D. Putnam, *Our Kids: The American Dream in Crisis* (New York: Simon and Schuster, 2015), 67.

48. Ibid., 68.

49. Sara McLanahan, "The Consequences of Single Motherhood," *The American Prospect* 5, no. 18 (June 1994), prospect.org/article /consequences-single-motherhood.

50. Valerie Polakow, *Lives on the Edge: Single Mothers and Their Children in the Other America* (Chicago: University of Chicago Press, 1993), 73.

51. Anna Gorman, "Caught in the Cycle of Poverty," *Los Angeles Times,* May 24, 2012, articles.latimes.com/2012/may/24/local/la -me-natalie-20120524.

52. Office of the Press Secretary, "Fact Sheet: Helping All Working Families and Young Children Afford Child Care," press release, The White House, obamawhitehouse.archives.gov/the-press -office/2015/01/21/fact-sheet-helping-all-working-families-young -children-afford-child-care.

53. "Study Shows Consistent Benefit of Early Daycare," Reuters, May 14, 2010.

54. *The NICHD study of Early Child Care and Youth Development: Findings for Children up to Age 4½ Years* (Washington, DC: NICHD, 2006), 11, nichd.nih.gov/publications/pubs/documents/seccyd_06 .pdf.

55. Jonathan Cohn, "The Hell of American Day Care," *The New Republic,* April 15, 2013, newrepublic.com/article/112892/hell -american-day-care.

56. Grover J. "Russ" Whitehurst, "Can We Be Hard-Headed About Preschool? A Look at Targeted Pre-K" (Jan. 23, 2013), Brown Center Chalkboard Series Archive, brookings.edu/research/can-we-be -hard-headed-about-preschool-a-look-at-universal-and-targeted -pre-k/.

57. Melissa Healy, "Day Care Kids Are More Impulsive, Bigger Risk Takers, Study Finds," *Los Angeles Times,* May 13, 2010, articles .latimes.com/2010/may/13/science/la-sci-kids-daycare-20100514.

58. Jay Belsky, "Effects of Child Care on Child Development: Give

Parents a Real Choice," Institute for the Study of Children, Family, and Social Issues, March 2009, mpsv.cz/files/clanky/6640/9_Jay_Belsky_EN.pdf.

59. N. J. Bergman et al., "Randomized Controlled Trial of Skin-to-Skin Contact from Birth Versus Conventional Incubator for Physiological Stabilization in 1200- to 2199-gram Newborns," abstract, *Acta Paediatrica* 96, no. 6 (June 2004), 779–85, PubMed.gov, ncbi.nlm.nih.gov/pubmed/15244227.

60. Baby Gooroo, "10 Benefits of Skin-to-Skin Contact," n.d., babygooroo.com/articles/10-benefits-of-skin-to-skin-contact.

61. Ruth Feldman et al., "Maternal-Preterm Skin-to-Skin Contact Enhances Child Physiologic Organization and Cognitive Control Across the First 10 Years of Life," abstract, *Biological Psychiatry* 75, no. 1 (Jan. 1, 2014), 56–64, biologicalpsychiatryjournal.com/article/S0006-3223(13)00764-6/abstract.

62. Mary Eberstadt, "The Real Trouble with Day Care," Humanum (Spring 2013), humanumreview.com/articles/the-real-trouble-with-day-care.

63. "Pelosi Remark at Press Conference Introducing Comprehensive Child Care and Early Learning Bill to Ensure Working Families Have Access to Affordable, High-Quality Child Care," press release, democraticleader.gov/newsroom/91417-2/.

64. Michael Baker, Jonathan Gruber, and Kevin Milligan, "Non-Cognitive Deficits and Young Adult Outcomes: The Long-Run Impacts of a Universal Child Care Program," National Bureau of Economic Research, NBER Working Paper No. 21571, Sept. 2015, nber.org/papers/w21571.

65. "Toxic Stress," Center on the Developing Child, Harvard University, developingchild.harvard.edu/science/key-concepts/toxic-stress/.

66. Aria Bendix, "How Universal Child Care Affects Boys vs. Girls," *The Atlantic,* March 21, 2017, theatlantic.com/education/archive/2017/03/how-universal-child-care-affects-boys-vs-girls/520266/.

67. Mark W. Lipsey, Dale C. Farran, and Kerry G. Hofer, "A Randomized Control Trial of a Statewide Voluntary Prekindergarten Program on Children's Skills and Behaviors Through Third Grade," Peabody Research Institute, Vanderbilt University, Sept. 2015, peabody.vanderbilt.edu/research/pri/VPKthrough3rd_final_with cover.pdf.

68. Andrew Flowers, "Is Pre-K All It's Cracked Up to Be?" FiveThirty-Eight, Jan. 5, 2016, fivethirtyeight.com/features/is-pre-k-all-its-cracked-up-to-be/.

69. Laura Sanders, "Staring into a Baby's Eyes Puts Her Brain Waves and Yours in Sync," *Science News,* Dec. 5, 2017.

70. Quoted in Peter Robinson, "Milton Friedman, Ronald Reagan and William F. Buckley Jr.," Forbes.com, Dec. 12, 2008, forbes.com/2008/12/11/friedman-reagan-buckley-oped-cx_pr_1212 robinson.html#2c3f86a371e0

71. Gretchen Livingston and Anna Brown, "Birth Rate for Unmarried Women Declining for First Time in Decades," Pew Research Center, Fact Tank, Aug. 12, 2014, pewresearch.org/fact-tank/2014/08/13/birth-rate-for-unmarried-women-declining-for-first-time-in-decades/.

72. Heather Wilhelm, "Closing the Marriage Gap," *Philanthropy,* Summer 2016, philanthropyroundtable.org/topic/philanthropic_freedom/closing_the_marriage_gap.

73. W. Bradford Wilcox and Wendy Wang, "The Millennial Success Sequence," AEI and Institute for Family Studies, June 14, 2017, aei.org/publication/millennials-and-the-success-sequence-how-do-education-work-and-marriage-affect-poverty-and-financial-success-among-millennials/.

74. "Family Relations, Low Income and Child Outcomes: A Comparison of Canadian Children in Intact, Step- and Lone-Parent Families," Canadian Research Data Center Network, crdcn.org/family-relations-low-income-and-child-outcomes-a-comparison-canadian-children-intact-step-and-lone.

75. Ron Haskins and Isabell Sawhill, *Creating an Opportunity Society* (Washington, DC: Brookings Institution Press, 2009).

76. "MADD History Impact of Mothers Against Drunk Driving," Elite Driving School, n.d., drivingschool.net/madd-history-impact-mothers-drunk-driving/.

77. Amanda Marcotte, "Surprise! Unwed Birth Rates Are Going Down," *Slate,* May 11, 2015, slate.com/blogs/xx_factor/2015/05/11/the_number_of_unwed_women_giving_birth_is_in_decline_not_that_you_d_know.html.

78. Rachel Lehmann-Haupt, "Single-Mother Families Aren't the 'Other,'" *Slate,* May 7, 2016, slate.com/articles/life/family/2016/05/for_mother_s_day_let_s_stop_shaming_and_stigmatizing_single_moms.html.

79. "Improving the Lives of Single Moms and Their Kids," *Talk of*

the Nation, NPR, June 12, 2012, npr.org/2012/06/12/154853988 /improving-the-lives-of-single-moms-and-their-kids.

80. Ibid.

81. Barack Obama, "Text of Obama's Fatherhood Speech," Politico, June 15, 2008, politico.com/story/2008/06/text-of-obamas-father hood-speech-011094.

82. Office of the Press Secretary, "Remarks by the President at More-house College Commencement Ceremony," press release, The White House, obamawhitehouse.archives.gov/the-press-office /2013/05/19/remarks-president-morehouse-college-commencement -ceremony.

SELECT BIBLIOGRAPHY

Allyn, David. *Make Love, Not War: The Sexual Revolution; An Unfettered History.* Boston: Little, Brown, 2000.

Baron-Cohen, Simon. *The Essential Difference: Men, Women and the Extreme Male Brain.* New York: Penguin Press/Classics, 2012. Originally published 2003.

Bell, Daniel. *The Coming of Post-Industrial Society: A Venture in Social Forecasting.* New York: Basic Books, 1973.

Bernard, Jesse. *The Future of Marriage.* New Haven, CT: Yale University Press, 1982. Originally published 1972.

Bogle, Kathleen A. *Hooking Up: Sex, Dating, and Relationships on Campus.* New York: New York University Press, 2008.

Brizendine, Louann. *The Female Brain.* New York: Three Rivers Press, 2006.

Brown, Helen Gurley. *Sex and the Single Girl.* New York: Bernard Geis Associates, 1962.

Brownmiller, Susan. *Against Our Will: Men, Women, and Rape.* New York: Simon and Schuster, 1975.

Caplow, Theodore, Louis Hicks, and Ben J. Wattenberg. *The First Measured Century: An Illustrated Guide to Trends in America, 1900–2000.* Washington, DC: AEI Press (American Enterprise Institute), 2001.

Cherlin, Andrew. *The Marriage-Go-Round: The State of Marriage and the Family in America Today.* New York: Knopf, 2009.

Coontz, Stephanie. *The Way We Never Were: American Families and the Nostalgia Trap.* New York: Basic Books, 2016. Originally published 1992.

Crews, Frederick. *The Memory Wars: Freud's Legacy in Dispute.* New York: New York Review of Books, 1995.

Eberstadt, Mary. *Adam and Eve After the Pill: Paradoxes of the Sexual Revolution.* San Francisco: Ignatius Press, 2012.

Eberstadt, Nicholas. *Men Without Work: America's Invisible Crisis.* West Conshohocken, PA: John Templeton Foundation, 2016.

Ehrenreich, Barbara, Elizabeth Hess, and Gloria Jacobs. *Re-Making Love: The Feminization of Sex.* New York: Doubleday, 1986.

Erwin, Edward. *A Final Accounting: Philosophical and Empirical Issues in Freudian Psychology.* Cambridge, MA: A Bradford Book, MIT Press, 1995.

Firestone, Shulamith. *The Dialectic of Sex: The Case for Feminist Revolution.* New York: William Morrow, 1970.

Flanagan, Caitlin. *Girl Land.* Boston: Little, Brown, 2012.

Fleming, Anne Taylor. *Motherhood Deferred.* New York: Putnam, 1994.

Freitas, Donna. *The End of Sex: How Hookup Culture Is Leaving a Generation Unhappy, Sexually Unfulfilled, and Confused About Intimacy.* New York: Basic Books, 2013.

Friedan, Betty. *The Feminine Mystique.* New York: W. W. Norton, 1963.

Friedan, Betty. *The Second Stage.* New York: Simon and Schuster, 1981.

Frum, David. *How We Got Here: The 70's; The Decade That Brought You Modern Life (For Better or Worse).* New York: Basic Books, 2000.

Furchtgott-Roth, Diana. *Women's Figures: An Illustrated Guide to the Economic Progress of Women in America.* Washington, DC: AEI Press (American Enterprise Institute), 2012.

Gilder, George. *Men and Marriage.* Gretna, LA: Pelican Publishing, 1986.

Graglia, Carolyn. *Domestic Tranquility: A Brief Against Feminism.* Dallas: Spence Publishing, 1998.

Greer, Germaine. *The Female Eunuch.* New York: Harper Perennial Modern Classics, 2008. Originally published 1970.

Grossberg, Michael. *Governing the Hearth: Law and the Family in Nineteenth-Century America.* Raleigh: University of North Carolina Press, 1988.

Grossman, Miriam. *Unprotected: A Campus Psychiatrist Reveals How Political Correctness in Her Profession Endangers Every Student.* New York: Sentinel, 2007.

Harden, Nathan. *Sex and God at Yale: Porn, Political Correctness, and a Great Education Gone Bad.* New York: Thomas Dunne Books, St. Martin's Press, 2012.

Hennessee, Judith. *Betty Friedan: Her Life.* New York: Random House, 1999.

Horowitz, Daniel. *Betty Friedan and the Making of the Feminine Mystique.* Amherst: University of Massachusetts Press, 1998.

Hymowitz, Kay. *Marriage and Caste in America.* Chicago: Ivan R. Dee, 2006.

Kass, Army, and Leon R. Kass, eds. *Wing to Wing, Oar to Oar: Readings on Courting and Marrying.* South Bend, IN: University of Notre Dame Press, 2000.

Kennedy, David. *Freedom from Fear: The American People in Depression and War, 1929–1945.* New York: Oxford University Press, 2001.

Kimball, Roger. *The Long March: How the Cultural Revolution of the 1960s Changed America.* San Francisco: Encounter Books, 2000.

Koedt, Anne, Ellen Levine, and Anita Rapone, eds. *Radical Feminism.* New York: Times Books, 1973.

Levy, Ariel. *Female Chauvinist Pigs: Women and the Rise of Raunch Culture.* New York: Free Press, 2005.

McElroy, Wendy. *Sexual Correctness: The Gender-Feminist Attack on Women.* Jefferson, NC: McFarland, 1996.

Millett, Kate. *Sexual Politics.* New York: Columbia University Press, 2016. Originally published 1970.

Mitchell, Susan. *Icons, Saints and Divas: Intimate Conversations with Women Who Changed the World.* New York: HarperCollins, 1997.

Moir, Anne, and David Jessel. *Brain Sex: The Real Difference Between Men and Women.* New York: Dell Publishing, 1989.

Morgan, Robin, ed. *Sisterhood Is Powerful: An Anthology of Writing from the Women's Liberation Movement.* New York: Random House, 1970.

Murray, Charles. *Coming Apart: The State of White America, 1960–2010.* New York: Crown Forum, 2012.

O'Beirne, Kate. *Women Who Make the World Worse.* New York: Sentinel, 2006.

Paglia, Camille. *Sexual Personae: Art and Decadence from Nefertiti to Emily Dickinson.* New York: Vintage Books, 1991.

Parker, Kathleen. *Save the Males: Why Men Matter, Why Women Should Care.* New York: Random House, 2010.

Paul, Pamela. *Pornified: How Pornography Is Damaging Our Lives, Our Relationships, and Our Families.* New York: Henry Holt, 2005.

Petigny, Alan. *The Permissive Society: America, 1941–1965.* New York: Cambridge University Press, 2009.

Pinker, Steven. *The Blank Slate: The Modern Denial of Human Nature.* New York: Penguin Books, 2003.

Pinker, Susan. *The Sexual Paradox: Men, Women, and the Real Gender Gap.* New York: Scribner, 2009.

Polakov, Valerie. *Lives on the Edge: Single Mothers and Their Children in the Other America.* Chicago: University of Chicago Press, 1993.

Putnam, Robert D. *Our Kids: The American Dream in Crisis.* New York: Simon and Schuster, 2015.

Regnerus, Mark, and Jeremy Uecker. *Premarital Sex in America.* New York: Oxford University Press, 2011.

Rhoads, Steven E. *Taking Sex Differences Seriously.* San Francisco: Encounter Books, 2004.

Ridley, Matt. *The Red Queen: Sex and the Evolution of Human Nature.* New York: Harper Perennial, 2003. Originally published 1994.

Roiphe, Katie. *The Morning After: Sex, Fear, and Feminism.* Boston: Little, Brown, 1993.

Rosin, Hanna. *The End of Men and the Rise of Women.* New York: Riverhead Books, 2012.

Sandberg, Sheryl. *Lean In: Women, Work, and the Will to Lead.* New York: Knopf, 2013.

Sax, Leonard. *Why Gender Matters: What Parents and Teachers Need to Know About the Emerging Science of Sex Differences.* New York: Doubleday, 2005.

Schulz, Nick. *Home Economics: The Consequences of Changing Family Structure.* Washington, DC: AEI Press (American Enterprise Institute), 2013.

Shalit, Wendy. *A Return to Modesty: Discovering the Lost Virtue.* New York: Free Press, 1999.

Sommers, Christina Hoff. *Freedom Feminism: Its Surprising History and Why It Matters Today.* Washington, DC: AEI Press (American Enterprise Institute), 2013.

Stepp, Laura Sessions. *Unhooked: How Young Women Pursue Sex, Delay Love, and Lose at Both.* New York: Riverhead Books, 2007.

Tiger, Lionel and Joseph Shepher. *Women in the Kibbutz*. New York: Harcourt Brace Jovanovich, 1975.

Torrey, E. Fuller. *Freudian Fraud: The Malignant Effect of Freud's Theory on American Thought and Culture*. New York: HarperCollins, 1992.

Tucker, William. *Marriage and Civilization: How Monogamy Made Us Human*. Washington, DC: Regnery, 2014.

Vance, J. D. *Hillbilly Elegy: A Memoir of a Family and Culture in Crisis*. New York: HarperCollins, 2016.

Whitehead, Barbara DaFoe. *The Divorce Culture: Rethinking Our Commitments to Marriage and Family*. New York: Vintage Books, 1998.

Wilson, James Q. *The Marriage Problem: How Our Culture Has Weakened Families*. New York: HarperCollins, 2002.

INDEX

ABOUT THE AUTHOR

Mona Charen, one of the most prominent conservative writers in the country, is the author of the *New York Times* bestseller *Useful Idiots*. She writes a critically acclaimed syndicated column that appears in more than two hundred newspapers, is a contributor for *National Review,* and is a senior fellow at the Ethics and Public Policy Center. She appears regularly on radio and television news shows and is a former panelist on CNN's *Capital Gang*.